Automating SRE and Operations on AWS

Understanding SRE practices for streamlined operations, implementing automations with native AWS services

Sushanth Mangalore

bpb

www.bpbonline.com

First Edition 2026

Copyright © BPB Publications, India

ISBN: 978-93-65895-216

LIMITS OF LIABILITY AND DISCLAIMER OF WARRANTY

To View Complete
BPB Publications Catalogue
Scan the QR Code:

www.bpbonline.com

Dedicated to

My wife, Ambika, and my children: Theia and Yuvaan for their love and encouragement,my parents: Pushpa Rao and Yashwanth Rao for my upbringing and education, my late grandfather: Bhaskar Rao–a published author himself and my grandmother Geetha Rao, for their blessings.

About the Author

Sushanth Mangalore is a seasoned software architect and technology leader with close to 20 years of experience. Having witnessed the world of technology evolve firsthand, he specializes in helping businesses adopt the cloud, build robust cloud-native architectures, and strategically implement technologies like AI to meet their success objectives. From his real-world experience of working as an architect with customers of varying sizes across numerous industries, Sushanth advises technology executives and the tech community,providing clear guidance on effective strategies for cloud adoption and maximizing the value from technology investments. A prolific author of technical blogs and whitepapers, he is also a regular and highly rated speaker at technology and industry conferences. Sushanth has mentored dozens of early career technologists, continually paying it forward to the community. He presently resides in a suburb of Chicago,IL, USA with his wife and two children.

About the Reviewers

❖ **Satish Prahalad Gururajan** is a passionate and highly skilled Solutions Architect with nearly two decades of professional experience in the tech industry. He has a strong foundation in application development, with a focus on Java technologies, and has played pivotal roles in software design, development, and delivery. Over the course of his career, Satish has excelled in diverse positions, ranging from developer to architect, product owner, and designer, which has allowed him to build a comprehensive understanding of both technical and business needs. Satish's expertise goes beyond development; he has consistently demonstrated a strong ability to bridge the gap between technical teams and business stakeholders, ensuring that solutions align with both strategic goals and user requirements. His experience spans a variety of industries, and he has a proven track record of successfully leading teams through the development lifecycle, from ideation and design to implementation and deployment. As a certified professional, Satish holds multiple industry-recognized certifications, including SAFe® Product Owner/Product Manager, Certified Scrum Product Owner (CSPO®), and Certified Scrum Master (CSM®), which have honed his skills in agile methodologies and product management. These certifications have not only enriched his technical acumen but also enhanced his leadership and project management capabilities, enabling him to guide teams in delivering high-quality software in a collaborative and efficient manner. Satish is especially passionate about problem-solving and has a natural talent for distilling complex technical concepts into easily understandable terms. His ability to simplify intricate topics allows him to communicate effectively with both technical and non-technical audiences.

❖ **Suresh Dodda** is a seasoned Java and cloud-native engineer with over two decades of experience in enterprise software development. He is currently a Lead Application Developer at ADP, focusing on designing and delivering scalable microservices and REST APIs using technologies like Java, Spring Boot, and PostgreSQL. His expertise spans AWS, containerization, and distributed systems, and he is committed to building high-availability platforms for global HR and payroll solutions.

Suresh is also passionate about automation, leveraging tools and practices such as CI/CD pipelines, TDD, and infrastructure as code to eliminate manual overhead and drive operational efficiency. He actively follows innovations in AI/ML, contributing to architecture discussions and mentoring teams on enterprise-grade solution design.

Acknowledgement

I extend my heartfelt gratitude to everyone who has contributed to the creation of this book. I am deeply thankful to my family and friends for their unwavering support and encouragement throughout the writing process. This work would not have been possible without their constant motivation.

I am equally grateful to my employer, Amazon Web Services, and my colleagues, whose experiences, guidance, and opportunities have significantly shaped the content of this book. I would also like to acknowledge my first employer, Infosys, for providing me with a strong foundation in the technology industry and for the invaluable learning during the early stages of my career.

My sincere thanks go to BPB Publications for placing their trust in me and for offering guidance and support at every step of this journey.

Finally, I wish to acknowledge the reviewers, technical experts, and editors whose insights and expertise have greatly refined this book and enhanced its overall quality.

Preface

As more organizations continue to build their businesses in the cloud, it is essential to understand and prepare to operate in a manner that differs markedly from the on-premises data center way. **Site reliability engineering** (**SRE**) is an essential practice in the cloud and helps keeps your systems in the cloud running swimmingly. Public clouds like AWS provides you several native tools to help with the SRE tasks, simplifying your experience as a cloud operations professional. This book is a primer on getting familiar with AWS tooling for SRE and how you can apply them to automate a range of tasks that you will routinely performas SRE. While no book is a substitute for the rich documentation that AWS provides for each of their services, you can use this as your guide for understanding what's available and where to start your operations journey on AWS. Through the automation ideas presented in the book, you will get a head start on applying the native AWS tooling to build your SRE practice on AWS.

The book is comprised of 10 chapters, covering topics necessary for understanding SRE responsibilities on AWS and using native AWS options to automate a large portion of your day-to-day operations tasks on AWS. The book starts with an overview of SRE responsibilities in general, contrasting traditional operations practices on-premises with how AWS native SRE practices.We then move into understanding how SRE and DevOps complement each other. Following this, we introduce SRE responsibilities on AWS and start mapping them to options natively available on AWS to address them across the remaining chapters. We use a simple application as our example workload in this book to demonstrate how the concepts discussed can be practically applied.

This book is designed to cater to professionals starting their cloud operations journey on AWS and students curious to learn about operational excellence on AWS. Basic prior knowledge of AWS is assumed, along with some familiarity executing shell scripts through command line and rudimentary coding with Python programming language.

Chapter 1: Site Reliability Engineering Responsibilities - This chapter introduces **site reliability engineering** (**SRE**) and IT operations, comparing traditional on-premises environments with modern cloud-native approaches. Readers learn about the challenges of on-premises operations, including compatibility issues, reactive firefighting, and limited automation. The chapter explains how SRE brings software engineering rigor to operations, focusing on automation, collaboration with development teams, and measuring reliability through metrics like SLOs, SLIs, and SLAs. The chapter concludes by introducing a sample three-tier web application that will be used throughout the book to demonstrate automation concepts on AWS, covering deployment, maintenance, security, monitoring, scaling, disaster recovery, and cost management. This foundation prepares readers to understand how cloud services can reduce manual toil while increasing operational efficiency and accuracy.

Chapter 2: SRE versus DevOps - This chapter explores the relationship between DevOps and **site reliability engineering** (SRE), presenting them as complementary disciplines with distinct focuses. Readers learn that DevOps emphasizes cultural collaboration and speed of changes across broader engineering teams, while SRE takes a more prescriptive, metrics-driven approach with rigorous engineering practices like SLIs/SLOs and error budgets. It introduces DORA metrics as indicators of DevOps performance that align with SRE principles. Readers will understand how DevOps processes and tools (version control, CI/CD, infrastructure as code, observability) support both disciplines, and how combining DevOps' cultural elements with SRE's technical rigor creates stronger operational capabilities for today's complex production systems.

Chapter 3: SRE on AWS - This chapter introduces SRE practices on AWS, explaining how cloud-native options enable more efficient automation of operational tasks. Readers learn about the shared responsibility model for resilience on AWS.The chapter explores the benefits of applying engineering principles to operations, including using AWS SDKs to build custom orchestration, implementing advanced resilience patterns, and automating security controls. It provides a comprehensive overview of AWS services that support SRE practices, categorized by functions such as infrastructure management, updates/maintenance, release engineering, observability, reliability engineering, incident response etc. The chapter concludes by explaining how to organize AWS workloads efficiently using multiple accounts, AWS Organizations, and Control Tower to achieve centralized governance and compliance. This knowledge prepares readers to leverage AWS services for implementing effective SRE practices that enhance reliability while reducing manual effort.

Chapter 4: Infrastructure as Code - The chapter introduces infrastructure as code (IaC) and its implementation on AWS. Readers learn about the significant benefits of IaC, including consistency, version control, automation, improved security, scalability, reduced downtime, and cost savings. The chapter provides a detailed exploration of AWS CloudFormation, explaining its key features like templates, stacks, provisioning, updates, rollbacks, and security. Through a practical example, readers see how to automate infrastructure for a sample workload using CloudFormation templates, with explanations of template sections. The chapter also covers alternative IaC approaches: AWS Cloud Development Kit (CDK) for defining infrastructure using familiar programming languages, AWS Serverless Application Model (SAM) for serverless applications, and Terraform as a multi-cloud option. By the end, readers understand how to choose the appropriate IaC tool for their needs and how to implement infrastructure automation, which is essential for modern cloud operations and a key aspect of SRE practices.

Chapter 5: Automating Infrastructure Maintenance - This chapter provides a comprehensive guide to automating infrastructure maintenance on AWS. Readers learn about the different categories of maintenance tasks (operations management, node management, change management, and application management) and how AWS Systems Manager serves as a central hub for these activities. The chapter introduces the AWS Systems Manager Agent (SSM Agent) as a lightweight component that enables centralized management across EC2 instances and on-premises servers. Through practical examples using the sample application, readers learn how to implement these features to perform tasks like restarting instances, gathering inventory, updating the SSM Agent, and creating patch baselines. By leveraging these capabilities, SREs can significantly reduce manual effort, improve consistency, and maintain more reliable infrastructure while focusing on strategic initiatives rather than repetitive maintenance tasks.

Chapter 6: Release Automation - Readers will be introduced to release automation on AWS, a critical component of modern DevOps practices. Readers learn about the various tasks involved in the release process, including code checkout, quality checks, build, test, release, deploy, operate, and monitor. The chapter explores AWS services for release automation such as CodeBuild, CodeDeploy and CodePipeline. Through a practical example, readers see how to implement a complete release pipeline for the sample application using CloudFormation templates, with detailed explanations of configuration files for services in use. The chapter also covers DevSecOps on AWS, showing how to integrate security practices throughout the software development lifecycle.

Chapter 7: Observability for Reliable Operations - This chapter provides a comprehensive guide to observability for reliable operations on AWS. Readers learn how observability differs from monitoring by enabling understanding of a system's internal state through external outputs. The chapter explores three key components of observability: metrics, logs, and traces. It details AWS services like CloudWatch for collecting metrics and logs, X-Ray for distributed tracing, and anomaly detection capabilities that use machine learning to identify unusual patterns. Through practical examples with the sample application, readers learn to implement custom metrics, set up CloudWatch agents, create metric math expressions, and instrument applications with X-Ray. By implementing robust observability practices, SREs can proactively detect issues, reduce costs through optimization, ensure compliance, and ultimately deliver more reliable applications with improved user experiences.

Chapter 8: Automating Resilience - This chapter explores automating resilience on AWS. Readers learn how to build robust, fault-tolerant applications that can withstand and recover from failures while maintaining service availability. The chapter distinguishes between high availability (HA) and disaster recovery (DR), explaining how they complement each other. For HA, readers discover AWS services and strategies like multi-AZ deployments, autoscaling, and application-level resilience techniques such as circuit breakers and retries. For DR, the chapter presents four strategies (backup and restore, pilot light, warm standby, and active-active) with increasing costs and availability benefits, helping readers select appropriate solutions based on Recovery Time Objectives (RTO) and Recovery Point Objectives (RPO). Practical considerations for cross-region backup copies, AWS Backup policies, and cell-based architecture are also covered. Through these approaches, readers learn to implement automated resilience that enables systems to survive disruptions by designing resilience upfront rather than reacting after failures occur, ultimately ensuring business continuity and maintaining customer trust.

Chapter 9: Incident Response Automation - In this chapter, readers learn the principles of effective incident response, including preparation, detection, containment, eradication, recovery, post-incident analysis, automation, notification, and continuous improvement. The chapter demonstrates how Amazon EventBridge can be used to respond to events by capturing and routing them to appropriate targets like Lambda functions or SNS topics. Through practical examples, readers discover how to create multi-step workflows using AWS Step Functions for complex incident response scenarios. The chapter also covers testing recoverability through disaster recovery drills, chaos engineering, backup testing, and other approaches. AWS Fault Injection Service (FIS) is introduced as a managed service for conducting controlled chaos engineering experiments to identify weaknesses in applications. By implementing these automation techniques, SREs can significantly minimize human error during critical situations, and build more resilient systems that can withstand and recover from failures with minimal business impact.

Chapter 10: Auditing, FinOps and Miscellaneous Automation - This chapter explains auditing, FinOps, and miscellaneous automation on AWS. Readers learn about auditing activities and infrastructure configurations using AWS CloudTrail and AWS Config, which provide comprehensive visibility into user actions and resource states. The chapter also covers Financial Operations (FinOps), introducing its principles of collaboration, business value-driven decisions, accessible reporting, shared ownership, centralized management, and cost variability benefits. Readers discover AWS cost management tools like Cost Explorer, Budgets, and Cost and Usage Reports, along with strategies for optimization including right-sizing, reserved capacity, and serverless architectures. The chapter concludes with an overview of additional automation opportunities for security operations, network operations, data operations, and ML operations. This knowledge helps SREs implement comprehensive auditing, optimize costs, and extend automation to specialized operational domains.

Code Bundle and Coloured Images

Please follow the link to download the
Code Bundle and the *Coloured Images* of the book:

https://rebrand.ly/e2e165

The code bundle for the book is also hosted on GitHub at
https://github.com/bpbpublications/Automating-SRE-and-Operations-on-AWS.
In case there's an update to the code, it will be updated on the existing GitHub repository.

We have code bundles from our rich catalogue of books and videos available at
https://github.com/bpbpublications. Check them out!

Errata

We take immense pride in our work at BPB Publications and follow best practices to ensure the accuracy of our content to provide with an indulging reading experience to our subscribers. Our readers are our mirrors, and we use their inputs to reflect and improve upon human errors, if any, that may have occurred during the publishing processes involved. To let us maintain the quality and help us reach out to any readers who might be having difficulties due to any unforeseen errors, please write to us at: errata@bpbonline.com

Your support, suggestions and feedbacks are highly appreciated by the BPB Publications' Family.

At www.bpbonline.com, you can also read a collection of free technical articles, sign up for a range of free newsletters, and receive exclusive discounts and offers on BPB books and eBooks. You can check our social media handles below:

Instagram

Facebook

Linkedin

YouTube

Get in touch with us at: business@bpbonline.com for more details.

Piracy

If you come across any illegal copies of our works in any form on the internet, we would be grateful if you would provide us with the location address or website name. Please contact us at business@bpbonline.com with a link to the material.

If you are interested in becoming an author

If there is a topic that you have expertise in, and you are interested in either writing or contributing to a book, please visit www.bpbonline.com. We have worked with thousands of developers and tech professionals, just like you, to help them share their insights with the global tech community. You can make a general application, apply for a specific hot topic that we are recruiting an author for, or submit your own idea.

Reviews

Please leave a review. Once you have read and used this book, why not leave a review on the site that you purchased it from? Potential readers can then see and use your unbiased opinion to make purchase decisions. We at BPB can understand what you think about our products, and our authors can see your feedback on their book. Thank you!

For more information about BPB, please visit www.bpbonline.com.

Join our Discord space

Join our Discord workspace for latest updates, offers, tech happenings around the world, new releases, and sessions with the authors:

https://discord.bpbonline.com

Table of Contents

CHAPTER 1
Site Reliability Engineering Responsibilities

Introduction

The first chapter of this book will introduce you to **IT operations (ITOps)** and **site reliability engineering (SRE)** and how these functions are organized within enterprises. We will look at how operations are performed in the traditional on-premises world and its challenges. Next, we will discuss modern cloud-native operations and categories of operational tasks. We will conclude this chapter by introducing the workload we will use throughout this book to explain different concepts, tasks, and automation scenarios.

Structure

The chapter covers the following topics:

- Introduction to operations and site reliability engineering
- Operations in on-premises environments
- SRE responsibilities for cloud workloads
- Categories of operational tasks
- Introduction to our sample workload

Objectives

By the end of this chapter, we will understand how operations were performed in the on-premises environment and how SRE practices and operations have evolved. We will discuss different operational tasks and how they can be categorized. We will also get familiar with the sample workload used throughout the book. Moreover, we will understand how the concepts in the chapters that follow will be explained with the help of this workload.

Introduction to operations and site reliability engineering

Operations or ITOps, also known as **systems administration (sysadmin)** is the broad practice of actively designing, deploying, and supporting an organization's diverse technology building blocks. This includes servers, networks, databases, storage systems, permissions, applications, and more, that enable employees to productively perform their work and assist the organization in attaining business goals. Operations engineers manage this infrastructure while continually administering upgrades, security patches, troubleshooting issues, and enhancing performance across on-premises and cloud-hosted systems. ITOps teams perform a mix of proactive and reactive tasks. They create, evolve, and support a high-functioning IT environment catered to an organization's needs and direction.

SRE has emerged as a discipline that targets reducing the manual toil involved in running operations. It uses engineering practices to automate operational tasks and provide the desired level of reliability. It builds on ITOps by implementing infrastructure management through automated, proactive practices that create scalable, resilient, self-healing technology stacks tuned for high-performance. It makes engineered software the basis for running operations in your environment, which helps perform tasks faster, with lower effort and fewer errors. SRE also collaborates closely with the development team to deliver reliability aligned to product requirements. Organizations have started investing more of their IT budget towards building an SRE practice to derive these benefits. With the overlap between ITOps and SRE, many organizations have started to absorb the ITOps responsibilities in the SRE teams.

We will explore operations and SRE responsibilities in more detail in this chapter. Let us first look at how operations were traditionally performed and the challenges this approach poses for workloads in the cloud.

Operations in on-premises environments

Operations in traditional on-premises environments involve building and maintaining technology across servers, networking, backup and storage, security, and more from various vendors. ITOps provides monitoring, troubleshooting, systems upgrades, capacity planning, and daily break/fix for infrastructure. ITOps is responsible for operations and maintenance, continually optimizing performance and availability so that technology delivers the services the business needs. They proactively predict and plan for future capacity demands. They reduce disruption from outages or disasters by implementing continuity plans and rapidly responding to unplanned incidents like cyberattacks. Whether it is rolling out new applications, preventing overloaded servers, building automation to reduce manual processes, securing data, or supporting users with their devices, the role of IT ops is to ensure all foundation technology pieces are in place for the organization to carry out its critical functions and be commercially successful.

The following figure summarizes some of the operational challenges on-premises:

Figure 1.1: *Operational challenges in traditional on-premises environments*

The disparate on-premises technologies can lead SRE teams to complicated hardware and software interdependencies and compatibility issues. This is further amplified by the difference in operating a combination of physical and virtualized infrastructure. By upgrading one component, SRE risks destabilizing others. Without visibility into interconnections, troubleshooting issues, and performance problems become difficult for SREs. This leads to a constant risk of outages that SRE teams must frequently *firefight*. The lack of options for automation, flexibility, and consolidation with on-premises infrastructure hampers SREs. Also, there is poor resource utilization and high operational overhead, which leads to cost inefficiencies. Ultimately, the business suffers from IT delivery delays and limited scalability, constrained by capital-intensive, siloed on-premises technology. Consolidating on standardized and programmable cloud infrastructure enables SRE teams prevent compatibility issues and outages.

The highly reactive nature of ITOps work can often negatively impact personnel satisfaction. While trained staff grow skilled at scripting fixes for some issues, the unpredictable ways in which problems manifest prepare for every failure mode infeasible. The lack of sufficient standardization causes a repetitive, stressful environment of technology fire drills. Even attempts at automation efforts falter due to infrastructure complexities and business demands for continuous uptime amidst frequent changes. As systems grow in complexity over time and demand higher attention and upkeep, the workload for ITOps teams increases proportionately. With the focus on minimizing service disruptions, there is little mindshare left to implement technology reliably, more thoughtfully and sustainably. There is very little input from ITOps into architecture planning and quality targets. The chasm between ITOps and developers expands, leading to mutual dissatisfaction and hurt organizational agility. Operating in a constant state of emergency makes the role demanding for those who seek to gain expertise through engineering challenges rather than repetitive maintenance. Instead of innovating better solutions, skilled staff get burdened with handling tedious tasks manually, which can burn them out over time.

By adopting SRE principles powered by cloud infrastructure programmability, organizations can help ITOps transition from fighting fires to proactively designing reliability into systems. SRE culture emphasizes engineering over repeated manual tasks, which helps attract and retain talent. With SREs involved early in system design and lifecycle planning, services can achieve sustainability goals for availability, performance, and agility. This allows ITOps staff to focus on higher-value objectives compared to perpetual reactive mitigation. This leads to an overall increase in the agility for organizations and increased job satisfaction for motivated operations staff who want to influence the success of the business through continuous quality improvements.

SRE responsibilities for cloud workloads

As we saw in the preceding section, the operations teams existed in isolation from the development teams traditionally and had limited inputs or collaboration during the architecture definition. They remained focused on keeping the lights on and had limited interactions with development teams during deployments, maintenance and fire drills. One of the biggest reasons for organization s failing to see the benefits of a cloud migration, is a tendency to operate in the cloud the same way did on-premises. In one of the conversations with a technology executive responsible for the success of a large cloud migration, we recall mentioning, *if you replicate your data center in the cloud, it is likely you will find cloud more expensive than your data center spend*. This is a by-product of not adopting cloud-native solutions and treating the cloud as a data center where you can procure infrastructure faster. The net result of this is you acquire infrastructure faster, but continue to use it in an unoptimized manner, like your data center. This can result in your cloud bills skyrocketing before you know it.

Adoption of cloud-native services help ease this quite a bit. Additionally, the responsibility of SRE evolves in the cloud too. SRE brings software engineering rigor to operations problems. As a result, SREs collaborate more closely with product developers and architects to design scalable and resilient architectures. While product engineering focuses on solving business problems, the engineering skills possessed by SRE is focused on solving operational challenges. Their expertise come together to yield benefits for the whole organization. SRE works to understand the business needs to formulate reliability and performance requirements of the workloads.

SRE does not eliminate manual operational tasks but strives to reduce them continuously. Team members are incentivized to find ways to spend less time doing manual work and doing more with automation. The idea is that more automation leads to better operations and, in turn, better service quality. This is more than just an aspirational goal but rather something which is continuously measured and improved upon. SRE uses these metrics to measure the quality of your service.

The following figure summarizes the important SRE metrics:

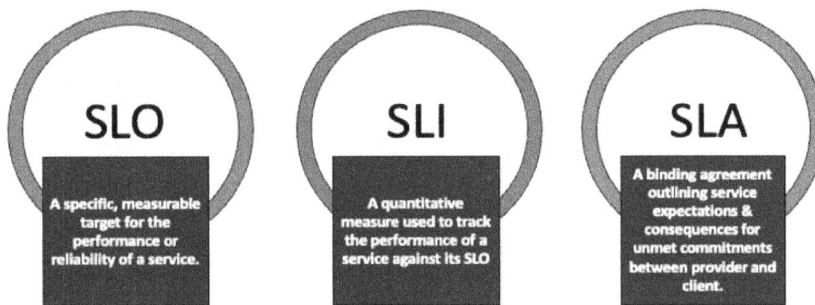

SLO
A specific, measurable target for the performance or reliability of a service.

SLI
A quantitative measure used to track the performance of a service against its SLO

SLA
A binding agreement outlining service expectations & consequences for unmet commitments between provider and client.

Figure 1.2: SRE metrics

Let us understand these SRE metrics in more detail.

- **Service level objectives (SLO):** SLOs measure the quality or health of your system. It is a measurable, agreed-upon target that your service can deliver within the cost constraints you want to set. Some examples of this could be:

    o Availability or uptime measures the time a system is in operation.

    o Business metrics include conversion rates, total traffic, and sales volume.

    o Performance metrics, such as the speed at which the application loads or responds.

SLO is expressed in terms of percentage. For example, an availability SLO of 99.9% equates to a downtime period of about 43 minutes over a 30-day month:

    o 30 days × 24 hours × 60 minutes = 43,200 minutes

    o 99.9% availability means the service should be up 99.9% of the time. To find the allowed downtime, we need to calculate 0.1% (100% - 99.9%) of the total time: 0.1% of 43,200 minutes = 0.001 × 43,200 = 43.2 minutes

An SLO is a promise to your customer about output or quality from your software that can be measured.

- **Service-level indicators (SLI):** SLIs are actual metrics in quantifiable terms that indicate if your SLO is being met. Your SLI may not match your SLO exactly. If the SLI exceeds the SLO, you are doing better than the promise you made to your customers. On the other hand, an SLI less than your SLO means there is corrective work your SRE team needs to do to deliver the experience you promised. For example, the SLI corresponding to an availability SLO of 99.9% could be the percentage of successful requests over the total number of requests in a 30-day period. If a service received 1,000,000 requests in a 30-day period, and 999,000 of those requests were successful (i.e., returned a valid response without errors), the SLI would be (999,000 / 1,000,000) $\times$ 100 = 99.9%.

- **Service-level agreements (SLA):** SLAs are contractual agreements between you and your customers about the measurable level of service to provide. The contract usually has information about financial consequences for failure to meet the service quality you are guaranteeing. For example, the SLA could state that your service guarantees 99.95% uptime. If your service is unavailable for more than 0.05% of the month or specified contract length, you may be obligated to compensate your customer up to what is stated in the contract language.

Additionally, error budgets are a closely related measure that SRE uses. Error budget refers to the amount of SLO miss that a service can accumulate over a period of time such as a month, without disrupting user experience. It is measured as 1 minus the SLO of a service. An SLO of 99.99% implies an error budget of 0.01%. Error budget sets realistic expectations for achieving a reliable SLO. While a 100% SLO sounds ideal in theory for the best user experience, it is often impractical and prohibitively expensive to achieve. This expense for an organization requires additional effort spent for negligible user benefit.

Service users expect high reliability, which gives them the confidence to continue using the service. It is a risk-reduction strategy for organizations to invest towards achieving these expectations. However, users also expect services to improve in value over time by adding new and improved features. Through realistic SLOs and error budgets, organizations can balance the risks of low reliability with the benefits of service improvements. Engineering resources can then be allocated effectively towards achieving both high reliability and better service quality without over-indexing at the expense of the other.

In cloud environments, the SRE practice becomes even more important to achieve the benefits advertised by migrating to the cloud. In the absence of an efficient SRE practice, organizations end up operating in the cloud, in the same manner as they are used to on-premises. Despite ambitions of agility and elasticity, continuing manual and reactive processes does not help reap the benefits. This leads to leadership questioning the move to the cloud when the agility, improved resiliency, ease of operations, and better utilization of resources are not realized. Operating in the cloud with a data center mindset can feel like additional recurring costs for little gain. The executives wonder if they could have avoided expenses by sticking with on-premises infrastructure despite other challenges. With the right level of automation enabled by the cloud operations, you will begin to unlock the potent benefits of your migration.

Cloud providers like **Amazon Web Services** (**AWS**) allow declarative infrastructure definition through code. This enables programmatic management at scale for greater resilience and consistency. It unlocks the automation and consistency required for seamless operations that can be applied predicably. This reduces dependency on one-off manual processes for operational tasks, which can be time consuming and error prone. Thus, cloud and SRE unlock a path where increased automation decisively drives better service quality and customer experiences. Beyond provisioning resources or recovering quickly from outages, automation unlocks even bigger benefits through continuous optimization. By codifying workflows rather than relying on tribal knowledge, SRE in cloud creates guardrails, so that changes can be applied with repeatability and consistency. The cloud allows SRE teams to build sturdy automation driven systems using metrics to get insights into usage and errors. These data insights allow you to gradually improve system reliability and efficiency. Rather than overpaying for more resources than required, you can run only what real usage demands. Performance problems can be spotted early without customers noticing slowdowns or drastic service degradation.

Automating the tedious manual work saves the SRE team time and energy. Instead of constantly fighting fires, they can use their skills to add value towards delivering business outcomes. Their expertise shifts from reactive fixes to proactively innovating better systems for the future. Defining infrastructure configurations, service behaviors, and reliability metrics as code and data paves the path for operations guided by evidence, not assumptions. This promotes a mindset of incremental improvements and an organizational realignment to sustained engineering over makeshift fixes. The cadence evolves beyond keeping the lights on towards willful automation for strategic gains.

Categories of operational tasks

Thus far, we have discussed SRE and operational responsibilities at a high level. We will now take a closer look at specific operational tasks the SREs are responsible for. These are applicable across on-premises and cloud but are usually easier to accomplish in the cloud due to the reasons we have mentioned in the preceding section.

Note: **Having introduced you to SRE, the rest of this book will use the terms SRE and operations interchangeably. This is intentional, as many organizations have chosen not to delineate rigidly between SRE and cloud operations. It is fairly common for SRE teams to take on the end-to-end ownership of operations. There may be some situations where your system administration roles may be separate from your SRE roles, even in cloud environments. However, there is value in looking at them through a unified lens due to the increasing crossover in responsibilities.**

A closely related discipline to SRE is platform engineering. Platform engineering focuses on providing self-service capabilities for infrastructure provisioning, especially for development environments. This focuses on self-service infrastructure with pre-baked compliance and governance as a product and improving the developer experience. Developers do not have to concern themselves with acquiring and setting up development infrastructure on a piecemeal basis. Instead, they can accurately provision exactly what they require for their project. Platform engineering is a deep and complex topic in itself. This book will not focus on platform engineering in much detail. Many of the services and techniques described in this book can be used as part of platform engineering (this book does not have chapters that dive deep into platform engineering directly).

We will see a combination of operational tasks and SRE as follows:

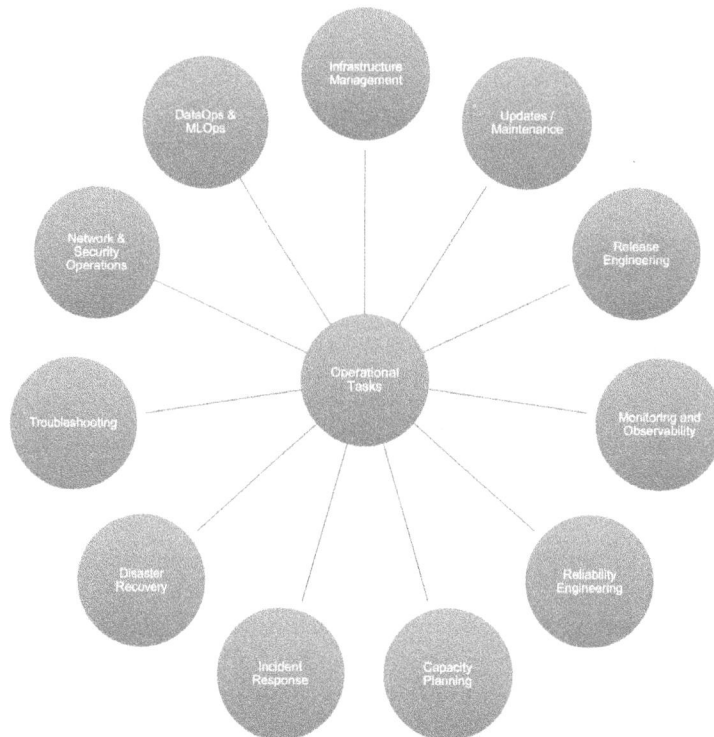

Figure 1.3: Operational tasks

Having set those expectations, let us now look at common categories of operational tasks:

- **Infrastructure management:** SREs are responsible for developing reusable code libraries and configurations to automate production infrastructure provisioning. This involves:

  o Utilizing **infrastructure as code** (**IaC**) frameworks like CloudFormation, AWS **Cloud Development Kit** (**CDK**), and Terraform to define infrastructure elements programmatically, allowing teams to provision resources much faster and more reliably without clicking around in a **graphical user interface (GUI)** like the AWS Console.

o Reviewing changes, rolling back bad changes, and evolving configurations over time in infrastructure code repositories, just like application code. Applying quality practices to IaC including linting, unit testing, regression testing and end-to-end validation. This prevents uncontrolled changes or downtime from rolling out faulty configuration.

o Developing tools and sandboxes for application teams to easily deploy pre-approved infra building blocks in a self-serve way in alignment with guardrails. As discussed previously, this responsibility generally falls under the focused discipline of platform engineering, but organizations may also accomplish this through SRE or operations teams.

- **Updates/maintenance:** Operations maintain systems through new patches, new software versions, hardware refresh cycles and handling version upgrades. This involves:

o Keeping track of essential patches and updates required to maintain desired security posture, reliability, and performance of workloads. This is followed on a well-established schedule and automated where possible.

o De-risking updates by deploying to a portion of the infrastructure first. This is followed by monitoring health and business metrics closely for problems before a broader rollout.

o Developing automated operational runbooks to perform routine procedures. By orchestrating changes, creating contingencies, and architecting for recoverability, updates, and upgrades can be applied without jeopardizing stability or uptime.

- **Release engineering:** This focuses specifically on the software release process and pipeline. SRE plays a central role in managing **continuous integration and continuous delivery (CI/CD)** pipelines. As part of this, they are responsible for:

o Designing and implementing the CI/CD workflow automation from the initial code push to eventual production deployment. This includes integrating testing tools, security checks, infrastructure provisioning actions, and release management controls.

o Incrementally deploying new versions to subsets of users via automation, with criteria defined for rolling forward or rolling back release changes using metrics if issues are detected.

o Standardizing the tools and environments in the release process for speed, safety, and consistency. CI/CD is an integral part of the SRE model for most modern technology organizations with cloud-native application architectures, allowing faster and more reliable delivery of software changes.

- **Monitoring and observability:** SRE depends on production telemetry for rapid issue detection and root cause analysis when problems occur. This involves the following:

  o Setting up metrics, logs, and alerts to track the health, performance, and availability of infrastructure and applications. This is key to detecting outages or degradation. The instrument systems emit logs, metrics, and traces and construct an observability nerve center to detect impending problems long before they occur.

  o Establishing adequate telemetry within apps and across microservices surfaces any possibilities of cascading failures. Tracing distributed interactions reduces the complexity of troubleshooting errors and performance issues.

  o Designing dashboards that consume metrics from applications and services, representing the state of your infrastructure in a graphical form for visual cues. The metrics, traces, logs, and dashboards give them the ability to perform rapid diagnoses and avoid prolonged post-mortems. These insights help SRE develop preventative engineering toward architectural enhancements and automated remediations instead of reactive firefighting.

- **Reliability engineering:** Reliability engineering is the heart of SRE, focused on ensuring quality of service and the desired level of resilience in your infrastructure. SREs perform the following tasks as part of reliability engineering:

  o Architecting environments for redundancy, fault tolerance, and continuity through peaks and valleys of traffic and usage. They observe patterns and develop solutions that yield sustainable operability.

  o Defining precise reliability goals through SLOs and error budgets and using observability data to measure quality and find improvement opportunities.

  o Employing practices such as scaling, throttling, load balancing, and load shedding. Eliminating single points of failure, decoupling dependencies, and isolating outages from propagating across integrated systems.

  o Stress testing and chaos experiments are performed to anticipate and guard against real-world situations. This helps in discovering weaknesses in staging, not production. Thereby, SRE bakes in resilience engineering from design, yielding highly available platforms ready to withstand steady-state usage and demand spikes.

- **Capacity planning:** Capacity planning is an important exercise that operations perform. This involves the following tasks:

  o Analyzing current workloads and usage trends to forecast future resource requirements. This is especially important in on-premises environments with long procurement cycles. With the cloud, operations can take advantage of the elasticity by scaling out and scaling in as loads vary.

o Being aware of workloads that need to react by scaling out when the load increases to ensure additional capacity is acquired to provide the expected user experience. To help save costs, the workloads must also be designed to scale in when the period of increased activity passes. Here, ensuring the workload is not scaled in prematurely is important. Removing resources before the load decreases will cause another scaling-out event and impact customer experience. This can be avoided by not scaling in too soon and favoring higher availability.

o Observing metrics and usage to find opportunities for the right size infrastructure to adjust for performance needs or bring down costs. SRE strives to prevent over or under-provisioning across heterogeneous resources.

- **Incident response:** SRE assesses issues when a service disruption happens. They perform the following tasks:

  o Mitigating the immediate impacts through failovers, understanding root causes, and implementing fixes to resolve and prevent recurrences. SREs start by assessing the blast radius of outages and take swift actions to ensure business continuity by preventing cascading failures.

  o Meticulously tracing error through logs and metrics to accurately identify root causes. Traditional operations resorted to rebooting servers when certain issues occurred. This leaves root causes undiscovered and causes the same issues to recur in the future. Root causes give you the information to resolve problems in a more permanent manner.

  o Eliminating single points of failure to strengthen the reliability of specific components. By building resilience along identified areas of failures, SREs uplift architectures to withstand inevitable disruptions. They transform insights into preventative reliability improvements and fallback mechanisms which allows systems to endure stress and unpredictable failure modes.

  o Escalating to the business leaders when outages occur, so proactive communications can be made to end users when there is unavoidable downtime. SRE also provides an estimated time for recovery and continuous status updates until the service recovers.

- **Troubleshooting performance:** SREs troubleshoot infrastructure bottlenecks and application latency which can impact user experience. As part of this, they perform the following tasks:

  o Navigating signals received from metrics and alarms to investigate degradation in performance. Symptoms like slow load times can emerge from different tiers like front-end code affecting browser performance, not scaling application servers fast enough to handle sudden traffic spikes, storage read contention, or cascading failures across microservices under sustained stress.

o   Analyzing insights via metrics, logs, dashboards, and distributed traces to pinpoint the root causes of issues. They examine all available telemetry data and evidence to diagnose reliability risks that may be signaled by an increased latency or a performance dip initially.

o   Thoroughly investigating potential bottlenecks across infrastructure resources, application code, and service dependencies to uncover factors contributing to degraded user experience. They also make proactive efforts to performance test systems, scale capacity planning, and establish reasonable performance baselines and indicators.

- **Data protection and disaster recovery:** Disaster in IT terms can strike suddenly through forces of nature, human errors, or cyber attackers seeking data ransom. SRE teams implement **disaster recovery (DR)** protections and ensure enterprise continuity. As part of this, the responsibilities involve:

o   Establishing rigorous business continuity management plans to meet **Recovery Time Objective (RTO)** and **Recovery Point Objective (RPO)** targets beyond quick failover to redundant infrastructure.

o   Conducting periodic DR testing to intentionally validate these plans rather than just relying on documentation, which could be outdated. SREs prioritize redundant backups both on-premises and across cloud regions for critical data, with regular restore validations to guarantee recovery effectiveness and avoid stale backups.

o   Maintaining strict access controls, least privilege permissions, vaulted credentials, and secrets to further shield data and DR controls from compromise. Information durability through comprehensive data retention policies is as important as infrastructure resilience, so policies are designed carefully with redundancy and compliance in mind. This way, when disasters inevitably occur, SRE teams have well-prepared business continuity provisions in place to enable resilience by design.

- **Network and security operations:** SRE teams actively ensure network and security operations to keep services fast, available, and safe from digital threats. At a basic level, the tasks involved here are:

o   Configuring policies in firewalls and rules in a virtual private cloud so resources can communicate with each other while blocking unauthorized access. By monitoring network traffic and activity, SREs quickly detect problems like overloaded links or unusual data flows that could signal an attack.

o   Patching security holes in servers, applications, and libraries to prevent hackers from exploiting vulnerabilities to steal data or install malware. By tracking new threats, SREs stay on top of protecting infrastructure and information.

- o Logging and analyzing access attempts to enable tracing issues when accounts get compromised, or data gets incorrectly changed. They lock down networks and systems, watch for risks, and respond swiftly to incidents to keep services operating safely. SREs work closely with security engineers and network engineers to provide the necessary support for secure and reliable operations. Implementing strong security and networking practices empowers SRE teams to confidently maintain service health and availability.

- **DataOps and MLOps:** DataOps and MLOps are newer disciplines that SRE teams adopt to manage **artificial intelligence/machine learning** (**AI/ML**) systems and data pipelines reliably. SRE provides the software engineering rigor needed to build reliable systems and observability around ML and data workflows. That way, as companies use more AI, SREs help ML teams ship and run systems properly. Without an SRE partnership, ML projects risk being unreliable or unsafe for customers. Together, they uphold stability and ethics standards at a model scale. As part of these, SRE performs the following tasks:

  - o Ensuring training data and models are managed smoothly from research to production rollout as AI and machine learning get integrated into more products.

  - o Automating and monitoring steps of data processing to quickly surface bugs-whether data cleaning, labeling for model training, or analytics. It helps keep bad data from crashing apps.

  - o Implementing MLOps to handle the machine learning model building, testing, and deployment pipeline specifically. This includes model experiment tracking, model drift detection if predictions degrade, and automation to refresh models. Both rely heavily on data and integration.

As you can see, there are varying facets to operations and SRE responsibilities. Each one of them is as important as the other. As we progress through this book, you will see how there are opportunities to apply automation to many of these tasks and how the cloud offers tools and services to ease the burden on the operations team to accomplish these tasks. While this book will not try to discuss cloud services in each of these tasks, you will understand how they can be used for automation. The services can be used in a variety of combinations to solve a range of problems. Depending on the nature of your workloads and the complexity involved, some, few, or all of the services we will discuss can be used in concert to accomplish your operational tasks in an automated manner.

Introduction to our sample workload

The preceding section introduced you to categories of operational tasks that most organizations hosting IT assets on-premises or in the cloud will need to perform. This book focuses on operating workloads in the cloud and using automation to reduce the manual toil while increasing efficiency and accuracy. Specifically, the book will focus on tooling available on AWS, to automate operational tasks. This book takes an approach of operating a workload in production on AWS and achieving the benefits of automation. The workload is intentionally kept simple, so the readers who want to experiment with the samples in this book do not incur a large bill. Every example will include a blurb about the cost impact, so you have information about the cost implications of implementing the solutions recommended in this book. While there are many complex workloads that run on AWS today, it is impractical to solve for every possibility that exists. For a reader looking to automate different aspects of their operations, this book will serve as a primer which provides a sampling of the options available on AWS to implement the automation. Even though the examples may appear simple on the surface, they can be combined and used in ways that solve large cross-cutting problems for very complex setups.

The workload we have picked is a three-tier web app that allows users to upload ratings and review comments for products across multiple vendors. Users will enter their comments using a web-based frontend. The information collected will be used to analyze the sentiment of the reviews.

Figure 1.4 depicts the logical architecture for the workload we will be using as our example in its simplest form:

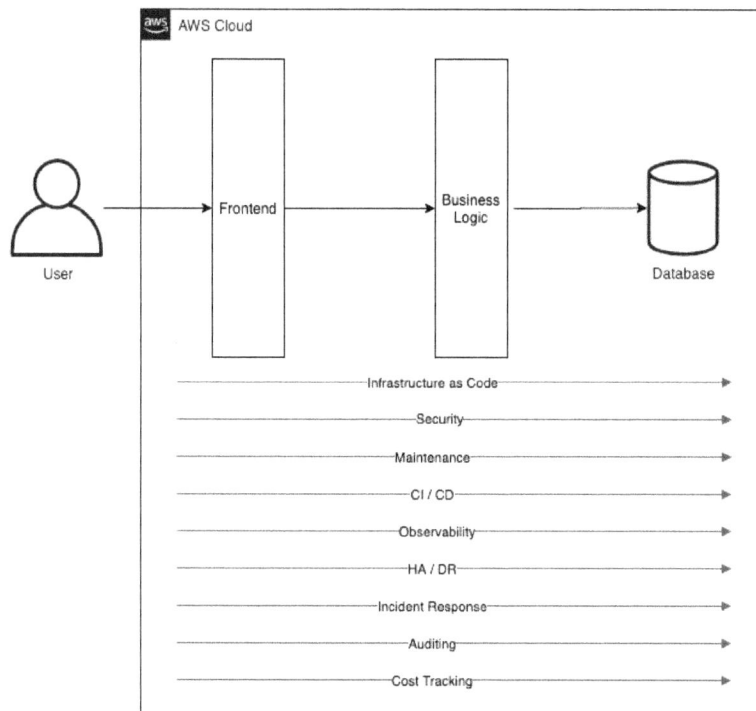

Figure 1.4: *Logical workload architecture*

You may notice that we have not listed the names of the AWS services that will be used for our implementation yet. This is intentional, as we will be introducing the different services we plan to use later in the book. As we introduce the AWS services, we will flesh out the architecture diagram more with details about the services that will be used to implement the functional requirements and the operational concerns. For now, we will focus on the logical architecture shown in the figure, which includes a frontend tier, a business logic tier, and a database tier. While this is a relatively straightforward use case on the surface, the figure also shows the different operational concerns that we plan to describe using this workload.

The example will cover the following concepts:

- **Deploying IaC:** All infrastructure used in the example will be codified.

- **Ongoing maintenance of the workload resources:** We will look at how to inventory, define maintenance windows, implement patching, and ensure compliance with the resources.

- **Continuously deploying changes to the application:** Any changes to the application will be applied through a continuous delivery pipeline.

- **Setting up security:** We will apply security at multiple layers using recommended practices to ensure that our application and infrastructure are protected.

- **Auditing API activity and cloud resources:** API activity at a resource level and any changes to the resource configuration will be audited and checked for compliance.

- **Monitoring metrics and logs:** We will monitor the metrics and logs from the cloud resources and the application to evaluate health and performance.

- **Setting up high availability and automatic scaling:** The application will be set up to be highly available and scale out and scale in response to varying loads.

- **Preparing a DR strategy and testing it:** We will define a DR strategy for the application and discuss how this will be tested.

- **Automating incident response:** We will look at how to respond to any incidents that occur while operating the workload.

- **Keeping track of infrastructure costs:** We will track costs incurred from running the workload on AWS and alert on excess usage.

There is more than one facet to each of these concerns, and we will use our sample to dive deep into each of them. We will look at challenges associated with each of the concerns, while drawing comparisons with how this varies from on-premises and implementing it without automation.

Conclusion

In this chapter, we introduced ITOps and SRE. We discussed the manner in which operations are implemented in traditional on-premises environments and the challenges associated with it. We saw how cloud operations differ from on-premises and how there are options available to simplify performing operational tasks. Next, we looked at the categories of operational tasks that are required to be performed for both on-premises and cloud workloads. We concluded the chapter by introducing the workload, which will be used as an example to explain the concepts covered in this book.

In the next chapter, we will compare SRE with DevOps and understand how they can work together to improve operations.

Points to remember

- Operations provides the technology required to support the business for an organization.

- Site reliability engineering brings engineering rigor to solve operational problems.

- Operations and SRE is easier to perform in the cloud compared to on-premises.

- There are various categories of operational tasks for both on-premises and cloud environments.

Multiple choice questions

1. **Which of the following is a key responsibility of SRE teams?**

   a. Designing product features

   b. Collaborating with business to understand reliability needs

   c. Focused only on development work

   d. Manual operations work

2. **Which of the following is an SRE responsibility around software releases?**

   a. Designing and implementing CI/CD workflows

   b. Production deployment automation

   c. Code development

   d. Architecture design

3. **What does an SRE team ensure through production monitoring?**

   a. Adoption of new technologies

   b. Revenue growth

   c. Stability and reliability of services

   d. Feature development speed

4. **Which of the following is included in disaster recovery protections established by SRE teams?**

   a. Meeting recovery time and point objectives

   b. Backup of critical data across regions

   c. Infrastructure management and support

   d. Incident communication

5. **What does an SRE team help with through capacity planning?**

   a. Software testing

   b. Infrastructure right sizing

   c. Disaster recovery testing

   d. Incident management

Answers

1.	b
2.	a
3.	c
4.	a
5.	b

Join our Discord space

Join our Discord workspace for latest updates, offers, tech happenings around the world, new releases, and sessions with the authors:

https://discord.bpbonline.com

CHAPTER 2
SRE versus DevOps

Introduction

This chapter will introduce you to DevOps and compare it with our learnings about SRE from *Chapter 1, Site Reliability Engineering Responsibilities*. We will understand how these disciplines are closely related but have semantic differences. Together, both ideas help maximize the value you get from your IT investments by improving how you operate. Although the automation techniques in this book can be applied to both operational and SRE tasks, comparing DevOps and SRE will give you a better appreciation of the intent behind them existing as separate disciplines.

Structure

The chapter covers the following topics:

- Understanding DevOps
- Comparing DevOps with SRE
- SRE's role in enhancing DevOps practices
- DevOps processes and tools
- Metrics for DevOps
- DORA and SRE

Objectives

By the end of this chapter, you will learn how DevOps and SRE are related but distinct disciplines that both aim to improve IT operations. DevOps emerged as a movement focused on breaking down silos between development and operations teams through cultural change, automation, and new processes like **continuous delivery** (**CD**). SRE was pioneered shortly after to solve issues with reliability and scale for massive internet services. While SRE incorporates some DevOps tooling and culture elements, it also applies more rigorous engineering practices around error budgets, SLIs/SLOs, capacity planning, and incident analysis. In this way, SRE can be seen as taking core DevOps collaboration principles to their fullest technical expression to meet the extreme demands of today's complex, rapidly evolving production systems.

Understanding DevOps

DevOps and **site reliability engineering** (**SRE**) are related philosophies and practices aimed at improving the operations of technology systems and services in organizations. Both emphasize culture, automation, measurement, and sharing responsibility for operational concerns between developers and IT operations teams. However, DevOps and SRE have some subtle differences in their intent and implementation. This chapter provides an overview of DevOps and SRE, how they compare, and how organizations can benefit from applying aspects of each. It is common to see technical articles or YouTube videos that claim, *DevOps is dead* or how *SRE has killed DevOps*. However, these claims tend to be sensationalist and not grounded. The reality is both DevOps and SRE have their place in the industry, and it is important to understand what they offer.

DevOps traces its roots back to earlier Agile software movements that emerged as alternatives to traditional waterfall development. Agile methodologies like Scrum and Kanban promoted faster iteration through lightweight cross-functional delivery teams, frequent working software releases, and adaptive planning. **Extreme Programming** (**XP**) expanded Agile values further through an emphasis on technical practices like test-driven development, **continuous integration** (**CI**), pair programming, and other forms of automation to improve software quality and velocity. However, these methodologies focused largely on application code and not the surrounding infrastructure and IT operations. As software systems and cloud platforms grew increasingly complex with the rise of Internet services, collaboration gaps between development and operations teams widened. This misalignment frequently manifested in the form of unearthed production defects or prolonged outages. DevOps philosophy took shape in response, expanding the scope of Agile software principles beyond just developers to bridge the gaps between infrastructure operators, quality assurance testers, security staff, and all other stakeholders involved in safely delivering software reliably at high velocity. In this way, DevOps builds upon the groundwork originating from Xtreme Programming and other Agile software movements while encompassing a wider circle of roles and concerns relating to holistic service delivery.

Prior to the DevOps movement, developers focused more on frequently developing new features and making updates, while operations teams were responsible for keeping systems stable and available. A lack of communication and collaboration between the two departments often led to a gap in shared understanding, bottlenecks in the software delivery process, and sometimes production outages. DevOps advocated for a culture of sharing responsibilities and processes between development and operations. The term **DevOps** was coined to reflect this blend of responsibilities. DevOps principles promoted adopting Agile development methods, implementing process automation, embracing infrastructure as code techniques, and monitoring/telemetry to create shared visibility. As DevOps matured, additional practices like continuous integration/continuous delivery, microservices architecture, and SRE have been incorporated into or associated with DevOps. At this point, you may start viewing SRE as a sub-practice under the larger DevOps umbrella. This is mostly accurate, but the next section compares DevOps and SRE in more detail.

DevOps is often misunderstood as simply an expanded toolchain or set of technical capabilities rather than a culture and mindset shift. People can mistakenly see it as making developers perform operations responsibilities or operations teams perform development work. In reality, DevOps eliminates siloed roles and encourages shared responsibility across the service delivery lifecycle. Handoffs are replaced by cross-functional collaboration. DevOps is often incorrectly manifested in an organization as a team or a job title. Instead, DevOps represents an organizational commitment to rapid experimentation powered by continuous automation. While Agile methodologies focus mainly on faster application changes, DevOps extends this velocity safely into production release processes. There are also misconceptions about costs, complexity, and maturity targets for DevOps. DevOps does not demand wholesale legacy modernization or rearchitecting, especially in the beginning. Investment in low-cost tooling and cloud resources allows incremental progress in the right direction. Streamlining deployment processes offers value well before reaching sophisticated practices like progressive delivery or SRE. Tailored adoption of cultural and technical elements of DevOps can pave an incremental transformation path for organizations without taking on large-scale disruptive changes.

While DevOps represents a cultural shift rather than a discrete team, organizations still require internal leadership and representation to help facilitate adoption. Some establish centralized DevOps centers of excellence or designate individual DevOps engineers acting as internal consultants guiding tool selection, automation strategies, metric dashboards, and training. However, the most effective structure empowers cross-functional product teams to own services end-to-end with embedded ops engineers paired with developers. These well-integrated teams share joint **key performance indicators** (**KPIs**) around customer value delivery, leaning on platform teams for internal tooling and best practice support. While Lean/ Agile methods still focus mainly on the software, SRE and DevOps expand responsibility to surrounding infrastructure critical to modern cloud-native applications. This collective ownership and unit autonomy model optimizes innovation velocity, even in highly regulated environments.

Comparing DevOps with SRE

SRE has close ties to DevOps but was formulated slightly later to address complex technical operations challenges that fast-growing technology organizations started to face. The overarching goal of SRE is to create very highly scalable and reliable technology systems and services. A key catalyst for SRE's creation was hyper-growth in these organizations, which required supporting hundreds of services and billions of users. Traditional IT operations teams struggled with this complexity, causing slow product iterations and instability issues. SRE pioneered the idea of bringing in systems engineers and software developers to establish a new discipline focused solely on reliability, capacity planning, and automation for their massive operations. Core SRE components include SLIs/SLOs/error budgets, blameless post-mortems, automation over manual tasks, and balancing feature velocity with system stability.

While DevOps and SRE share some similarities in culture and technical tooling, SRE takes a more prescriptive, metrics-driven approach grounded in systems engineering. SRE emerged more recently than DevOps and was necessitated by extreme-scale challenges. The DevOps movement emerged across a wider range of industries to solve a cultural challenge of gaps between engineering and operations. SRE teams have deep technical skills, often dedicated to a single service family, operating with a high-level of autonomy. DevOps encourages cross-functional upskilling across the broader engineering org to break the silos. SRE's systematic process is somewhat prescriptive by design. DevOps stays focused more on general culture and principles and avoids being overly prescriptive about the implementation.

Blending the human-focused cultural element of DevOps with the technical rigor of SRE allows organizations to create vastly improved service operations. They can use ongoing measurement to obtain the feedback needed to continue evolving operational maturity over time.

Let us look at how aspects of DevOps and SRE compare with each other. The following figure compares these disciplines on a high level:

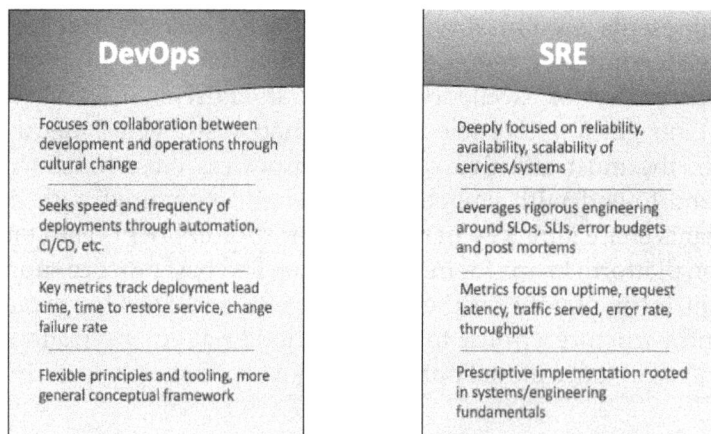

DevOps	SRE
Focuses on collaboration between development and operations through cultural change	Deeply focused on reliability, availability, scalability of services/systems
Seeks speed and frequency of deployments through automation, CI/CD, etc.	Leverages rigorous engineering around SLOs, SLIs, error budgets and post mortems
Key metrics track deployment lead time, time to restore service, change failure rate	Metrics focus on uptime, request latency, traffic served, error rate, throughput
Flexible principles and tooling, more general conceptual framework	Prescriptive implementation rooted in systems/engineering fundamentals

Figure 2.1: Comparing DevOps and SRE

DevOps teams use various automation tools to improve the speed and reliability of building, testing, and deploying software. The details are as follows:

- For managing code, developers collaborate on version control systems like track changes and updates in a central code repository.

- Continuous integration tools are used to build the code into software packages automatically whenever changes get merged in.

- They run automated tests to catch issues early on. Teams also employ infrastructure as code tools to automatically manage infrastructure like cloud servers, networks, and databases that the software needs to run on.

- Configuration management software lets engineers install and set up all the dependencies for the applications to operate properly across environments.

- Monitoring tools help teams track performance metrics and logs to make sure everything is working well for users. If any problem crops up, on-call incident response platforms notify engineers to fix it.

All these robust automation tools work together to improve the development lifecycle. This allows faster delivery of software while still keeping quality and maintaining agility.

SRE's role in enhancing DevOps practices

DevOps and SRE are two disciplines that take different but equally important approaches to improving IT operations. While DevOps focuses more on the speed of software changes and cultural collaboration, SRE addresses the reliability and scalability of large, complex systems. DevOps emerged from the need to break the chasm between developers iterating on new features and operations teams trying to maintain system stability. It bridges this through share ownership. SRE became popular a few years later when companies brought in software engineers to create a role focused on reliability and feature velocity through automation techniques. Traditional operations teams who followed elaborate change management processes and manual deployments found it challenging to handle the complexity of massive scale and frequent software changes without working overtime and fighting fire. DevOps provided the initial blueprint for cultural inroads by advocating shared goals, collective ownership, and automation to accelerate delivery while preserving reliability. However, more rigorous practices were needed for internet-scale systems. For this, hyper scalers defined the site reliability engineer role focused solely on balancing feature velocity with reliability through advanced automation techniques.

Both philosophies promote the use of data and metrics over assumptions and gut feelings. DevOps measures improvements in release cycle times as indications of smoothly flowing delivery pipelines. SRE analyzes detailed logs, error budgets, and system metrics to quantitatively model, forecast, and improve system behavior. SRE also employs formal SLIs and SLOs to help quantify availability targets based on business costs. SRE teams often serve as internal consulting partners across the broader engineering org, providing subject matter expertise in designing large-scale systems for reliability and evolutionary architecture. Combining SRE's relentless engineering focus with DevOps' collaborative blameless culture provides organizations with a potent blend to improve IT operations. This approach combines both the human and technical challenges that modern digital businesses demand to succeed.

DevOps processes and tools

DevOps represents a combination of cultural philosophies, practices, and tools aimed at increasing an organization's ability to deliver applications and services faster and with greater reliability. Critical practices like continuous integration and continuous delivery, along with source control, test automation, and monitoring tools, form the technical backbone enabling high-performing DevOps.

Version control systems like Git, GitHub, GitLab, and Bitbucket allow developers to collaborate on code in a common repository, track changes, catch defects early, and enable collaboration via pull or merge requests before pushing to the application mainline. Continuous integration incorporates frequent code commits into a shared mainline paired with automated builds and tests. CI tooling like Jenkins, CircleCI, TravisCI, TeamCity, or AWS CodeBuild spin up agent-based build workflows which can be triggered on every code merge to generate build artifacts. Tools like code linting and static code analysis during code push uncover quality issues that could impact reliability or security down the line if not promptly remediated. Integrating sophisticated test automation frameworks within the build process, allows performing unit and integration testing. You can also perform other tests like stress testing and security testing for the multiple configurations an application needs to support. This promotes the idea of *shifting-left* quality control processes in the release process. Catching issues early in the release cycle prevents problems from cascading and compounding.

Infrastructure provisioning and configuration tools help take environments and their dependencies out of human hands as much as possible and shift left into the development realm. Tooling such as Kubernetes, Docker, AWS CloudFormation, and Terraform allow version-controlled, repeatable infrastructure deployments, including underlying databases, networking, or storage. Containerization encapsulates and decouples what applications require to run successfully from the underlying operating environments. Options such as Ansible, Puppet, and Chef handle configuration management once resources are provisioned.

Deployment automation and continuous delivery pipelines pick up where continuous integration ends to streamline the releases. Jenkins, Spinnaker, AWS CodePipeline, and other CD platforms take applications through staging, canary, and production releases. Along the way, you can automate functional testing, performance testing, and approvals. Successful signals determine if applications pass onward through gates or need to be rolled back. Progressive delivery techniques like feature flags, blue-green deployments, and incremental rollout percentages allow granular control over downstream impacts an application change may cause.

Observability toolsets complete the delivery chain by verifying that applications operate with the desired quality of service after changes are released to users. Monitoring provides visibility into error rates, response times, and other metrics that impact user experience. Log management consumes streams of operational events, which contains information that is useful for troubleshooting any mishaps at application runtime. Tracing tools capture paths of communication between distributed services, which can help rapidly identify bottlenecks and sources of errors. Dashboards provide a view into trends over time and help distinguish healthy and unhealthy systems states. Alerting helps notify the right responsible personnel through the right channels when logs and metrics signify potential problems. When put together, this telemetry provides incident response capabilities and longer-term observation of trends to expose technical debts that may require architectural refactoring.

All these technical capabilities require careful cultural change within teams to gain traction. Organizations can become efficient in producing valuable change by aligning purpose across the broad. This is achieved by bringing together people participating in the software delivery to foster participative responsibility and decision models. This optimizes collaborative outcomes over local efficiencies. Small, empowered teams can be loosely coupled with external dependent teams through shared mental models and communication mechanisms. This helps achieve better efficiencies over large, centralized planning hierarchies, which can become an obstacle to agility. DevOps based solution delivery promotes the adaptability of decentralized authority with the coordination of validated learning cycles.

Metrics for DevOps

In *Chapter 1, Site Reliability Engineering Responsibilities,* we looked at the metrics that SRE measures their effectiveness on. DevOps also tries to standardize a set of metrics. **DevOps Research and Assessment (DORA)** metrics refer to a targeted set of measurements identified by DevOps industry research to strongly correlate with high performance. DORA outlines a data-driven way for engineering teams to evaluate and improve their DevOps capabilities.

Based on research conducted by technology professionals from different companies and verticals, it was observed that organizations excelling at certain key metrics have a significant edge in achieving their goals around productivity, profitability, market share, and employee satisfaction, as shown in the following figure:

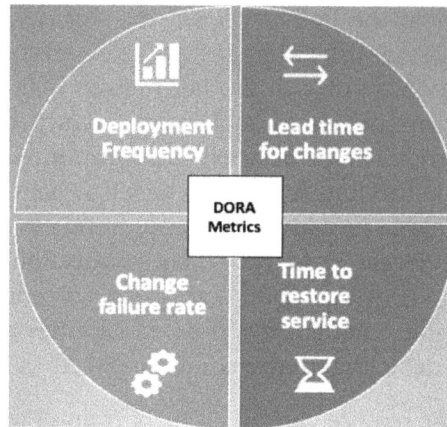

Figure 2.2: DORA metrics

The key DORA metrics that statistically indicate DevOps maturity include:

- **Deployment frequency**: It deals with how often code gets released into production environments. Organizations with the most mature DevOps capabilities deploy on-demand multiple times per day, whereas less mature organizations deploy between once per month and once every six months. Frequent releases require high test and deployment automation to maintain stability.

- **Lead time for changes**: Lead time for changes refers to the duration it takes new code commits to go from requirement identification to running in production. High-performing DevOps organizations have lead times of under one day, while lower-performing ones can have lead times of over six months. Rapid feedback loops and closer collaboration between development and operations teams enable this.

- **Time to restore service**: This measures how long it takes to recover from incidents. Mature DevOps organizations aim to have a mean time of under one hour to restore service (MTTR) compared to many hours for less mature organizations. Rigorous preparation for failures enables rapid incident response and recovery.

- **Change failure rate**: This is the percentage of deployments causing unexpected downtime or service degradation that requires remediation. The best-performing organizations have this percentage as close to 0% as possible, while lesser-performing organizations often exceed 30% failures from deficient testing, lack of automation, and immature release procedures.

Successful implementation of DORA metrics is enabled by cultural, architectural, and engineering capabilities of an organization. Here are some of the capabilities exhibited by high-performing DevOps organizations:

- Teams are cross-functional and share responsibilities. This enables better communication by giving them the ability to launch and maintain services more reliably with a broader perspective.

- There is a comprehensive test automation coverage built into unit, integration, performance, and security tests. This helps catch issues before production is impacted, and chances of outages are significantly reduced.

- Software changes flow from development to production rapidly in a robust manner with the help of automation provided by continuous delivery workflows.

- Changes are released in small incremental batches. This minimizes risk and enables faster feedback cycles.

- System health and performance are constantly monitored. This helps engineers understand operational status and detect incidents early.

- There is a shared vision, and goals established for the organization. This increases trust and empowers teams to deliver with motivation and velocity.

DORA provides data-driven metrics to define clear targets for your software teams to objectively assess and continually improve DevOps practices. It combines stable frequent deployments, rapid service restoration after incidents, and minimization of failed changes. These serve as markers of operational excellence, which can be quantified. Reliably achieving these markers delivers much better business agility and improved outcomes. Organizations can position themselves for competitive advantage by guiding culture transformation and systems thinking using these DevOps measures.

DORA and SRE

DORA highlights key metrics that serve as indicators of high performance and success in DevOps. The correlated measures from DORA, such as deployment frequency, lead time for changes, time to restore service, and change failure rate, directly influence availability and reliability outcomes, which are central to SRE. Thus, DORA metrics and capabilities provide a lens to examine parallels with disciplined SRE principles.

The following figure summarizes SRE responsibilities associated with each DORA metric:

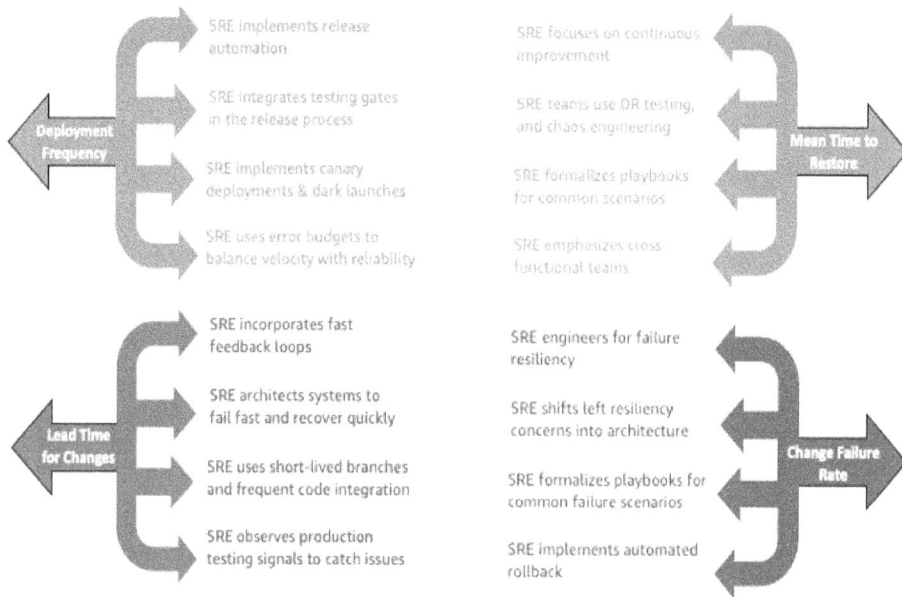

Figure 2.3: SRE responsibilities corresponding to DORA metrics

One of the findings by DORA is that elite DevOps organizations release code to production much more frequently - sometimes multiple times per day as compared to their lower-performing peers, who typically release changes in monthly, quarterly, or even longer cycles. This velocity and safety at scale are enabled by extremely high levels of test automation coverage, CI/CD pipeline automation, mature architecture patterns, and rigorous release procedures. High performing organizations have a lower change failure rate despite moving faster due to these scalable practices. They are also able to recover from production incidents faster than low performers through extensive investments in automated monitoring, logging, and incident response capabilities. SRE teams set quantitative SLOs designed to meet business outcomes. They use error budgets to determine an acceptable rate of production issues while aiming to keep the overall user-facing reliability high. Automated continuous delivery techniques like canary deployments, dark launches, or gradual rollout percentages limit the blast radius of changes that cause problems. SREs further build runbooks and playbooks documenting steps for the detection, diagnosis, and mitigation of incidents that still slip through preventative measures. Blameless post-mortems ensure failures become learning opportunities. Together, these SRE reliability practices allow exceptionally fast and safe code deployments at the highest scales.

The lead time for changes is measured as how long it takes from code commit to code successfully running in production. It is a key metric that separates high and low DevOps performers. Engineering teams who can complete entire cycles of planning requirements, coding, testing, and releasing changes into production environments in less than one day have a much higher likelihood of exceeding organizational performance goals, according to DORA. This is in contrast with low performers who take between 1-6 months for changes to funnel through stages while waiting for multiple approvals and handoffs with slow, disjointed cycles, brittle software delivery, and significantly delayed customer feedback. SRE incorporates principles around implementing fast feedback loops in IT operations. SREs architect systems to fail fast and recover fast when issues do occur. Shorter change lead times give prompt visibility into any availability, latency, or reliability issues from changes before small problems cascade into user-facing outages. This is applicable to both new feature rollout and regular runtime. SRE observes production testing signals to catch hotspots that require attention. Using short-lived branches combined and frequent code integration helps move changes faster. Post-mortems help with the detection and investigation steps for known classes of system failures to accelerate restoration. These SRE techniques optimize for fast feedback essential to stabilizing complex, rapidly evolving production systems.

DORA has also established that superior DevOps organizations are significantly better at recovering from incidents and outages, as reflected in their **mean time to restore service (MTTR)** metric. High performing DevOps organizations exhibit MTTR of under one hour compared to lower performing organizations, who often exceed 12 hours before service resumption. DORA data reveals a strong link between rapid MTTR rates and organizational performance. SRE teams focus intently on continuous improvement of failure detection and mitigation capabilities, even for complex systems. Techniques like disaster recovery testing, fire drills, game days, and chaos engineering exercises aim to uncover weaknesses in incident response through controlled injections of real-world impairment scenarios like CPU spikes, database outages, DNS failures, or overloaded APIs. SREs formalize the playbooks documenting steps for identification, containment, root causing, and issue resolution for common classes of system failures based on post-mortem analysis. Streamlining these runbooks and automating restoration procedures institutes a continuous incident learning culture. Both DORA metrics and SRE highlight that preparation for worst-case scenarios through advanced training separates resilient operations organizations from lower-achieving organizations. Cross-functional teams with unified urgency and well-established recovery mechanisms can overcome even the most chaotic of outages.

An elevated rate of failed deployments indicates that a team does not have the necessary checks in place to maintain reliable operations as changes are released continuously. DORA has observed less than 15% change failure rates for elite DevOps teams vs. 30% or higher for organizations on the other end of the scale. SRE treats the entire software delivery lifecycle itself as a system to engineer failure resiliency. Comprehensive version control, monitoring, testing at multiple levels, and staged rollout processes aim to fail fast and small. SRE believes in reliability not being an afterthought and must be shifted left in defining the system architecture.

DORA identifies a clear correlation between deployment failure rates and overall organizational effectiveness in DevOps transformations. Elite DevOps performers experience less than 15% of releases resulting in degraded service, unplanned downtime, or major reliability issues in production. In contrast, low-performing organizations, as measured by these business metrics, see over 30% of deployments incurring significant operational problems. A high failure rate points to deficient test automation, release procedures, rollback functionality, and cross-team collaboration. These gaps allow unintended changes or defects to cascade into customer-impacting incidents all too frequently. SRE treats the entire software delivery lifecycle itself as a complex system requiring continuous improvement to resilience failures early and often. SREs establish extensive unit, integration, load, and production testing framework coverage to catch issues pre-release. Canary rolls out are used to release incremental percentages of traffic to minimize the blast radius of new features before reaching full saturation. Observability measures provide visibility into system impacts when issues slip past preventative methods. Automated rollbacks are configured to be triggered by error rate or metrics thresholds to recover from outages. SRE recognizes that stability must be shifted left into the overall architecture to reduce the failure rate from deployments.

In summary, DORA metrics substantiate DevOps behaviors that enable stability, availability, and seamless iteration. This correlates very closely to the SRE principles that we have already learned about. Leading practices from DORA, such as deployment rates, align with and expand upon error budget-driven development and operational cycles. Monitoring time to restore and failure percentages highlights the delivery pipeline robustness that SREs architect.

They also substantiate key cultural and technical behaviors that directly enable stability, availability, and seamless iteration at the highest-performing IT organizations. These capabilities closely correlate with many SRE principles and practices we have learned about. DORA's examination of rapid restoration timelines and minimized failure percentages also spotlights the entire delivery pipeline robustness running from commitment to monitoring that SRE architectures specialize in fortifying for resilience.

As DORA metrics continue to mature and expand, they serve to validate that key priorities SREs have championed operationally for over a decade and also deliver superior business results when embraced properly. Measurements capturing system stability, feature velocity, and service continuity provide the necessary feedback loop for technology teams to continuously improve.

Conclusion

As modern internet-scale applications have become increasingly complex and distributed, DevOps and SRE have emerged to overcome the challenges of traditional siloed IT engineering models. DevOps encourages cultural alignment, shared ownership, and automation across the entire service delivery lifecycle. SRE incorporates systems thinking, data-driven management, and software engineering to create ultra-reliable services. Both disciplines offer impactful yet distinct approaches that organizations should consider tailored to their specific goals and culture. By learning from complementary philosophies, teams can form even stronger site operations capabilities over time.

In the next chapter, we will look at the options available for the implementation and automation of SRE tasks on AWS.

Points to remember

- DevOps focuses more on cultural collaboration and the speed of changes, while SRE addresses reliability, scalability, and balancing feature velocity of large, complex systems.

- DevOps emerged earlier to solve gaps between development and operations teams, while SRE was created later at internet-scale companies to handle the complexity of massive scale and frequent changes.

- DevOps encourages cross-functional upskilling across engineering teams, while SRE takes a more prescriptive approach with systematic processes.

- SRE applies more rigorous engineering practices, such as SLIs/SLOs and capacity planning, to meet the demands of today's production systems, building on the cultural elements of DevOps.

Multiple choice questions

1. **Which of the following best describes the main focus of DevOps?**

    a. Reliability and scalability of large complex systems

    b. Speed of software changes and cultural collaboration

    c. Balancing feature velocity with system stability

    d. Designing large-scale systems for reliability

2. **Which of the following led to the creation of SRE?**

    a. Solving gaps between development and operations teams

    b. Handling complexity of massive scale and frequent changes

    c. Breaking silos between engineering teams

    d. Meeting demands of today's production systems

3. **Which approach encourages cross-functional upskilling across broader engineering teams?**

    a. DevOps

    b. SRE

    c. Both encourage upskilling

    d. Neither encourage upskilling

4. **Which applies more rigorous engineering practices like SLIs/SLOs and capacity planning?**

   a. DevOps

   b. SRE

   c. Both apply the same level of rigorous practices

   d. Neither apply rigorous practices

Answers

1.	b.
2.	b.
3.	a.
4.	b.

Join our Discord space

Join our Discord workspace for latest updates, offers, tech happenings around the world, new releases, and sessions with the authors:

https://discord.bpbonline.com

CHAPTER 3
SRE on AWS

Introduction

In this chapter, we introduce the options available on AWS to perform SRE tasks. With the cloud-native options available on AWS, your SRE tasks can be automated more efficiently. We will understand how to use automation through engineering to ensure reliable operations, incident response, and recovery procedures. We will also be introduced to AWS services that we will be using in this book to automate operations and SRE tasks. Additionally, we will discuss how to lay the groundwork for efficient operation of AWS. This involves organizing your workloads by accounts and following well-architected recommendations from AWS.

Structure

This chapter will cover the following topics:

- Introduction to SRE practices on AWS
- Benefits of applying engineering to operations
- AWS services for operations and SRE practices
- Organizing for efficient operations on AWS

Objectives

By the end of this chapter, we will understand how AWS simplifies operations and SRE by providing native options to help you automate many common responsibilities. We will discuss the benefit of applying engineering discipline to operations and SRE tasks. We will also be introduced to services (discussed in detail in the subsequent chapters). Moreover, we will also discuss how to organize your workloads in a landing zone to ensure you have centralized governance and compliance capabilities.

Introduction to SRE practices on AWS

Amazon Web Services (**AWS**) provides you with a highly flexible and scalable public cloud to run your applications reliably. AWS delivers a range of services and tools to help build solutions with less effort and more efficiency than on-premises. This makes it suitable for organizations that aspire to establish an efficient SRE function. As SRE, the options available natively on AWS to simplify your tasks can feel both exciting and overwhelming. Knowing what is available and when to use them can help you navigate your AWS journey as SRE efficiently.

Real-world production systems require careful architectural planning and the implementation of operational practices on basic infrastructure to achieve extreme reliability at scale. Diverse workloads such as batch processing, enterprise applications, media streaming, e-commerce, and more run on AWS infrastructure reliably. These applications serve millions of customers, with billions of requests each day. SRE focuses on sustainably managing high scale, velocity, and complexity over the long-term immense growth of internet-scale systems. AWS offers an ideal foundation for implementing SRE methodologies with flexible and composable infrastructure components, which can be defined as software. This allows authoring scripts and code to orchestrate the software-defined infrastructure to accomplish various tasks, including many SRE responsibilities.

While AWS provides a highly reliable cloud infrastructure with built-in redundancy and fault tolerance, SREs must still implement additional resilience measures to fulfill their responsibilities under the **shared responsibility model**. AWS ensures the reliability of the underlying infrastructure like data centers, global connectivity and the physical hardware, but cannot account for how organizations specifically architect, deploy, and operate their applications within this infrastructure. Even with AWS's robust infrastructure, applications can still fail due to misconfiguration, software bugs, unexpected load patterns, or improper error handling. While AWS services offer several resilience features, they must be enabled and correctly configured. Some examples of this are multi-AZ deployments, auto-scaling, cross-region replication and setting up backups and recovery. The reliability of a cloud-based system is ultimately determined by how well both AWS and customer-side responsibilities are fulfilled, making it essential for SREs to implement comprehensive reliability measures despite AWS's underlying infrastructure reliability. The following figure depicts the shared responsibility model for resilience on AWS:

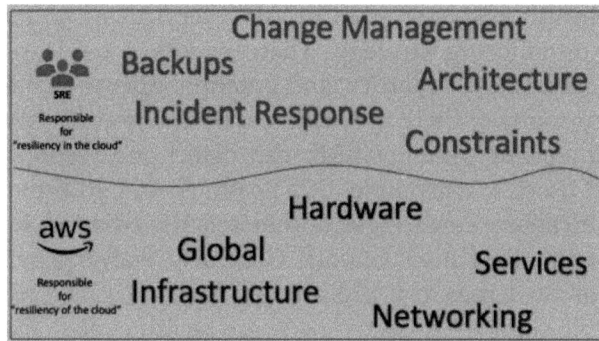

Figure 3.1: *Shared responsibility for resilience on AWS*

The following section looks at the different concerns that SRE needs to address while operating workloads on AWS. (In the subsequent sections, we will look at the services available on AWS to address these concerns):

- SRE needs to control access to new application features on AWS. This includes implementing custom traffic routing policies to roll out updates incrementally, as well as geographic or latency-based routing during incidents. To avoid performance issues and failures, SRE must deploy APIs while throttling call volumes. They shift traffic across primary and secondary backup clusters and use canary testing to assess the impact of new features. By configuring pre-production environments to mimic infrastructure, software versions, configurations, and even data, SRE enables realistic validation well before code reaches customers. By performing rigorous stress testing on systems by employing techniques like chaos engineering, SRE helps uncover weaknesses beyond what can be discovered from steady-state testing.

- SRE implements detailed telemetry to provide the observability required for timely incident identification and mitigation on AWS. They establish baselines to track key health indicators across all layers of the technology stack and surface them visually using dashboards. SRE uses granular custom application metrics to supplement out-of-the-box signals from AWS services and provide additional perspectives when necessary. They configure routing and aggregation of high-volume application and infrastructure logs to derive insights and analytics for isolating and troubleshooting issues. They further supplement metrics and logs with distributed tracing to gain visibility into inter-service application flows.

- SREs use proven distributed systems design patterns to build resilience against runtime failures, which can occur even within a highly reliable environment like AWS. For example, when transient exceptions temporarily disrupt event processing, SREs use dead letter queues to replay processing. They implement retry logic with back-offs when there is throttling and submit requests to try reprocessing them. Mechanisms like queueing and automated retries are among the several techniques in the SRE toolbelt, that can be employed for situations that require them.

- SREs leverage health events emitted by AWS services as an important indicator for their proactive monitoring strategy. These events provide real-time insights into service health, performance metrics, and potential operational issues across the AWS infrastructure supporting their applications. By integrating AWS health events with monitoring and alerting systems, SREs can detect and respond to anomalies before they impact end users. For example, EC2 health checks, RDS events, and AWS Health Dashboard notifications can trigger automated remediation workflows or alert on-call teams for immediate intervention. This early warning system enables SREs to implement automated recovery procedures, redirect traffic away from problematic resources, or scale capacity proactively. These health events also aid in post-incident analysis, helping teams understand failure patterns and implement preventive measures. By building operational procedures around AWS health events, SREs can maintain higher system reliability and reduce mean time to recovery when incidents occur.

- When things break, SREs need to act quickly and tactfully. Their first order of business is to understand what's broken and how it's affecting the users. This involves checking monitoring dashboards, recent alerts, and any error reports. The next step is to decide if this needs an immediate fix or if it requires a longer-term mitigation plan. This decision is usually based on how many users are affected and whether core business functions are down. During the incident, SREs work to both fix the immediate problem and keep stakeholders informed about what's happening. This might mean posting regular updates in an incident channel, sending emails to affected teams, or updating status pages. After the issue is mitigated, it is expected that SRE learns from it to improve their operational posture. SREs lead post-incident reviews where teams discuss what broke, why it broke, and how to prevent similar issues in the future. This is done in a blameless manner, with the intention of making the system better. These learnings then feed into improving monitoring, adding new automated fixes, or updating operation procedures to handle similar problems better next time.

Together, these proven SRE reliability capabilities allow cloud-hosted systems to survive disruptions by designing resilience upfront instead of reacting after the fact. With strong SRE controls in place, system behaviors can be made predictable even when there is volatility. Technical capabilities also must be supplemented with cultural capabilities. SRE employs blameless post-mortems to focus remediation efforts on systemic conditions causing outages rather than individuals. They learn from incidents and outages to identify root causes. They document troubleshooting and recovery steps, which can be codified into smooth procedures.

Benefits of applying engineering to operations

AWS provides a range of cloud services that allow you to run applications efficiently. By combining and integrating AWS services through software engineering approaches, you can unlock exponential capabilities for streamlining IT operations and implementing robust

SRE practices. Most AWS services provide native integration points with other services out-of-the-box. These native integration capabilities get operations teams started quickly with techniques like infrastructure as code. However, maintaining these largely static integrations and configurations may not be adequate as complexity scales. This can be addressed with more custom integration patterns.

The following are some of the benefits:

- AWS provides **software development kits** (**SDKs**) in several programming languages, enabling developers and SREs to build custom orchestration around AWS services. For example, you can write code to define dynamic behaviors based on incoming events and contextual variables instead of just static configuration. This allows advanced operations capabilities to evolve with changing application requirements and organizational goals over time. Most AWS services emit events detailing important lifecycle changes like deployment completions, auto-scaling actions, security findings, and more. Basic event-driven workflows let you trigger cross-service actions like logging events and sending notifications. However, more intricate event processing often requires writing custom code using AWS SDKs to handle events with arbitrary logic and contextual awareness. Operational tasks like automated incident response, health analysis across distributed systems, capacity forecasting and autoscaling, continuous validation pipelines and more all become programmable using code flexibly defining desired behaviors based on discrete runtime events.

- AWS services provide monitoring basics through metrics, logs, and minimal tracing, but focused operational excellence requires moving beyond basic telemetry data. Custom instrumentation through AWS SDKs exposes rich observability signals across your environments. For example, you can engineer code and publish custom metrics surfacing key business processes and application metrics mapped to SLIs, like order processing durations or e-commerce checkout flow measurements. You can mine deeper insights using advanced log routing, custom subscription filters, analytics, and machine learning techniques. Code extracts events or measurements into analytics for correlation and pattern detection that optimizes operations.

- AWS services inherently provide high security, but operational compliance requires additional safeguards. You can programmatically apply best practices across environments, resources, and changes by engineering security automation through code. Injecting security verification steps into CI/CD pipelines like static code analysis and container image scanning provides preventative quality gates ahead of production deployments. You can use security operations centers to automate incident response playbooks for mitigating threats through scripted remediation or containment actions against compromised resources.

- AWS services operate in a highly reliable and available manner. However, to achieve production grade resilience for complex multi-service applications, you need explicit patterns accounting for various failure modes. You can implement patterns like circuit breakers, bulkheads, load shedding, retries with exponential backoff, and queue-based idempotent processing in front of downstream systems to provide insulation from cascading failures. Deploying these higher-order resiliency measures through infrastructure as code and SDKs offers an architectural approach to fault isolation. Implementing self-healing capabilities like automated restarts, recovery, and rebalancing across fault domains can help return systems to safe states quickly. Techniques like chaos engineering can be further used to harden the resilience through controlled fault injection. SRE teams build comprehensive resiliency by continuously simulating failures, operationalizing failure learnings, and placing systemic safeguards against repeat outages.

- Continuous integration and continuous delivery pipelines increase release velocity and quality through process automation. You can streamline CI/CD on AWS at scale by using code to instrument pipelines to incorporate additional processes like repository scans, automated test suite execution, and artifact promotion across environments. Environment context can be injected into pipelines to dynamically provision short-lived infrastructure like building workers. You can further use release management layers with compliance controls to achieve approvals chaining, downtime coordination, and promotion criteria. Feature flags and canary configurations enable zero-downtime deploys without disrupting production operations. Using blue/green deployments, you can help balance risks across complex deployment transitions. Release engineering in SRE optimizes for velocity, quality, and governance across multiple delivery streams comprised of hundreds of pipelines and processes.

- SRE engineer infrastructure platforms to provide guardrails and self-service for application developers consuming cloud resources. These platforms abstract and optimize cloud services through standard configurations, APIs, tooling, and automated provisioning governed by policies. They implement quotas and service control constraints suitable for different trust boundaries between organizations. Engineering around SLIs and status monitoring can alert platform owners to health conditions to automatically trigger response scenarios. Change management workflows are baked into platforms to simplify cost management, compliance verification, and scheduling of routine actions.

- AWS services provide autoscaling capabilities to address varying capacity requirements for applications. They can be engineered to react to different dimensions of your application's scaling characteristics and account for burst conditions, ramp-up, steady peak loads, and ramp-down. SREs can instrument AWS environments to measure and extrapolate key scaling parameters. By using data analytics on captured telemetry, forecasting tools, and anomaly detection models can be applied to predict when resources are about to reach exhaustion. By using automated processes for scaling hot partitions, buffering, and throttling surge loads, SRE prepares for any unexpected demand spikes. Capacity engineering ensures availability and optimized resource allocation that matches demand. This avoids over or under-provisioning.

Cost management-focused engineering defines budgets, forecasts, and automated controls. This helps map technology spending to business value, which determines your business's profitability.

- While AWS continues providing powerful cloud service capabilities, building software to orchestrate, customize, and amplify those capabilities provides operational leverage beyond out-of-the-box functionalities of services. The principles of reliability engineering, release engineering, automated incident response, and infrastructure as code all prescribe combining AWS services with code to safely deliver highly available, secure, and scalable distributed systems.

By viewing operations through the lens of software engineering, organizations avoid simplistic cloud service configurations that may be unable to handle complexity at scale. Instead, they gain the automation of resilient self-service platforms, cost optimization engines driven by analytics, flexible release engineering processes, and layered defenses hardened by chaos testing. Human operators supplement automated workflows for governance and oversight rather than repeatedly fielding tactical issues.

AWS services for operations and SRE practices

AWS provides many cloud services that are perfectly suited for implementing SRE methodologies and capabilities. This section explores key AWS services through the lens of SRE, examining how they enable crucial areas like release management, observability, capacity planning, resilience engineering, and more. This book will not dive deep into all aspects of these services and does not intend to be a replacement for AWS official documentation for these services. Instead, the book will focus on the value of these services and provide examples of how you can make use of these services to achieve your SRE objectives.

AWS services can be used to accomplish a wide array of tasks. The following figure shows the services commonly employed for SRE tasks on AWS.

While this is not an exhaustive list, the services in the figure represent commonly utilized options for specific SRE tasks as follows:

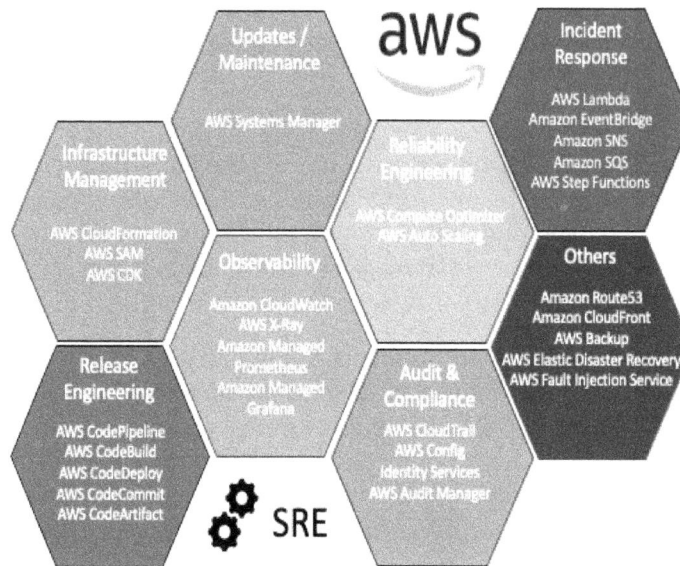

Figure 3.2: *AWS SRE services*

- **Infrastructure management:** SRE defines infrastructure as code for repeatability, ease of provisioning, and avoiding errors. **AWS CloudFormation** is a service that AWS offers to help define infrastructure in the form of JSON or YAML templates. With a CloudFormation template, you can create a stack, which is a collection of resources that are grouped as a unit. This usually represents the whole application or a logically separate portion of the application. CloudFormation support generally coincides with or very closely follows the release of any new service on AWS. This enables operations teams within organizations to start using IaC to script resources that make use of these services. CloudFormation allows you to establish dependencies between resources and control the order in which they are created. You can also implement security controls to ensure that the right users of your AWS environments can create, update, or delete resources using CloudFormation. Closely related to CloudFormation is the AWS **Serverless Application Model** (**SAM**). SAM is an extension of CloudFormation, which provides a shorthand IaC syntax optimized for serverless applications. We will look at CloudFormation in more detail in the upcoming chapters.

AWS Cloud Development Kit (CDK) provides a developer-centric approach to defining AWS resources as code. This helps use familiar programming languages like Python, TypeScript, Java, etc., to define AWS resources. The code is written with CDK compiled with *JSON/YAML* templates, is submitted to CloudFormation, and is used to create the resources. As CDK is similar to application code, it makes it easier to be tested with unit testing frameworks for that programming language.

- **Updates or maintenance:** AWS Systems Manager provides a valuable suite of tools for SRE. Systems Manager allows you to define maintenance windows and automate the process of ensuring consistent and timely patching across your resources. Additionally, it provides tools for gathering fleet inventory, running automated runbooks for incident response, and managing configurations. These are all crucial tasks for maintaining reliable and secure applications. AWS Systems Manager gives operations the ability to perform similar tasks across multiple resources together without the need to log into each host or VM directly. By streamlining these activities, the Systems Manager empowers SREs to focus on higher-level problem-solving and proactive infrastructure management. This translates to faster incident resolution, improved system uptime, and, ultimately, a more reliable and efficient cloud experience.

- **Release engineering:** SRE thrives on facilitating frequent updates and innovation. This is where release engineering-focused services on AWS come into play. These services automate the release pipeline, transforming manual processes into a smooth, efficient flow. Here are the services that you can use for this:

    o **AWS CodePipeline**: This fully managed service orchestrates the entire release pipeline, from code push to deployment. CodePipeline triggers automated builds, runs tests, and deploys your application to various environments.

    o **AWS CodeBuild**: This service builds your application code according to your specifications. CodeBuild integrates with your source control repository and runs build commands. CodeBuild automatically triggers a build whenever you push code changes, ensuring your application is ready for deployment.

    o **AWS CodeDeploy**: CodeDeploy service automates application deployments to various AWS targets like *Amazon EC2 instances, Amazon ECS clusters,* or *AWS Lambda* functions. Define deployment configurations and rollback strategies, and CodeDeploy handles the heavy lifting.

    o **AWS CodeArtifact**: This managed artifact repository service provides secure storage and management of your application code packages. You can integrate CodeArtifact with your build process, and it securely stores your build artifacts, making them readily available for deployments.

  By leveraging these AWS services, SREs can collaborate effectively with developers throughout the release process. SREs can define guardrails and automated tests within the pipeline, ensuring deployments meet security and performance standards. This promotes a culture of **continuous integration and continuous delivery (CI/CD)**, leading to faster innovation and a more reliable cloud experience.

- **Monitoring and observability:** Your AWS environment needs comprehensive monitoring and observability tools. These tools provide the visibility you need to identify potential issues, troubleshoot problems, and ensure the smooth operation of your applications and infrastructure.

The following is a breakdown of some key AWS services that empower you to see what is happening within your cloud:

○ **Amazon CloudWatch**: This service acts as your central hub for monitoring. CloudWatch collects and aggregates metrics (data points like CPU usage or network traffic) and logs. Logs represent detailed records of events within your resources. It uses dashboards to display resource utilization, performance data, and operational health in real-time. It also provides alarms, which automatically fire alerts based on anomalies or thresholds defined by SREs.

○ **Amazon X-Ray**: This service provides a view into application performance. X-Ray traces the path of a request as it flows through your application, allowing you to pinpoint bottlenecks, identify errors, and optimize performance. It provides a visual representation of your application's inner workings, helping you understand how different components interact and identify where optimizations can be made.

○ **Amazon Managed Grafana**: This service allows you to create interactive dashboards to visualize the data collected by CloudWatch and other monitoring tools. It will enable you to build customizable dashboards displaying key metrics and logs, which helps monitor your environment and quickly identify anomalies.

○ **Amazon Managed Service for Prometheus**: Prometheus is an open-source monitoring tool. This service provides a fully managed approach to leveraging Prometheus for collecting and storing metrics, specifically from containerized environments. It integrates Prometheus seamlessly with your AWS environment, providing necessary scaling, security, and management for monitoring containerized applications.

You gain a comprehensive view of your AWS environment by leveraging these tools. This empowers you to quickly pinpoint the root cause of performance problems or errors within your application or infrastructure. You can dive deeper into resource usage patterns and identify opportunities to scale up or down based on actual demand. Investing in a robust monitoring and observability strategy is crucial for any organization running on AWS. These tools empower you to maintain a healthy and efficient cloud environment, ultimately leading to a more reliable and cost-effective cloud experience.

• **Reliability engineering:** There are a few different services that help achieve reliability on AWS. This goes hand-in-hand with the concern of capacity planning, where you can utilize AWS Compute Optimizer to first right size your compute resources to ensure an adequate level of performance at a reasonable cost for a unit of work. In doing this, you may need to vertically scale your compute to achieve the right level of performance. However, when you have a surge of activity and the load increases proportionately, vertical scaling is no longer feasible. To rapidly perform additional work, you are better served by scaling capacity horizontally by adding additional resources that can absorb the load. AWS Auto Scaling provides the ability to scale compute based on metrics that are proportional to your application's load. AWS Auto Scaling works together with CloudWatch alarms to determine when metrics emitted by your application or services have reached a threshold, which requires adding more compute capacity to absorb the additional load.

On this opposite end, AWS Auto Scaling also gives the ability to save you costs by scaling in resources when the period of high activity is over. The same metric that enabled you to scale out to additional demand can be tracked to scale in resources. Additionally, Compute Optimizer may indicate that you are over-provisioned for the unit of work you are trying to perform. If the provisioned computing is not utilized appropriately, it helps you vertically scale down and reduce your spending. So, while reliability engineering focuses on ensuring continued operations with a certain level of performance, you also want to ensure that you achieve this while keeping your costs in control. Maintaining reliable system performance while optimizing for cost comprises a fundamental SRE consideration.

- **Incident response:** Incident response is achieved through a combination of multiple services on AWS. It goes together with monitoring and observability, which provides the signals that indicate the occurrence of an incident. This can come in the form of performance bottlenecks or outages observed through metrics and traces, error messages or API activity in the logs that indicate suspicious security behavior, or an event emitted by a service that indicates an incident. Events emitted by AWS services can be consumed and processed using *Amazon EventBridge*.

  When an incident is identified, SRE needs to determine its severity and decide on a course of action. Systems Manager also offers Ops Center and Incident Manager, where you can record your incidents. This allows an operator to view the incidents in a central place to analyze, prioritize, and determine the right action.

  The action could be notifying an email list or a group of people on your preferred communication tooling. Amazon SNS is a service that helps with this notification. Another incident response action could be to execute some code in response to the incident, which would perform a remedial action or a reversal of the situation that led to the incident. This is enabled by AWS Lambda, which allows you to run arbitrary code without having to pre-provision compute. When multiple actions need to be chained together, you can use AWS Step Functions to build an incident response workflow.

- **Traffic management:** Managing production traffic exposure for new application versions represents a key SRE focus area. AWS provides rich capabilities for safe deployment through incremental rollouts and failure isolation to minimize cutover risks. Services like Route 53, CloudFront and AWS Load Balancing offer granular traffic control through weighted routing policies, session stickiness, and custom request filtering rules. SREs define percentage-based deployment strategies ramping new versions from 0% to 100%. You can implement protection like static IP blocking and geographic isolation to safeguard user populations from blast radius. Traffic mirroring can be used to perform validations with near-real production traffic.

You can configure quick rollback options to restore previous baselines if issues emerge. CloudFront provides edge locations which can be used to extend advanced cache and traffic control policies to front door applications closer to end users. API Gateway provides corresponding capabilities for orchestrating API endpoint deployments through versioning, stages, and Canary release patterns. Traffic management capabilities empower SREs to model worst-case failure scenarios and adjust dynamically based on feedback signals like health metrics. Immense flexibility handles even the most complex requirements around load balancing, content routing, or zero-downtime migrations many teams struggle with in private data centers.

- **Audit and compliance:** Auditing, compliance validation, and security controls rank among the most critical ongoing SRE operational duties for protecting production availability and data integrity. AWS supplies a wide array of governance capabilities addressing these protection domains as follows:

    o **Amazon CloudTrail**: This service captures your API calls and related AWS account activity into event history for security analysis and operational auditing. This allows you to track user activity, troubleshoot issues, and achieve a compliant security posture. CloudTrail is the fastest way to find the answer to the question of what happened within your AWS environment, when it happened, and who took the action. CloudTrail integrates with Amazon CloudWatch Logs for storage, access control, and analytics.

    o **AWS Config**: Config Rules continuously track resource configurations against policies defined as code and help you trigger remediation actions on the non-compliant drift. For *PCI-DSS, HIPAA, NIST,* and other accreditation needs, AWS Config-managed rules help accelerate governance. It is also used by services such as *AWS Security Hub* to implement security controls and help surface security findings from your AWS environment.

    o **Identity services**: AWS **Identity and Access Management (IAM)**, IAM Identity Center, and Directory Services provide SREs centralized control planes governing authentication and authorization policies. You can use IAM Credential Reports to audit your IAM principals. This can help determine information such as the last password change time, MFA status, and time since the last access key rotation. IAM Access Analyzer helps achieve the least privilege security posture by validating permissions and continuously refining them by reducing access.

    o **AWS Audit manager**: It assists with the preparation of an ongoing audit cycle surrounding continuous compliance monitoring. It integrates with services such as AWS CloudTrail and AWS Config to accelerate evidence collection for specific compliance frameworks such as **Payment Card Industry Data Security Standard (PCI DSS)**, the **Service Organization Control 2 (SOC 2)**, and *FedRAMP*.

- **Data protection and disaster recovery:** AWS offers a comprehensive suite of data protection and disaster recovery services to safeguard your information and ensure business continuity. These services include options for automated backups across various AWS resources, from databases to file systems. Disaster recovery features enable you to replicate your data to separate regions or even back to your on-premises infrastructure, providing redundancy in case of outages. With tools for point-in-time recovery and granular restores, you can retrieve lost data with flexibility.

  By leveraging AWS data protection and disaster recovery services, you can achieve your **Recovery Point Objective (RPO)** and **Recovery Time Objective (RTO)** goals, minimizing downtime and data loss. AWS Backup, AWS Elastic Disaster Recovery, and AWS Application Recovery Controller help you build self-healing recovery assurances for entire application stacks or composite multi-tier resources. You can implement automated backup and DR scheduling, drift detection, and runbook executions to handle major disruptions ranging from corruption, deletion, or complete data center outages. Powered by these self-preservation capabilities, your applications can withstand disruptive real-world situations. SREs establish self-healing guardrails that provide higher levels of uptime and availability that align with SLOs.

- **Chaos engineering:** While observability provides awareness of your system's health and functioning, chaos engineering takes a more disruptive approach to pre-emptive operations improvement. AWS **Fault Injection Simulator (FIS)** exposes a broad range of actions for intentionally disrupting resources to assess resilience. It allows you to simulate various failure conditions with services like *EC2, EBS volumes, network, and Amazon RDS*. SREs validate resiliency assumptions, capacity planning tolerances, and failure mitigation responses through controlled failure injection. Security teams simulate data breaches, measuring containment procedures. Developers embed insights into improving application architecture, configuration, and monitoring. From pre-production sandboxes to production drills, chaos engineering on AWS proactively and continuously safeguards against systemic weaknesses.

In this section, we discussed AWS services, which can be used to perform SRE tasks that address various concerns. If you expected to see a service covered above and did not see it, it is not by oversight. AWS offers over 200 services as of this writing, and there is a possibility that many of these services can be used for performing SRE tasks. What we have covered above represents the most regular set of services to perform SRE tasks of a certain type. Some services, like Amazon CloudWatch, AWS System Manager, AWS Lambda, Amazon EventBridge, etc., are so versatile they can be used in multiple ways to perform a range of tasks. It is thus important to understand that how you use AWS services to perform your SRE tasks will completely depend on your specific needs. This book explores a few different patterns that have proved successful with some of the services we have discussed above. You do not need to restrict your SRE implementation to only what this book describes. Finding the right solution for your needs is always a good idea, as well as finding creative ways to utilize these services.

AWS equips SRE teams with a comprehensive portfolio of services supporting the operational pillars underpinning reliable, secure, and compliant systems. From delivery automation and traffic control to observability and capacity optimization, SREs derive powerful capabilities atop AWS infrastructure. Various engineering techniques utilizing these services further elevate the resilience of these AWS-hosted applications to withstand the intense demands of global internet-scale operation. With services continuously expanding and maturing, SREs creatively apply them in novel combinations and tailor solutions to your unique organizational needs around reliability. Organizations that take advantage of these building blocks and engineering techniques use technology efficiently to achieve their business outcomes.

Organizing for efficient operations on AWS

For enterprises migrating to AWS, it is often easy to fall into the trap of creating all your resources in a single AWS account. It might seem simple initially, but this can be disadvantageous for a few reasons. This approach can quickly become unwieldy and introduce security risks. If a single account is compromised, all the resources in that account could be exposed. This can be especially damaging if the account contains sensitive data or critical applications. As the number of resources in an account grows, managing and tracking them becomes more challenging. You run the risk of constantly running up against the account level service quotas, and some of these can have limits that cannot be increased by contacting AWS support.

The foundation of efficient AWS operations rests on isolating workloads. This essentially means creating boundaries between different applications or functionalities within your environment. You can achieve workload isolation on AWS in a few different ways.

The following are some of the methods:

- **IAM users and roles:** This approach involved achieving granular control with IAM By defining specific users and roles with permissions tailored to specific application needs. This ensures developers only have access to resources they need for their projects, enhancing security. However, managing a large number of users can be time-consuming and requires

- **Amazon Virtual Private Cloud (VPC):** VPCs help you create logically isolated networks within the AWS cloud. You can spin up multiple VPCs for development, testing, and production across your different applications, ensuring traffic from one VPC doesn't interfere with another. This approach offers better security and network control but requires additional configuration overhead.

- **AWS resource groups**: AWS resource groups allow you to group resources by tags. You can group resources based on function (e.g., web server group) or application (e.g., e-commerce application resources). This enables easy identification, management, and application of policies across related resources. While this is not technically isolating workloads, it can greatly help manage your resources.

- **Accounts:** This approach proposes using separate AWS accounts for different purposes. This offers clear segregation, for example, a development account for building and testing, a staging account for pre-production environments, and a production account for live applications. This is a highly effective approach and works very well in most situations. However, managing multiple accounts can become cumbersome, especially for large organizations.

- **AWS Organizations**: This approach simplifies and streamlines workload segregation by accounts. This managed service allows you to create a hierarchical structure across multiple accounts. This enables easier management and helps enforce centralized policies across accounts. It is ideal for large organizations with complex deployments but requires careful planning and understanding of its functionalities.

Choosing the most suitable method depends on your specific needs. The key is to achieve a balance between security, manageability, and cost-effectiveness. Structuring your AWS environment for efficient and secure operations paves the way for a smoother SRE.

Let us discuss AWS Organizations in detail. As your AWS footprint expands, managing multiple accounts requires careful planning. AWS Organizations helps with multi-account management with the features that it provides.

The following are its advantages:

- **Simplified account management**: It helps you create new accounts within your Organization with a few clicks, eliminating the need to manually provision and configure them. This streamlines the onboarding process for new projects or teams. You can also invite any existing accounts to your organization.

- **Centralized policy management**: It allows you to define security policies using **Service Control Policies (SCPs)**. SCPs do not grant any permissions but are used to set limits on permissions available to IAM principals within individual, **organizational units (OUs)** and accounts. You can configure these policies to automatically apply to all accounts within the hierarchy, ensuring consistent security standards across your environment.

- **Cost allocation and billing**: It enables you to consolidate your AWS bill under a single Organization payer account. This simplifies cost tracking and allocation to specific departments or projects within your organization.

- **Simplified resource sharing**: It enables resources in one account to be accessed by applications in another account within the organization. This facilitates collaboration between teams and allows for efficient resource utilization. You can share your savings instruments, such as Savings Plans and Reserved Instances, across your accounts within your organization.

Implementing AWS Organizations fosters a well-organized and secure cloud environment and lays the foundation for streamlined operations. AWS Control Tower further acts as the mission control for your AWS environment. This managed service builds on top of organizations, providing additional automation and governance capabilities. To setup Control Tower, you need to designate a management account, which is the payer account for your organization. In addition to this, you also start off with an AWS account for logs called Log Archive account and an AWS account for your Audit needs.

This results in a multi-account step as follows:

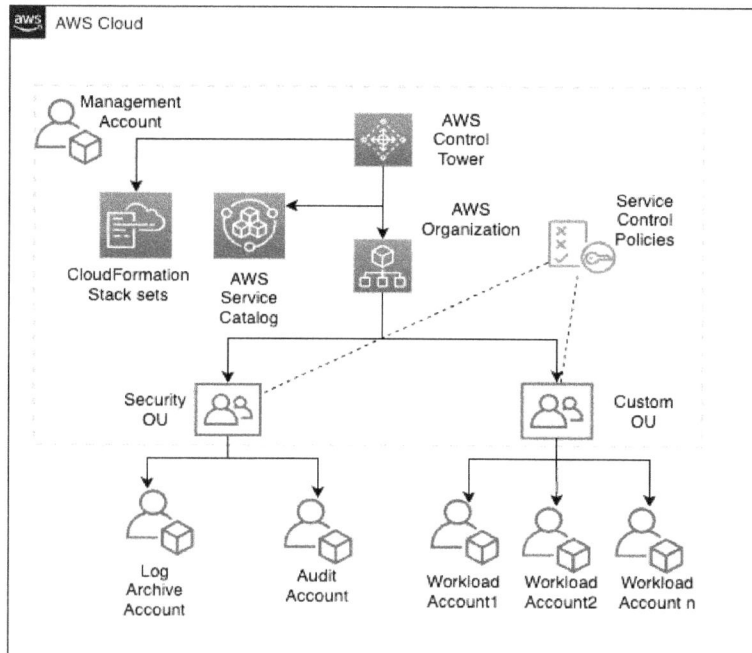

Figure 3.3: AWS Control Tower Account Structure

As you can see in *Figure 3.3*, it is common to organize your AWS accounts in your organization by organizational units or OUs. AWS Control Tower recommends the name Security OU to hold your log archive and audit accounts. Besides this foundational Security OU, you can create other OUs that can be used to hold your workload specific accounts. Although the figure depicts only one additional OU with the name Custom OU, this name is something you can pick and you can have more OUs which you can name based on your organizational structure.

The following are some examples of common OUs:

- *Sandbox OU* to hold accounts for individual developers. This enables developers to learn and experiment with AWS services within fixed spending limits.

- *Workload OU* holds accounts for specific workloads. Each of your major workload can be its own OU, within specific accounts for Dev, Production and any other lifecycle stages you choose to have accounts for. It is a good practice to separate your production workloads from your non-production workloads.

- *Policy staging OU* is used to test SCPs by applying it to accounts in a safe manner without impacting any workload accounts.

- *Shared services OU* is used to hold accounts specific to cross cutting infrastructure services such as deployment, management etc.

- *Suspended OU* can be used to hold accounts which have been closed and are waiting to be cleaned up.

The Control Tower elevates your cloud operations as follows:

- **Automated controls**: Control Tower allows you to define automated checks and validations against your organization's security and compliance policies. It helps you define rules that automatically flag any account that is non-compliant with the set of controls that Control Tower comes preconfigured with. This proactive approach empowers SREs to identify and address potential issues before they can lead to major problems.

- **Landing zone automation**: Landing zone is a term that refers to a well-architected multi-account setup on AWS. Control Tower takes landing zones to the next level by automating their deployment and enforcement. This eliminates manual configuration errors and ensures consistent security across your entire environment, freeing up valuable SRE time for more strategic initiatives.

- **Standardized account creation**: Control Tower streamlines account provisioning and management. Using the account factory, you can provision accounts from Control Tower, which are preconfigured with baselines customized for your needs.

- **Audit logging and reporting**: Control Tower provides comprehensive audit logs detailing all actions taken within your organization. This empowers SREs to track changes, investigate potential security incidents, and demonstrate compliance with regulations. It enables logs for every account creation, policy change, or resource provisioning within your organization. This level of transparency allows SREs to maintain a secure and accountable cloud environment.

By leveraging Control Tower, SREs gain a powerful tool for automating governance, enforcing security best practices, and ensuring compliance across their entire AWS landscape. This translates to less time spent on manual configuration tasks, faster incident response, and a more proactive approach to maintaining a healthy and secure cloud environment. Speaking to the cloud operations leader at a company who recently implemented AWS Control Tower, they wish they had done this much sooner. Having spent a few years managing infrastructure in the cloud, AWS Control Tower significantly boosted their ability to maintain compliance across accounts and apply targeted controls to accounts based on their importance to the business. Ultimately, a well-organized AWS environment fostered by account segregation, Organizations, landing zones, and Control Tower empowers SREs to focus on their core responsibilities: ensuring the high availability, performance, and scalability of your cloud applications. This translates to a more reliable and efficient cloud experience for your entire organization.

Conclusion

AWS provides you with a range of services that enable you to perform SRE tasks with ease. This chapter provided you with an introduction to applying SRE practices on AWS. We discussed how we could enhance the capabilities offered by individual services with custom code to orchestrate these services for achieving more complex objectives. We understood the benefits of applying engineering principles to operations. Next, we briefly introduced the important AWS services for operations and SRE tasks. We also looked at how we can organize our workloads on AWS for efficient operations and the services available on AWS to help with this.

Note: **The examples covered in this book do not use AWS Organizations and AWS Control Tower with the intent of keeping the examples simple. This will help you follow along with a single AWS account.**

However, in a real-world scenario, you will likely need a multi-account setup powered by AWS Organizations and possibly AWS Control Tower. The book will include notes about where it makes sense to use a separate account or a specific AWS Organization concept, such as SCPs, to accomplish a particular task that we are working on, but our examples will remain focused on working within a single account.

In the next chapter, we will discuss infrastructure as code, using our example workload.

Points to remember

- AWS provides native services and tools to help build solutions with less effort and more efficiency than on-premises environments, making it suitable for organizations to establish an SRE function.

- Engineering techniques using AWS services can further elevate the resilience of applications hosted on AWS infrastructure to withstand the intense demands of internet-scale operations.

- Key AWS services like *Amazon CloudWatch, AWS Systems Manager, AWS Lambda,* and *Amazon EventBridge* enable capabilities for delivery automation, traffic control, observability, and optimization, which SRE teams can utilize.

- Using separate AWS accounts isolates different workloads, such as development, staging, and production environments. Each account has independent resources and access controls.

- Organizing workloads using AWS Organizations and AWS Control Tower helps achieve centralized governance and compliance.

Multiple choice questions

1. **What is one key benefit of applying engineering to operations on AWS?**

   a. Automating many common operational responsibilities

   b. Achieving centralized governance and compliance

   c. Introducing new services and tools

   d. Building solutions with less effort

2. **Which AWS service helps you gain visibility into inter-service flows for troubleshooting?**

   a. AWS Lambda

   b. AWS CloudTrail

   c. AWS X-Ray

   d. Amazon EC2

3. **Which among these is a legitimate approach to segregate workloads on AWS?**

   a. Using a different S3 bucket for each workload

   b. Separating resources by regions

   c. Segregating workloads by time zones

   d. Using different AWS accounts for workloads

4. **Which among these is a benefit provided by AWS Control Tower?**

   a. Automated controls

   b. Reduced costs

   c. Increased reliability

   d. Better performance

Answers

1.	a
2.	c
3.	d
4.	a

Join our Discord space

Join our Discord workspace for latest updates, offers, tech happenings around the world, new releases, and sessions with the authors:

https://discord.bpbonline.com

CHAPTER 4
Infrastructure as Code

Introduction

In this chapter, we will be introduced to the concept of **infrastructure as code** (**IaC**) and how you can achieve this on AWS. IaC is an important operations concern in the cloud. AWS offers services that allow you to define your cloud resources as code. We will also be introduced to **AWS CloudFormation** and its capabilities. We will cover AWS **Cloud Development Kit** (**CDK**) and how this offers a way to define your IaC using familiar programming languages. We will briefly look at the AWS **Serverless Application Model** (**SAM**) and how this improves the IaC experience for serverless applications. Hashicorp's Terraform is a popular IaC tool that is not native to AWS but allows you to define AWS resources as code, too. We will introduce Terraform and how this can be another option to consider for your IaC needs. We will conclude the chapter by automating the infrastructure for our sample workload.

Structure

The chapter covers the following topics:

- Benefits of automating infrastructure as code
- AWS CloudFormation basics
- Automating infrastructure for our sample workload

- Using Cloud Development Kit

- AWS Serverless Application Model

- Terraform

Objectives

By the end of this chapter, we will understand the concept of IaC and its benefits. We will understand the different options for IaC available to define your infrastructure on AWS as code and the considerations in making your choice. Will we begin by looking at AWS CloudFormation and its features. Next, we will work through our first practical example in this book by defining the infrastructure for our sample workload architecture as code. We will also look at options such as CDK, SAM and Terraform as alternatives to working CloudFormation directly.

Benefits of automating infrastructure as code

IaC is a practice that involves managing and provisioning infrastructure resources such as virtual machines, networks, and storage through code and configuration files rather than through manual processes. This is an important advantage of running workloads in the cloud. By defining your resources as software code, you gain several benefits. These benefits can have a significant impact on the efficiency, security, and scalability of your organization's infrastructure.

In this section, we will explore some of the key benefits of IaC and why it is becoming an essential tool for organizations of all sizes, as follows:

- **Consistency and reusability**: IaC enables you create consistent and reusable infrastructure configurations. By defining infrastructure configurations as code, you can easily reuse configurations across different environments, such as development, testing, and production. This consistency and reusability can help reduce errors and improve the overall efficiency of infrastructure management.

- **Version control and collaboration**: One of the primary benefits of IaC is that it gives you the ability to manage infrastructure configurations using version control systems. This allows your teams to collaborate on infrastructure configurations and track changes over time. With IaC, you can use Git or other version control tools to manage your infrastructure configurations in a manner very similar to how you would manage your application code. This makes it easier to collaborate and rollback changes if necessary.

- **Automation and orchestration**: IaC helps you automate and orchestrate infrastructure provisioning and configuration management tasks. By defining infrastructure configurations as code, you can automate the process of deploying and configuring infrastructure resources, such as virtual machines, databases, networks, and storage. This saves time and reduces the risk of errors while improving the overall efficiency of infrastructure management.

- **Improved security**: IaC can improve the security of your organization's infrastructure by providing a centralized and controlled way to manage access to infrastructure resources. By defining access controls and security policies as code, teams can ensure that only authorized users have access to sensitive infrastructure resources. This can help reduce the risk of security breaches and improve the overall security posture of your organization.

- **Scalability and agility**: IaC can help you scale your infrastructure more quickly and easily. By defining infrastructure configurations as code, you can easily scale their infrastructure up or down to meet changing business needs. When you need to quickly stand-up new infrastructure resources to respond to a business need, it is easier and faster to do it with IaC. This helps you respond more quickly to changing market conditions and customer demand.

- **Reduced downtime and improved availability**: IaC can help reduce downtime and improve the availability of your infrastructure. By automating the process of deploying and configuring infrastructure resources, you can quickly and easily recover from failures or outages. This can help improve the overall reliability and availability of your organization's infrastructure.

- **Improved compliance and governance**: IaC can help you improve your compliance and governance posture by providing a centralized and controlled way to manage infrastructure resources. By defining compliance policies and procedures as code, you can ensure that infrastructure resources are configured and deployed in compliance with regulatory requirements and organizational policies.

- **Cost savings**: IaC can help you reduce the costs of managing and maintaining infrastructure resources. By automating the process of deploying and configuring infrastructure resources, you can reduce the cost of manual labor and improve the overall efficiency of infrastructure management.

- **Improved collaboration and communication**: IaC can improve collaboration and communication between teams by providing a centralized and controlled way to manage infrastructure resources. With IaC, your teams can easily share and collaborate on infrastructure configurations, improving communication and collaboration between teams.

- **Better visibility and monitoring**: IaC provides better visibility and monitoring of your organization's infrastructure resources. By defining IaC, you can easily monitor changes to infrastructure resources, improving visibility and control over the infrastructure.

IaC offers numerous benefits for organizations of all sizes and this practice has started to become a necessary aspect of operating in the cloud. The alternative to this is creating/updating resources by clicking links and buttons in the AWS Console, also referred to as *ClickOps*. While ClickOps can artfully handcraft precious infrastructure snowflakes, this is akin to creating your favorite recipe from memory. The exact ingredients can be disproportionate, and results vary with each attempt. In the real world, this approach proves labor-intensive, unpredictable, and error prone. By adopting IaC practices, you can improve the efficiency, security, and scalability of your infrastructure while also reducing costs and improving collaboration and communication between teams.

The following figure shows the IaC options for your AWS environment. Other options exist too, but the ones represented in the following figure are the most common:

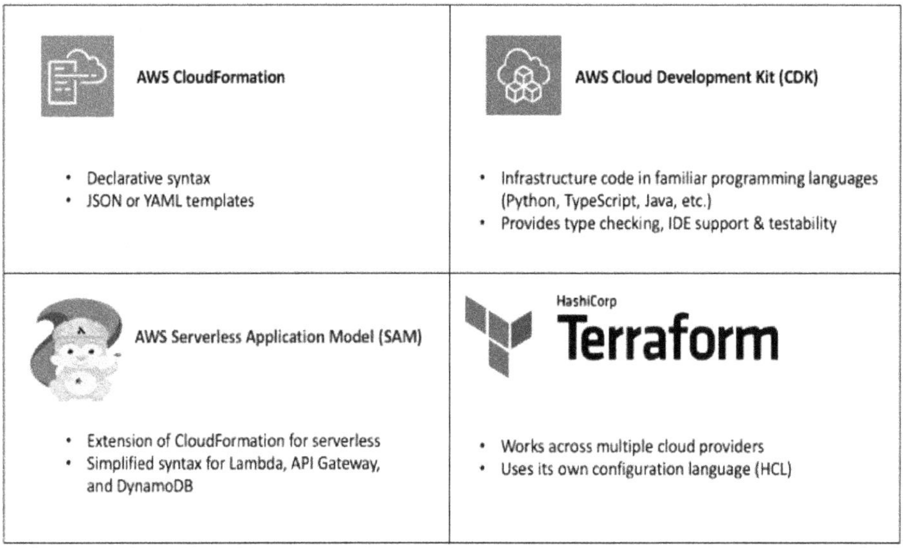

Figure 4.1: IaC options for your AWS environment

AWS CloudFormation

AWS CloudFormation is a powerful service offered by AWS, that enables users to create and manage AWS resources. You can manage something as simple as a single AWS resource to complex applications involving multiple services across regions. There is no additional cost to using CloudFormation. You only pay for the costs associated with the resources you create with it. This section will provide a detailed overview of AWS CloudFormation, including its features, benefits, and guidelines you can employ while using it.

The following are some features of AWS CloudFormation:

- **Templates**: CloudFormation templates are YAML or JSON files that define the structure and configuration of a stack. Templates describe your AWS resources and their properties. Templates can be used to create stacks in a repeatable and consistent manner, making it easier to manage and update infrastructure across multiple environments. By using templates, you can version control your infrastructure and quickly and repeatably replicate your infrastructure stack. CloudFormation is also useful for moving between lifecycle stages, like development and production. You can recreate the stack, but name it for its intended purpose. If your workload needs to be deployed to another region, you can easily and consistently set this up with your CloudFormation templates. Your templates will include your resource definitions once, but this can be used to create a stack in another region to provision the same resources.

- **Stacks**: A stack is a collection of related AWS resources which are created, updated, or deleted together, as a single unit. The resources in a stack are defined by the AWS CloudFormation template for the stack. CloudFormation creates or deletes the stack resources as required. To create, update, or delete a set of related resources, you can create, update, or delete the corresponding stack. The stack's resources are defined by using a CloudFormation template.

- **Provisioning**: CloudFormation's provisioning capabilities help specify how your resources should be created or updated. Dependencies between your resources is automatically managed by CloudFormation during provisioning. This feature ensures that resources are created in a consistent and predictable manner, reducing the risk of errors or conflicts. Stack resources created by AWS CloudFormation are treated as atomic. All resources must be created or deleted successfully for the stack to be considered provisioned.

- **Stack updates**: When you need to make changes to a stack's resources or modify its settings, you can update the stack without deleting and creating a new stack. CloudFormation updates only the modified resources by comparing the submitted changes with the current state of your stack. The update process does not impact any resources that have not changed, so they continue to run without disruption. AWS CloudFormation picks from these update behaviors for updated resources, depending on which property is updated for a given resource type, *Update with No Interruption*, *Updates with Some Interruption*, or *Replacement*. For updates that result in replacement and interruption, it is important to prepare to ensure continuity in operating your application and minimize disruption for the end user. How you prepare will depend on the resource type. For example, if the update results in a database instance being replaced, you would take a snapshot, handle any interruption to the application, and restore the snapshot to the new instance.

There are two methods for updating stacks with AWS CloudFormation:

- o **Direct update**: For directly updating a stack, you submit changes, and CloudFormation deploys them immediately. This option works well when you want to quickly deploy updates.

o **Change sets**: Change sets allow you to preview changes that will be applied to your stack by CloudFormation. This gives you the opportunity to ensure that your updates won't cause unintended consequences. To create and manage change sets, you can use the CloudFormation console, AWS CLI, or CloudFormation API. Change sets do not guarantee a successful stack update, as they do not check for account limits, unsupported resource updates, or insufficient permissions. If an update fails, AWS CloudFormation attempts to roll your resources back to their original state.

- **Rollbacks**: CloudFormation provides a rollback feature that enables you to undo changes to a stack in the event of an error or unexpected outcome. This feature ensures that users can quickly recover from mistakes and maintain a consistent state of their infrastructure. When a resource cannot be created, CloudFormation performs a rollback on the stack creation by default. You can, however, configure the stack failure options to preserve successfully provisioned resources. This allows you to retry the failed stack creation or update. This is also helpful in troubleshooting stack creation issues. Using rollbacks can help reduce the risk of errors and conflicts and make it easier to maintain and update infrastructure.

- **Security**: CloudFormation integrates with IAM for security. You can control what your users can do with AWS CloudFormation. In addition to the actions associated with CloudFormation, you can also specify which resources can be accessed using the service. The permissions that users have to create any AWS resource directly are the same permissions they have when they use CloudFormation to perform any actions. It provides a secure way to create and manage AWS resources, ensuring that resources are created and updated in a secure and compliant manner.

Automating infrastructure for our sample workload

Now that we understand how CloudFormation works, let us use it to automate the infrastructure of our sample application. For this, we will provision and configure the stack resources using an AWS CloudFormation template. Templates can be formatted in JSON or YAML. We will be using YAML as an example. In *Chapter 1, Site Reliability Engineering Responsibilities,* we looked at the high-level architecture of our sample workload. We will now flesh out the services that make up this architecture and define the resources for it using AWS CloudFormation.

The following figure depicts the solution architecture for our example workload:

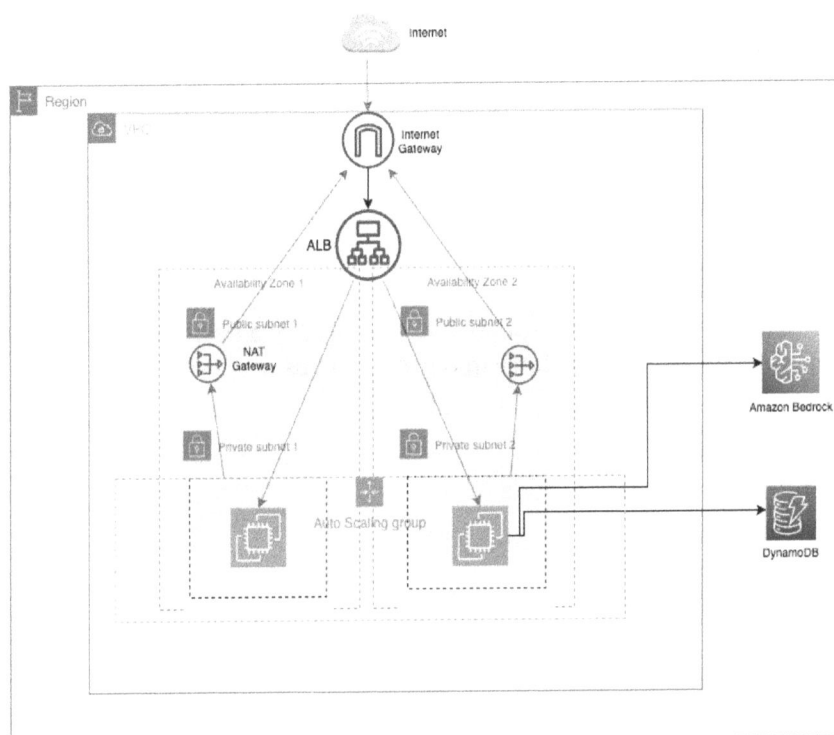

Figure 4.2: *Solution architecture for our example workload*

Let us begin with a quick summary of this architecture. We need an application that takes user inputs, processes information, and displays the output. We will use EC2 instances to provide the compute for this application. The EC2 instances are deployed into private subnets in a VPC in an auto scaling group. An Application Load Balancer allows the application to be accessible over the internet from a browser. The application's data store is provided using an Amazon DynamoDB database. We also use Amazon Bedrock, a generative AI service on AWS, which allows you to quickly perform tasks such as summarization of user reviews and sentiment analysis.

Let us now understand how you can use CloudFormation to set up your infrastructure. You should try deploying this CloudFormation template in your own AWS account to see this in action. You may pick a t3.micro instance to keep your costs low, as this template creates two load-balanced EC2 instances. There are also costs associated with the Application Load Balancer, NAT Gateways, and DynamoDB table created as part of this template.

The starter CloudFormation template for the aforementioned architecture in YAML format is as follows. We will update this template as we introduce new services in the subsequent chapters. We will look at each section of this template definition after introducing the template here. We have omitted sections of the CloudFormation YAML here for brevity. (The complete code will be made available as part of the GitHub repository accompanying this book.)

We begin the template definition with the optional **AWSTemplateFormatVersion** and **Description** values. More information about **AWSTemplateFormatVersion** follows later. Description is useful to provide an understanding of what infrastructure this CloudFormation template is defining, as shown:

```
AWSTemplateFormatVersion: "2010-09-09"
Description: "Load balanced autoscaled EC2 instances in a VPC with DynamoDB"
. . .
```

Next, we can include the **Parameters** section. You can define one or more parameters that will be used in other places within the template. One example of a parameter we have determined is **InstanceType**, which we will use later in our **Resources** section.

```
Parameters:
  InstanceType:
    Description: EC2 instance type
    Type: String
    Default: t3.micro
    AllowedValues:
      - t3.micro
      - t3.small
      - t3.medium
. . .
```

The **Mappings** section can optionally follow to include a lookup option for values that can change conditionally based on variations such as AWS Regions. We use it here to create a map of **Amazon Machine Image** (**AMI**) for different regions to which we can deploy our workload. If the AMI Ids have changed when you run this example, you can update the AMI ids in your mappings section.

```
Mappings:
  RegionAMIMap:
    us-east-1:
      AMI: ami-0a1179631ec8933d7
    us-east-2:
      AMI: ami-080e449218d4434fa
    us-west-2:
      AMI: ami-086f060214da77a16
. . .
```

The **Resources** section, which is the only mandatory section in a CloudFormation template, follows next. This section includes the definition of AWS resources and any custom resources that you need for your workload. This section will reference parameters and mappings you may have defined in the template.

Our **Resources** section begins with the VPC definition. The VPC includes other resources such as security groups, subnets, and NAT gateways, which are not shown here, but you will find them in the full version of this code.

```
Resources:
  #VPC
  VPC:
    Type: AWS::EC2::VPC
    Properties:
      CidrBlock: 10.0.0.0/16
      EnableDnsSupport: true
      EnableDnsHostnames: true
      InstanceTenancy: default
      Tags:
        - Key: Name
          Value: !Ref AWS::StackName
```

. . .

We follow this by defining the building blocks of the auto scaling group, such as the launch template, the instance profile, the IAM role associated with it, and the auto scaling group itself.

```
  # Launch Template for the Auto Scaling Group
  ASGLT:
    Type: AWS::EC2::LaunchTemplate
    Properties:
      LaunchTemplateName: "ASG_LaunchTemplate"
      LaunchTemplateData:
      ImageId: !FindInMap [RegionAMIMap, !Ref "AWS::Region", AMI]
      IamInstanceProfile:
        Name: !Ref AppEc2InstanceProfile
      InstanceType: !Ref InstanceType
      NetworkInterfaces:
        - DeviceIndex: 0
          AssociatePublicIpAddress: false
          Groups:
            - !Ref WebServerSG
          DeleteOnTermination: true
```

```yaml
    UserData:
      Fn::Base64: !Sub |
        #!/bin/bash
        yum update -y
        yum install -y httpd
        systemctl start httpd
        systemctl enable httpd
        echo "<h1>Temporary Content</h1>" > /var/www/html/index.html
    TagSpecifications:
      - ResourceType: instance
        Tags:
        - Key: App
          Value: Sample
AppEc2InstanceProfile:
  Type: 'AWS::IAM::InstanceProfile'
  Properties:
    InstanceProfileName: AppEc2InstanceProfile
    Roles:
      - !Ref AppEc2Role
AppEc2Role:
  Type: 'AWS::IAM::Role'
  Properties:
    AssumeRolePolicyDocument:
      Version: 2012-10-17
      Statement:
        - Effect: Allow
          Principal:
            Service: ec2.amazonaws.com
          Action: 'sts:AssumeRole'
    RoleName: AppEc2Role
    Description: Allows EC2 instances to call AWS services on your behalf.
    ManagedPolicyArns:
      - ' arn:aws:iam::aws:policy/AmazonSSMManagedInstanceCore'
    Tags:
      - Key: Name
        Value: app-ec2-role
```

```
ASG:
  Type: AWS::AutoScaling::AutoScalingGroup
  Properties:
    MinSize: 2 # Set minimum number of instances to 2
    MaxSize: 4 # Set maximum number of instances to 2
    TargetGroupARNs:
      - !Ref ALBTG
    VPCZoneIdentifier:
      - !Ref Private1Subnet
      - !Ref Private2Subnet
    LaunchTemplate:
      LaunchTemplateId: !Ref ASGLT
      Version: !GetAtt ASGLT.LatestVersionNumber
    HealthCheckType: ELB
```

. . .

We follow this by defining our DynamoDB-based data store for the workload. We also include a custom resource that helps populate the DynamoDB table with some preliminary seed data. While this is not always required, in our case, it helps our application display some information from when it is deployed.

```
DynamoProductTable:
  Type: AWS::DynamoDB::Table
  Properties:
    TableName: ProductTable
    BillingMode: "PAY_PER_REQUEST"
    AttributeDefinitions:
      - AttributeName: "Product"
        AttributeType: "S"
      - AttributeName: "Reviewer"
        AttributeType: "S"
    KeySchema:
      - AttributeName: "Product"
        KeyType: "HASH"
      - AttributeName: "Reviewer"
        KeyType: "RANGE"
InitializeDynamoDB:
  Type: Custom::InitFunction
```

```
    DependsOn: DynamoProductTable
    Properties:
      ServiceToken:
        Fn::GetAtt: [DynamoDBInitFunction, "Arn"]
      DynamoTableName: DynamoProductTable
  DynamoDBInitFunction:
    Type: AWS::Lambda::Function
    Properties:
      Code:
        ZipFile: >
          const { DynamoDBClient } = require(«@aws-sdk/client-dynamodb»);
          const {
            DynamoDBDocumentClient,
            PutCommand,
          } = require(«@aws-sdk/lib-dynamodb»);
          const response = require("cfn-response");
          const client = new DynamoDBClient({});
          const dynamo = DynamoDBDocumentClient.from(client);
          exports.handler =  (event, context) => {
            dynamo.send(
                  new PutCommand({
                        TableName: event.ResourceProperties.DynamoTableName,
                        Item:{
                          Product: "iPhone 15 Pro",
                          Reviewer: "john.doe@email.com",
                          Review: "Light weight, good performance. Slow
charging, heats easily, expensive"
                        }
                  })
              ).then(()=> {
                  response.send(event, context, "SUCCESS", {});
              }).catch((err) => {
                  console.log(err);
                  response.send(event, context, "FAILED", {});
              });
          };
```

```
      Handler: index.handler
      Role:
        Fn::GetAtt: [DynamoDBInitLambdaRole, "Arn"]
      Runtime: nodejs20.x
      Timeout: 60
  DynamoDBInitLambdaRole:
    Type: AWS::IAM::Role
    Properties:
      AssumeRolePolicyDocument:
        Version: "2012-10-17"
        Statement:
          - Effect: Allow
            Principal:
              Service:
                - lambda.amazonaws.com
            Action:
              - sts:AssumeRole
      Path: "/"
      Policies:
        - PolicyName: dynamodbAccessRole
          PolicyDocument:
            Version: "2012-10-17"
            Statement:
              - Effect: Allow
                Action:
                  - dynamodb:BatchWriteItem
                Resource: !Sub
arn:aws:dynamodb:${AWS::Region}:${AWS::AccountId}:table/DynamoProductTable
              - Effect: Allow
                Action:
                  - logs:*
                Resource: "*"
```

After our **Resources** section concludes, we include the optional **Outputs** section. Here, we have included the DNS name of the load balancer that we created in the **Resources** section. This will be used as the entry point into our application and will be accessible over the public internet.

```
Outputs:
  LoadBalancerDNSName:
    Description: DNS name of the Application Load Balancer
    Value: !GetAtt ALB.DNSName
```

You can author AWS CloudFormation templates in JSON or YAML formats. All AWS CloudFormation features and functions are supported for both formats. You can pick the format in which you are most comfortable working. We have used YAML in our example.

The following figure shows the anatomy of a typical CloudFormation template. The anatomy is the same for both JSON or YAML formats as follows:

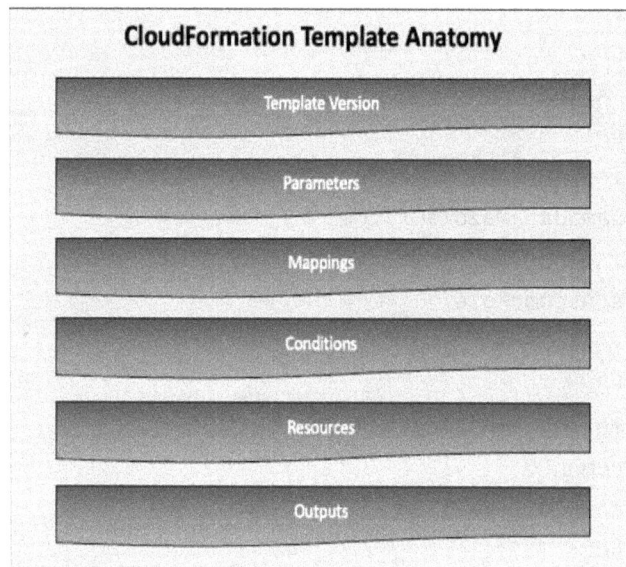

Figure 4.3: CloudFormation template anatomy

Let us break down some of the sections in this template to provide more information as follows:

- **AWSTemplateFormatVersion:** This section is used to identify the capabilities of the template. The latest template format version is 2010-09-09, and it is currently the only valid value. This is an optional section, but when used, it must be the first line of the template. If omitted, AWS CloudFormation assumes you're using the latest template format. It helps AWS determine how to parse and process the template. It ensures forward compatibility while enabling AWS to maintain consistent template processing across their services. This version identifier allows AWS to introduce new features and capabilities to CloudFormation while maintaining backward compatibility with existing templates, and it helps the service validate both template structure and syntax during deployment. Despite its 2010-09-09 date designation, this version continues to serve as the foundation for all modern CloudFormation features and functionality.

- **Template parameters:** The optional parameters section is used to pass values into your template. It provides a powerful way to make your infrastructure code reusable and flexible. Parameters can be used to create templates customized for each stack creation. You must provide a value for each parameter when you create a stack. You can specify a default value to make the parameter optional, so you do not need to pass in a value when creating a stack. In the following example, we see a parameter that selects the **InstanceType** with a **String** type and a default value of **t3.micro**. The only values allowed are from the list of **AllowedValues** of instance types are as follows:

```
Parameters:
    InstanceType:
      Description: EC2 instance type
      Type: String
      Default: t3.micro
      AllowedValues:
        - t3.micro
        - t3.small
        - t3.medium
        - t3.large
        - m5.large
        - m5.xlarge
```

The following are allowed for a parameter type attribute:

o **String**: Text values

o **Number**: Integers or floating points

o **List<Number>**: Array of numbers

o **CommaDelimitedList**: Comma-separated values

o **AWS-specific parameters**: Like AWS::EC2::KeyPair::KeyName

o **SSM parameter types**: For accessing existing parameters in Parameter Store

You can use the intrinsic function **Ref** to reference the parameter's value in other places within the template. For example, later in the full template definition, you see that the **LaunchTemplate** resource refers to the **Instance Type** parameter as shown:
InstanceType: !Ref InstanceType

The following are some important properties of **Parameters** to keep in mind:

o **Default:** Specifies an optional default value

o **AllowedValues**: List of valid options

o **AllowedPattern:** Regex pattern for validation

o **MinLength/MaxLength**: Specifies minimum or maximum lengths for string parameters

o **MinValue/MaxValue**: Specifies minimum or maximum values for number parameters

o **NoEcho**: Prevent parameter values from being displayed in the console, command line tools, or API. You can use this for sensitive values (like passwords)

o **Description**: Explains the parameter's purpose

When working with CloudFormation template parameters, these guidelines ensure robust and maintainable infrastructure code. Always provide clear descriptions for each parameter to aid users during stack creation and implement appropriate constraints to prevent input errors and maintain security standards. For better usability, group related parameters together and set sensible default values where applicable to streamline the deployment process. When dealing with sensitive information such as passwords or API keys, utilize the `NoEcho` property to protect these values from being displayed or logged. Additionally, consider leveraging SSM Parameter Types for dynamic values, which allows for centralized parameter management and easier updates across multiple stacks.

• **Template mapping**: The `Mappings` section in AWS CloudFormation templates serves as a powerful lookup table mechanism that enables developers to create versatile and region-aware infrastructure deployments. This optional section allows you to establish relationships between keys and their corresponding named values, where both keys and values must be literal strings, making it particularly useful for scenarios requiring conditional resource configurations. Each mapping consists of a unique key that acts as an identifier for a collection of name-value pairs, with the constraint that key names must contain only alphanumeric characters to maintain template validity. One of the most common and practical applications of the `Mappings` section is managing AMI IDs across different AWS Regions, where you can define region-specific AMI IDs and reference them dynamically based on where the stack is being deployed. For example, you might create a mapping that correlates AWS Region codes with their corresponding AMI IDs, instance types, or other region-specific configurations, allowing your template to automatically select the appropriate values based on the deployment context. This approach not only makes templates more maintainable and reduces the likelihood of errors but also eliminates the need for multiple templates for different regions or environments, as you can conditionally reference the appropriate values using intrinsic functions such as `!FindInMap`. Additionally, mappings can be used for environment-specific configurations, operating system selections, or any other scenario where you need to maintain a structured set of key-value relationships within your template.

The following is an example snippet from our template example, which shows how the **Mappings** section can be used to create a lookup for AMI IDs by region:

```
Mappings:
    RegionAMIMap:
      us-east-1:
        AMI: ami-0a1179631ec8933d7
      us-east-2:
        AMI: ami-080e449218d4434fa
      us-west-2:
        AMI: ami-086f060214da77a16
```

The **Fn::FindInMap** intrinsic function is a fundamental component in AWS CloudFormation that enables dynamic value lookups within template mappings. This function can be written either as **!FindInMap [MapName, TopLevelKey, SecondLevelKey]** in YAML short form or as **{"Fn::FindInMap": [MapName, TopLevelKey, SecondLevelKey]}** in JSON, requires exactly three parameters to operate. The first parameter identifies the mapping section name where the lookup should occur, the second parameter specifies the top-level key to match, and the third parameter determines which specific attribute should be returned from the matched mapping.

The following is an example of how you would use the **FindInMap** function:

```
ImageId: !FindInMap [RegionMap, !Ref "AWS::Region", AMI]
```

In this scenario, **FindInMap** will automatically select the appropriate AMI ID based on the deployment region, making the template dynamically adaptable to different AWS Regions. This function is particularly valuable for creating portable templates that can be deployed across multiple regions or environments while maintaining the correct resource configurations for each context.

- **Template resources**: The resources section is the only required section in a CloudFormation template. In this section, you declare the AWS resources that you want to define in the stack. Each resource is declared separately, but multiple resources of the same type can be declared together by separated by commas. Each resource within this section should have a unique alphanumeric (A-Za-z0-9) logical ID. The logical ID can be used to reference the resource in other parts of the template. For example, the **RouteTable** definition is as follows, referencing the logical ID of the VPC resource defined in the template.

```
PublicRT:
  Type: AWS::EC2::RouteTable
  Properties:
    VpcId: !Ref VPC
```

Some resources, such as an Amazon S3 bucket name, represent a physical ID, which is the actual assigned name for that resource. Physical IDs can identify resources even outside of AWS CloudFormation templates after the resources have been created. Because the physical ID of a resource is not known until the stack is created, you need to use references to associate resources within a template. Each of the hundreds of different **CloudFormation** supported AWS resources have their own set of properties. When CloudFormation does not support an AWS resource directly, you can use custom resources. You can develop logic for custom provisioning in templates for the custom resources you create. AWS CloudFormation runs this logic when you create, update, or delete stacks. Custom resources in your templates can be defined using the **AWS::CloudFormation::CustomResource** or **Custom::String** resource type. The service token property of the custom resource is used to specify the service, such as **Amazon Simple Notification Service (Amazon SNS)** topic or AWS Lambda, which receives the request from CloudFormation.

The following code is an example of a custom resource, which defines an initialization function to insert items into our DynamoDB table. The service token points to a Lambda function, which is also defined in our template. The Lambda function definition is not included here for brevity. The Lambda function is written in Node.js and performs the task of inserting a sample item in our DynamoDB table as follows:

```
InitializeDynamoDB:
  Type: Custom::InitFunction
  DependsOn: DynamoProductTable
  Properties:
    ServiceToken:
      Fn::GetAtt: [DynamoDBInitFunction, "Arn"]
    DynamoTableName: DynamoProductTable
```

Another thing you may have noticed here is the **DependsOn** property for this resource. Normally, CloudFormation does a very thorough job of establishing dependencies between the resources being created and ensuring that the resources are created in the right order. In the case of a custom resource, it becomes a challenge to deduce the relationship with the DynamoDB table from just the resource definition. The actual dependency with the DynamoDB table is established inside the Lambda function code. In such a case, it becomes important to explicitly establish a relationship between the custom resource and the resource on which it depends. Without this, CloudFormation may try to create the custom resource before the DynamoDB table. This can lead to unexpected errors.

- **Template outputs**: The **Outputs** section is optional and can be used to declare values to be output from the stack that is created by the template. You can create cross-stack references by importing these values into other stacks. These values can also be viewed in the AWS CloudFormation console for quick access, or you can return them in response to describe stack calls. For example, you can specify the DNS name of a load balancer in the **Outputs** section. This makes it easy to find the load balancer DNS name to access the application using an internet browser. The **Outputs** section consists of a unique alphanumeric logical identifier for each output. Optionally, you can specify the type of the output. The output values can be literals, references to parameters, pseudo parameters, mapping values, or intrinsic functions. Outputs can also include an export field. The exported values are useful to create cross-stack references.

In the following example, the output named **ALBDNSName** returns the DNS name of the Application Load Balancer resource with the logical ID ALB:

```
Outputs:
  ALBDNSName:
    Description: DNS name of the Application Load Balancer
    Value: !GetAtt ALB.DNSName
```

You can create the infrastructure using the above CloudFormation template using the AWS Console, AWS CLI, or by directly invoking the CloudFormation API. However, we will take the AWS CLI approach for now.

```
aws cloudformation create-stack \
  --stack-name app-stack \
  --template-body file://template.yaml \
  --region us-west-2 \
  --capabilities CAPABILITY_NAMED_IAM
```

We are making use of the create-stack AWS CLI command to create the infrastructure using our template, which we have saved in a file named **template.yaml**. We specify the region where we want to create our stack using the region parameter. Lastly, we use the **capabilities** parameter with the value **CAPABILITY_NAMED_IAM** to specify that this template will create IAM resources with custom names.

Other sections that you may see in a CloudFormation template, which we did not use in our example template, are as follows:

- **Template metadata**: This optional section can include arbitrary JSON or YAML objects that provide additional details about the template. For example, you can include template implementation details about specific resources. During a stack update, the **Metadata** section cannot be updated by itself. It can only be updated when there are changes that add, modify, or delete resources.

```
Metadata:
  Instances:
    Description: "Information about the instances"
```

```
Databases:
  Description: "Information about the databases"
```

Some AWS CloudFormation features retrieve settings or configuration information that you define from the **Metadata** section. You define this information in AWS CloudFormation-specific metadata keys. **AWS::CloudFormation::Init** defines configuration tasks for the **cfn-init** helper script. This script is useful for configuring and installing applications on EC2 instances. **AWS::CloudFormation::Interface** is a metadata key that defines how parameters are grouped and ordered in the CloudFormation console. When you create or update stacks in the console, the console lists input parameters by their logical IDs in alphabetical order. Using this key, you can define your own parameter grouping and ordering. Additionally, you can define labels for parameters, which are user-friendly names or descriptions the console displays in place of a parameter's logical ID. Labels are useful for helping users understand the values to specify for each parameter.

```
Metadata:
  AWS::CloudFormation::Interface:
    ParameterGroups:
      - ParameterGroup
    ParameterLabels:
      ParameterLabel
```

- **Template conditions**: Conditions are an optional section that includes statements that define when a resource is created or when a property is defined. For example, you can compare a value to another value to see if they are equal. Based on the result of that condition, you can create resources. You can separate multiple conditions with commas. You can use conditions when you want to reuse a template that can create resources in different contexts, such as a test environment versus a production environment. For example, you can add an input parameter that represents an **EnvironmentType** in your template, which could take the value of prod or test. For the test environment, you may choose to use smaller-sized resources to save costs. For the production environment, however, you may choose to use higher-powered resources.

Input parameter values during stack creation or update determine how the conditions are evaluated. A condition can reference another condition, a parameter value, or a mapping. After defining your conditions, you can associate them with resources and resource properties in the **Resources** and **Outputs** sections of a template.

During stack creation or stack update, AWS CloudFormation evaluates all the conditions in your template before creating any resources. A true condition results in resources being created. Resources for conditions that are evaluated as false are ignored. During a stack update, you cannot update conditions by themselves. You can update conditions only when you include changes that add, modify, or delete resources. To create resources conditionally, you need to include statements in at least three different sections of a template - Parameters, Conditions, and Resources. In the parameters section, you will define the input values that you want to evaluate in your conditions. Based on the values of these input parameters, the conditions will result in a true or false evaluation. The **Conditions** section is where you define the conditions using intrinsic condition functions. In the resources section, you will associate conditions with the resources that you want to create conditionally. Use the condition key and a condition's logical ID to associate it with a resource or output.

You can use the following intrinsic functions to define conditions as follows:

- o **Fn::And**: Returns true if all the specified conditions evaluate to true. Returns false if any of the conditions evaluate to false.

- o **Fn::Equals**: Returns true if the two values are equal or false if they are not.

- o **Fn::If**: Returns one value if the specified condition evaluates to true and another value if the specified condition evaluates to false.

- o **Fn::Not**: Returns true for a condition that evaluates to false or returns false for a condition that evaluates to true.

- o **Fn::Or**: Returns true if any one of the specified conditions evaluates to true, or returns false if all the conditions evaluate to false.

For best results, it is recommended that you use the lifecycle and ownership of your AWS resources to help you decide what resources should go in each stack. In our example, we put all our resources in one stack. However, as your stack grows in scale and broadens in scope, you may find that managing a single large stack can be cumbersome and time-consuming. You can group resources with common lifecycles and ownership. This allows owners to make changes to their resources using their own processes and schedules without affecting other resources. When you organize your AWS resources based on lifecycle and ownership, you can build a stack that uses resources that are in another stack. This can be achieved using cross-stack references to export resources from a stack so that other stacks can use them. Stacks can use the exported resources by calling them using the **Fn::ImportValue** function.

- **Nested stacks**: As your AWS infrastructure expands, you may repeat the same configurations across multiple CloudFormation templates, making infrastructure management increasingly complex. Nested stacks provide a powerful way to break down these common elements into reusable building blocks, effectively addressing the challenges of large-scale infrastructure management. With nested stacks, you define reusable templates containing common infrastructure components and then reference these templates within your main templates using the AWS::CloudFormation::Stack resource type. This approach offers several significant benefits: reduced redundancy by eliminating the need to duplicate configurations across multiple templates, which streamlines maintenance and reduces the risk of errors; improved reusability by making common infrastructure components self-contained units that can be easily incorporated into various stacks as needed; and enhanced maintainability since changes to a nested stack automatically propagate to all referencing stacks, simplifying updates and promoting consistency across your infrastructure.

Nested stacks also provide additional advantages such as improved error handling through stack rollbacks that include nested components, better resource organization with the ability to manage up to 200 resources per nested stack (helping circumvent the 500-resource limit of standard stacks), and simplified parameter management through parameter passing between parent and nested stacks. Furthermore, nested stacks support versioning through template URLs stored in S3, allowing you to maintain different versions of your infrastructure components and roll back to previous versions if needed. Teams can also implement change management practices more effectively by controlling access to nested stack templates and managing updates through a centralized process. By leveraging nested stacks, you can create modular, reusable, and easier-to-maintain CloudFormation templates. This promotes efficiency, scalability, and better organization in your infrastructure management while reducing the potential for configuration drift across different environments.

With nested stacks, you define reusable templates containing common infrastructure components and then reference these templates within your main templates using the **AWS::CloudFormation::Stack** resource. This approach offers several benefits:

o **Reduced redundancy**: Eliminate the need to duplicate configurations across multiple templates, streamlining maintenance and reducing the risk of errors.

o **Improved reusability**: Common infrastructure components become self-contained units, easily incorporated into various stacks as needed.

o **Enhanced maintainability**: Changes to a nested stack propagate to all referencing stacks, simplifying updates and promoting consistency.

By leveraging nested stacks, you can create modular, reusable, and easier-to-maintain CloudFormation templates, promoting efficiency and organization in your infrastructure management.

• **StackSets:** AWS CloudFormation StackSets extends the capability of traditional stacks by enabling you to create, update, or delete stacks across multiple accounts and AWS Regions with a single operation, providing a powerful tool for managing infrastructure at scale. You create the stack set in an Administrator account, which typically serves as the management account within your AWS Organization, establishing a central point of control for multi-account infrastructure deployment. A target account is any AWS account into which you create, update, or delete one or more stacks in your stack set, allowing for consistent resource deployment across your organization. Before implementing StackSets, you must establish a trust relationship between the administrator and target accounts, which can be accomplished either through self-managed permissions (using IAM roles) or service-managed permissions (leveraging AWS Organizations). StackSets supports sophisticated deployment options, including the ability to set maximum concurrent operations, failure tolerance thresholds, and region deployment order, ensuring controlled and reliable infrastructure rollouts.

Additionally, StackSets provides automatic drift detection and remediation capabilities, helping maintain consistency across your infrastructure by identifying and correcting unintended changes. The service also supports stack sequence operations, allowing you to define dependencies between stacks across accounts and regions, and offers deployment options like retain stacks (keeping resources when removing accounts from a stack set) and automatic deployment to new accounts added to an organization. Furthermore, StackSets maintains detailed operation history and status tracking, enabling administrators to monitor deployment progress and troubleshoot issues across their multi-account environment. This makes StackSets particularly valuable for enterprises managing complex, multi-region applications, implementing compliance requirements across accounts, or maintaining consistent infrastructure configurations throughout their organization.

• **CloudFormation hooks:** Compliance with your cloud resources is an important SRE concern. As we will see in future chapters, the AWS Config service enables compliance checking for resources in your AWS environment. However, Config and other methods of checking compliance inform about compliance posture after the non-compliant resources have been in existence. It is sometimes better to implement proactive checks to check if resources are being created in a compliant manner. CloudFormation hooks helps you maintain compliance proactively.

By running code prior to creating, updating, or deleting a CloudFormation managed resource, hooks help prevent the creation or be warned about non-compliant resources. You can implement a series of checks at the time of provisioning to automatically enforce business requirements proactively with CloudFormation hooks. As a result, you can be sure that any provisioned resources have already passed these checks. This reduces risks related to security and compliance and the overhead of fixing non-compliant resources after they are live in your environment. A hook includes a JSON-based specification and handlers. Handlers execute custom logic at different invocation points. PreCreate, preUpdate, and preDelete are three invocation points that hooks provide, where handler code can be executed. Hander code can be implemented in Java or Python. Hook targets are the resources for which the hooks are invoked. For each resource, the handler can implement specific checks related to that resource. For example, a pre-create handler, an `AWS::S3::Bucket` resource, will only pass if the Amazon S3 bucket encryption is set.

CloudFormation provides a flexible and customizable way to create and manage AWS resources, enabling users to tailor their infrastructure to meet their specific needs. Before using a template in a production environment, it is important to test and validate it in a non-production environment. By using recommended CloudFormation features such as templates, provisioning, change sets, and rollbacks, you can ensure that their infrastructure is created and maintained in a secure, scalable, and compliant manner.

Using AWS Cloud Development Kit

The AWS CDK is an open-source framework developed by AWS. It represents a significant evolution in IaC, offering developers a sophisticated framework to define cloud resources using familiar programming languages, including Python, JavaScript, TypeScript, Java, Go, and C#. We introduce CDK in this section to give you an idea about how you can use this for your IaC needs. A detailed discussion of CDK is outside the scope of this book, as we are using CloudFormation to create our resources. There is extensive AWS documentation that gives you more details on CDK.

Unlike traditional CloudFormation templates that use YAML or JSON, CDK allows developers to leverage their existing programming expertise, complete with modern IDE features like code completion, syntax highlighting, and inline documentation. The framework translates these high-level programming constructs into CloudFormation templates through a process called synthesis, ultimately deploying the same reliable CloudFormation stacks. CDK introduces powerful concepts such as Constructs (reusable cloud components), Stacks (unit of deployment), and Apps (collection of stacks), enabling developers to build complex cloud infrastructure with object-oriented programming principles.

The framework provides significant advantages, including type safety, reusable component libraries, and the ability to implement custom logic and validation rules directly in your infrastructure code. Additionally, CDK offers built-in security best practices, automatic dependency management, and asset bundling capabilities for applications. The framework's compatibility with standard software development workflows means teams can implement infrastructure changes using familiar tools and practices, including version control, code review, and **continuous integration/continuous deployment (CI/CD)** pipelines. While CloudFormation remains the underlying deployment technology, CDK abstracts much of its complexity while adding powerful features like the ability to create custom constructs that encapsulate architectural patterns and best practices, making them easily shareable across teams and projects. Furthermore, CDK's integration with AWS Services is continuously updated, providing developers with the latest service features and capabilities as they become available.

CDK provides pre-built constructs that encapsulate configurations for various AWS services. These constructs eliminate the need to write repetitive code, saving you time and effort. You can leverage the features of your chosen programming language for version control, testing, and collaboration. This makes your infrastructure configurations more maintainable and reliable. You can define the resources you need and their configurations with programming code and avoid directly dealing with the low-level details of AWS CloudFormation templates.

Since CDK uses common programming languages, it seamlessly integrates with your existing development tools and workflows. You can write your application code and define your infrastructure in the same environment. You can write unit tests to test your CDK application code the same way you would test your regular application code. This is a distinct advantage over CloudFormation, as testing YAML or JSON-based CloudFormation templates is not straightforward.

The following are the key concepts in CDK:

- **Apps**: A CDK app is a collection of one or more CDK stacks.

- **Stacks:** Stacks represent a logical grouping of constructs that define AWS resources. Each CDK stack maps to a CloudFormation stack as part of the app you define using CDK.

- **Constructs:** Constructs are reusable building blocks representing one more CloudFormation resource and its configuration. You can import CDK constructs into your CDK apps from the Constructs library. The constructs are organized into a *construct tree* using the *scope* argument. The scope allows constructs to be defined inside other constructs. The root of the tree is the app. The construct tree defines the order in which the constructs will be synthesized into the resulting CloudFormation template.

  AWS Construct Library constructs have three levels:

  o **Level 1 (L1) constructs (or CFN resources)** in AWS CDK are the most basic level of constructs that map directly to individual CloudFormation resources, offering no additional abstraction. They are named with a 'Cfn' prefix (e.g., CfnBucket for S3 buckets) and are automatically generated from the CloudFormation resource specification, making them ideal for developers who need precise control over resource properties and are already familiar with CloudFormation.

  o **L2 constructs** in AWS CDK, developed by the CDK team, provide a higher-level abstraction over L1 constructs with built-in best practices, sensible defaults, and automated boilerplate code generation. These curated constructs (like s3.Bucket) include helpful methods for managing properties and permissions, making them the most commonly used construct type for production environments, while experimental L2 constructs are available in separate modules during development.

  o **L3 constructs** (or patterns) in AWS CDK represent the highest level of abstraction, combining multiple AWS resources into pre-configured solutions for specific use cases. These constructs (like `ecsPatterns.ApplicationLoadBalancedFargateService`) provide opinionated, complete system designs that require minimal input to deploy entire architectures, making them ideal for quickly implementing common cloud patterns with established best practices.

For example, here is how you would define the DynamoDB table from our CloudFormation template aforementioned using CDK code in Python as follows:

```
table = dynamodb.Table(
            self, "DynamoDBTable",
            table_name="Product",
            billing_mode=dynamodb.BillingMode.PAY_PER_REQUEST,
            partition_key=dynamodb.Attribute(
            name="Product",
            type=dynamodb.AttributeType.STRING
            ),
            sort_key=dynamodb.Attribute(
            name="Reviewer",
            type=dynamodb.AttributeType.STRING
            )
)
```

Constructs in use in this example are:

- **dynamodb.Table**: An L2 construct that represents a DynamoDB table.
- **dynamodb.Attribute**: A helper construct for defining table attributes.
- **dynamodb.BillingMode**: An enum construct defining billing options.
- **dynamodb.AttributeType**: An enum construct for attribute data types.

The following figure shows the workflow of a CDK application:

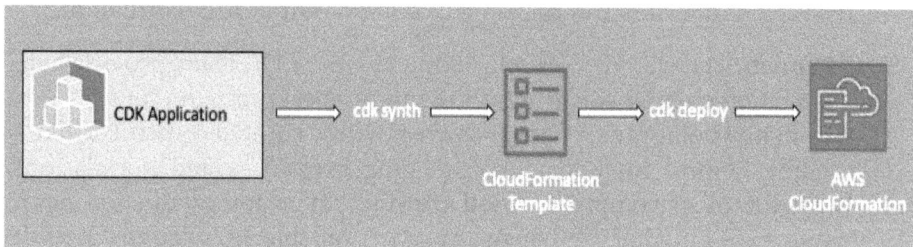

Figure 4.4: CDK application workflow

First, the CDK code is used to synthesize the CloudFormation template. From there, you use the template to create your AWS resources with the help of the AWS CloudFormation service.

The details are as follows:

- **Define IaC:** When defining IaC using AWS CDK, developers can write their infrastructure code using their preferred programming languages, such as Python, TypeScript, or Java, while importing the necessary CDK constructs from the AWS Construct Library. This approach allows teams to define resource configurations using familiar object-oriented programming principles and implement complex logic for resource relationships and dependencies. The process benefits from built-in validation and type-checking native to the chosen programming language while enabling teams to apply custom business logic and compliance rules directly in their infrastructure code. Developers can create reusable components through class inheritance and composition, making the infrastructure code more maintainable and scalable. Additionally, they can leverage modern IDE features such as code completion and inline documentation, significantly improving the development experience and reducing the likelihood of configuration errors.

- **Synthesis:** The synthesis process in AWS CDK begins when developers execute the `cdk synth` command, initiating a series of automated steps where CDK first validates the construct tree for logical consistency. During this phase, the framework converts high-level programming constructs into CloudFormation templates, generating the necessary JSON/YAML files and storing them in a `cdk.out` directory along with all synthesized assets. The process includes automatic dependency resolution between resources, validation of resource configurations against AWS service limits, and generation of unique identifiers for each resource. Additionally, the synthesis phase handles asset bundling for components like Lambda functions or container images, ensuring all necessary artifacts are properly packaged and prepared for deployment.

- **Provisioning:** Next, you deploy the CDK stack. The provisioning phase of AWS CDK begins when developers execute the `cdk deploy` command, triggering CloudFormation to read the synthesized templates and initiate the deployment process. CloudFormation first creates a change set to identify necessary resource modifications, then executes the deployment in the correct order based on established dependencies, creating, updating, or deleting AWS resources as needed. Throughout this process, the system provides real-time feedback on deployment progress and automatically handles rollbacks if any errors occur, ensuring infrastructure integrity. The deployment process also updates stack outputs and exports, maintains a comprehensive deployment history for change tracking, and validates the successful creation and configuration of all resources, providing a robust and reliable infrastructure deployment mechanism.

Overall, AWS CDK provides a powerful and flexible way to define and manage your AWS infrastructure using familiar programming languages. It simplifies infrastructure management, improves maintainability, and integrates seamlessly with your development workflow. By leveraging CDK, you can focus on building and deploying your applications faster and more efficiently.

AWS Serverless Application Model

AWS SAM templates provide a short-hand syntax optimized for defining IaC for serverless applications. SAM provides a higher level of abstraction than CloudFormation. It offers specific resources for serverless components (Lambda functions, API Gateway, DynamoDB tables) with a more concise and readable syntax compared to raw CloudFormation. SAM integrates well with development tools and frameworks, enabling local testing, packaging, and deployment functionalities for streamlined serverless development. Its simplified syntax and developer tools accelerate the development process for serverless applications. CloudFormation can define virtually any AWS resource, providing greater flexibility for complex deployments involving both serverless and traditional components. A SAM template file is a YAML configuration that represents a serverless application. You use the template to declare all of the AWS resources that comprise your serverless application in one place. AWS SAM templates are an extension of AWS CloudFormation templates, so any resource that you can declare in an AWS CloudFormation template can also be declared in an AWS SAM template. During deployment, SAM transforms and expands the SAM syntax into AWS CloudFormation syntax.

The following figure shows the workflow of how a SAM template:

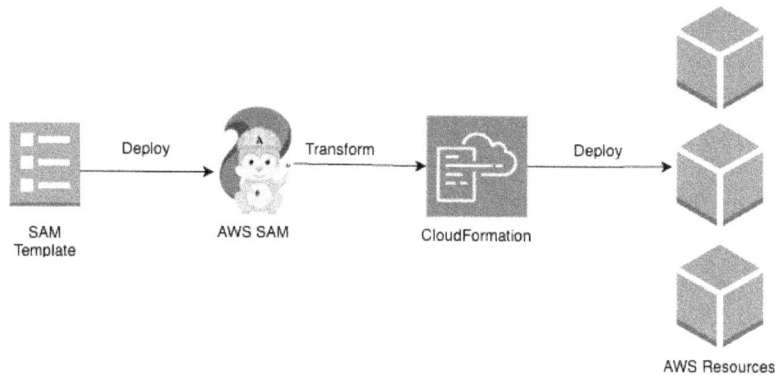

Figure 4.5: *Workflow of SAM template generating AWS resources*

First, the SAM template is transformed into CloudFormation. From there, CloudFormation is used to create the AWS resources that are defined in the template.

For example, you can define the DynamoDB table in the aforementioned example, as shown, using SAM:

```
ProductTable:
  Type: AWS::Serverless::SimpleTable
  Properties:
    TableName: Product
    PrimaryKey:
```

```
      Name: Product
      Type: String
  SortKey:
      Name: Reviewer
      Type: String
```

Here, you can see that **AWS::DynamoDB::Table** changed to **AWS::Serverless::SimpleTable** To compare to the corresponding CloudFormation template. This resource indicates a SAM resource for a DynamoDB table with a primary key for a single attribute. The **TableName** property remains the same. The primary key in the SAM template matches the HASH key, and the Sort key matches the RANGE key in the CloudFormation DynamoDB definition. The CloudFormation template includes BillingMode. SAM does not require this property definition explicitly, as the BillingMode will be specified as **PAY_PER_REQUEST**, if the **ProvisionedThroughput** property of **SimpleTable** is not specified.

In general, you should use SAM if you are building a pure serverless application and you don't require extensive customization beyond basic serverless resources. On the other hand, if your application involves a mix of serverless and traditional resources and you need fine-grained control over your infrastructure configurations, you may want to use CloudFormation.

Terraform

Terraform is a popular non-AWS IaC tool created by HashiCorp. Terraform became popular because of its ability to work across multiple cloud providers (AWS, Azure, GCP) and on-prem infrastructure. It uses a human-readable syntax for defining infrastructure using a configuration language called **HashiCorp Configuration Language** (HCL). This configuration file, known as a Terraform configuration, specifies the resources you need (e.g., virtual machines, databases, security groups) along with their desired configuration settings. Terraform then interacts with the relevant cloud APIs to provision and manage these resources according to your specifications. Configurations can be version-controlled and reused, ensuring consistent infrastructure deployments across environments. The declarative nature of the language minimizes manual configuration errors and promotes infrastructure automation. Terraform supports a wide range of cloud providers and infrastructure platforms, allowing you to manage resources across different environments. Terraform integrates well with security tools and can enforce security controls within your infrastructure deployments.

Terraform offers a large community-driven library of modules for various services and configurations. It makes use of a state file to track infrastructure changes. The state file allows Terraform to plan, manage, and apply infrastructure changes efficiently. The state file contains the bindings of resources already provisioned and the resources defined in your configuration.

We have not extensively discussed Terraform in this book. However, here are some considerations if you want to decide between Terraform and CloudFormation for your infrastructure automation. CloudFormation is designed and optimized to provision and manage resources within AWS. It provides native integration with AWS services and features like IAM roles and CloudTrail. It manages the state of your infrastructure and helps simplify deployments. Both CloudFormation and Terraform do a good job of providing support for new AWS service releases and feature updates. You may prefer Terraform if you need multi-cloud or hybrid cloud infrastructure management with some code reusability across different cloud environments. CloudFormation may be a better fit if it works exclusively within AWS and benefits from tight integration with other AWS services. With Terraform, you need to be comfortable managing your own infrastructure state, whereas CloudFormation manages the state for you. Another consideration is that Terraform will require you to learn HCL, a new language syntax. CloudFormation, on the other hand, uses familiar data formats such as JSON and YAML. However, JSON and YAML can also be hard to work with and are not preferred by everyone. Both CloudFormation and Terraform do a good job of keeping up with new releases of services and features. This means you will not often find yourself in a situation where you cannot automate your infrastructure due to a lack of IaC support.

There is no one option which is right for all situations. Terraform and CloudFormation solve similar concerns but with varying flexibility and syntactical aspects. The choice depends on your specific needs and environment.

Conclusion

In this chapter, we discussed the benefits of IaC. We were introduced to AWS CloudFormation, the primary service for creating cloud resources on AWS. We also discussed the features of CloudFormation and how to apply them to different situations. You saw how the architecture for our sample application can be defined as a CloudFormation template. You understood the different sections that make up the CloudFormation and their purpose. Next, we saw alternate IaC options to CloudFormation on AWS. We learned when you can use CDK and SAM as an alternative to directly writing CloudFormation syntax. Lastly, we briefly looked at Terraform, which is a non-AWS option for IaC, that works across multiple cloud providers.

In the next chapter, we will learn how you can perform maintenance tasks on your AWS infrastructure using native AWS options.

Points to remember

- IaC is a practice that involves managing and provisioning infrastructure resources through code and configuration files, rather than manual processes. This provides several benefits, including consistency and reusability of infrastructure configurations, version control and collaboration, and improved security and compliance.

- AWS offers various IaC tools and services, such as CloudFormation, AWS CDK, and AWS SAM, that allow you to define your cloud resources programmatically.

- Terraform is a popular open-source IaC tool that can also be used to manage AWS resources.

- Automating infrastructure through IaC can significantly improve the efficiency, scalability, and reliability of cloud-based workloads.

- Understanding and implementing IaC is a crucial skill for effective cloud infrastructure management.

Multiple choice questions

1. **What is the primary benefit of using IaC compared to manual infrastructure provisioning?**

   a. Improved security through complex password management

   b. Increased cost due to additional software licensing

   c. Faster and more consistent deployments through automation

   d. Reduced need for technical expertise in cloud platforms

2. **Which AWS service allows you to define your cloud resources programmatically?**

   a. Amazon EC2

   b. AWS CloudFormation

   c. Amazon S3

   d. Amazon RDS

3. **What is the expansion of the acronym CDK in the context of AWS IaC tools?**

   a. Cloud Development Kit

   b. Cloud Deployment Kit

   c. Cloud Delivery Kit

   d. Cloud Deployment Toolkit

4. **Which IaC tool can be used to manage cloud resources across multiple cloud providers?**

   a. AWS SAM

   b. AWS CloudFormation

   c. Terraform

   d. AWS CDK

5. **What is the primary advantage of automating infrastructure through IaC?**

   a. Reduced manual effort

   b. Improved security

   c. Increased scalability

    d. All the above

6. **Which of the following is NOT a key benefit of using version control with IaC?**

    a. Improved collaboration

    b. Increased manual processes

    c. Easier rollback and auditing

    d. Consistent infrastructure configurations

7. **Which of the following statements is most accurate about CloudFormation templates?**

    a. They are written in a compiled programming language like Java.

    b. They define infrastructure resources using a graphical user interface.

    c. They utilize a declarative syntax to specify the desired infrastructure state.

    d. They require real-time connection to the cloud platform for resource creation.

8. **CloudFormation templates can reference other CloudFormation stacks. What is the main advantage of using this feature?**

    a. To create redundant copies of infrastructure resources for increased availability

    b. To promote modularity and reusability of common infrastructure components across deployments

    c. To simplify the process of deleting resources when a stack is no longer needed

    d. To enforce strict access controls and limit user permissions to specific resources

Answers

1.	c
2.	b
3.	a
4.	c
5.	d
6.	b
7.	c
8.	b

CHAPTER 5

Automating Infrastructure Maintenance

Introduction

This chapter helps you understand your options for infrastructure maintenance on AWS. Having taken the first steps to create your AWS infrastructure in the previous chapter, you will now see how AWS provides options to simplify the maintenance of the AWS resources that you have created. In this chapter, we start by looking at the different maintenance concerns you will often encounter and compare how infrastructure maintenance on AWS can be simpler than traditional on-premises hardware environments. We will look at the services and features you can use on AWS to perform your maintenance tasks.

Structure

The chapter covers the following topics:

- Maintenance tasks for your infrastructure
- AWS Systems Manager basics
- Operations management
- Application management
- Change management
- Node management

Objectives

By the end of this chapter, you will learn your options for maintaining your AWS infrastructure. You will be introduced to AWS Systems Manager and its capabilities. Although this is an AWS service, it is made up of several sub-services or features that allow you to perform a range of maintenance tasks. Understanding how to use this service and its features will elevate your SRE practice and save you several hours a month in manual effort. We begin by talking about the different maintenance tasks for your cloud infrastructure. From there, we begin with the basics of AWS Systems Manager and introduce the Systems Manager Agent. Next, we branch into different functionalities offered by Systems Manager in the form of operations management, application management, change management, and node management. We will also look at some examples you can try with the sample application we are using in this book.

Maintenance tasks for your infrastructure

Regular maintenance tasks are essential for the optimal performance of your cloud infrastructure. Through routine checks and updates, you can ensure your systems operate efficiently, maintain compliance standards, and establish effective monitoring for timely incident detection and response. These ongoing maintenance activities form the foundation of a robust and reliable cloud environment.

Maintenance tasks can be grouped into four high-level categories, as shown in the figure:

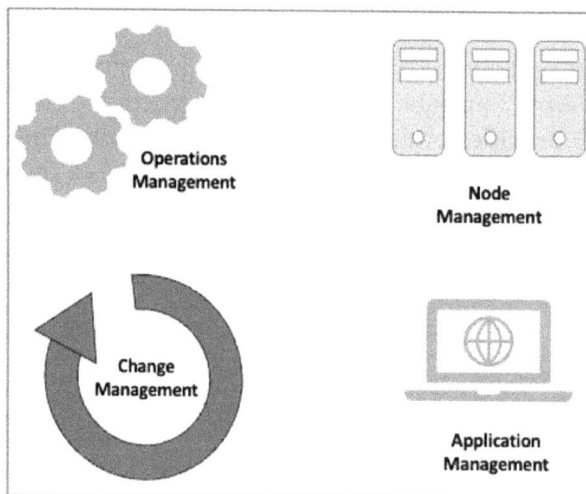

Figure 5.1: High-level categories of maintenance tasks

Let us understand the high-level categories for maintenance tasks:

- **Operations management**: In AWS operations management, incident handling forms a critical component of infrastructure maintenance that requires a systematic and well-structured approach. As an operations manager, you must implement a robust incident management framework that begins with precise incident classification based on factors such as business impact, service disruption scope, and customer effect, typically categorized as SEV1 (critical) through SEV4 (low impact). This classification drives the response timeline and resource allocation. You will need to develop and maintain playbooks for common incidents, incorporating automated responses where possible, while ensuring manual intervention protocols are clearly defined for complex scenarios. Operational data tracking should be centralized. This enables you to establish **key performance indicators (KPIs)** and **service level objectives (SLOs)**. This data-driven approach allows for the prioritization of operational tasks based on quantifiable metrics such as impact radius, resource utilization trends, and compliance requirements, ensuring that critical infrastructure components receive immediate attention while maintaining a balance between proactive maintenance and reactive problem-solving.

- **Node management**: Node compliance management in AWS infrastructure requires a comprehensive and automated approach to maintain security, stability, and operational efficiency. You can implement automated inventory tracking that maintains detailed records of installed software, running services, and configuration settings across your cloud instances and on-premises nodes. You can enable systematic patch deployment through patch baselines and maintenance windows, ensuring that security updates and bug fixes are applied consistently and within defined change management windows. Configuration compliance can be enforced to automatically monitor and remediate drift from your defined baseline configurations. For software installation control, you can centrally manage and deploy software packages while maintaining version control. **infrastructure as code (IaC)** principles ensure that new nodes are provisioned with consistent configurations, while runbooks can orchestrate complex maintenance tasks across your fleet. This automated approach not only reduces human error and operational overhead but also provides audit trails, making compliance documentation and reporting significantly more streamlined.

- **Change management**: Effective change management in cloud infrastructure requires a methodical approach that minimizes service disruption while maintaining system reliability. Operational changes, whether they involve configuration updates, security patches, or system modifications, should follow a well-defined process that includes risk assessment, impact analysis, and rollback planning. The implementation of these changes should leverage automation pipelines that include proper testing phases, staged deployments, and health checks to validate success at each step. Change windows should be carefully selected based on historical traffic patterns, business requirements, and geographical user distribution to minimize potential impact on end users. A robust change management strategy incorporates clear documentation, stakeholder communication, and approval workflows while maintaining detailed audit trails of all modifications. The ability to execute changes progressively across the infrastructure, often referred to as rolling updates, allows for immediate validation and rapid rollback if issues are detected. This systematic approach should also include post-implementation verification steps and performance monitoring to ensure the changes achieve their intended outcomes without unintended consequences. The key advantage of cloud-based change management lies in the ability to standardize these processes through automation, reducing human error, increasing deployment speed, and maintaining consistency across the entire infrastructure landscape while adhering to compliance requirements and operational best practices.

- **Application management**: Effective application management on AWS requires a holistic approach that maps individual resources to their respective business services and applications. This mapping begins with a comprehensive resource tagging strategy that clearly identifies application ownership, environment type, cost centres, and business criticality for every cloud component. When operational issues arise, this contextual information enables rapid impact assessment and prioritization based on business significance rather than isolated technical metrics. This application-centric approach to infrastructure management requires maintaining detailed service maps that document dependencies between components, data flows, and integration points. When troubleshooting or performing maintenance, operators can quickly understand the broader implications of their actions on business services, ensuring that maintenance windows and remediation efforts align with business priorities. Furthermore, capacity planning, cost optimization, and scaling decisions should be made with a full understanding of application patterns and business requirements rather than individual resource utilization. This comprehensive view enables more informed decision-making about resource allocation, performance optimization, and risk management while maintaining clear lines of responsibility for each component within the larger application ecosystem.

Together, these categories of maintenance tasks cover a lot of ground, and AWS provides a range of tooling to perform these tasks. In the next section, we will look at AWS Systems Manager and the wide-ranging features offered by this service.

AWS Systems Manager basics

AWS Systems Manager is a hub of operational tooling that brings together many features that help you accomplish your maintenance tasks. You can view this as an umbrella service which provides sub-services that accomplish specialized tasks. In this section, we will start by understanding the features offered under AWS Systems Manager, and in later sections, we will dive deeper into specific key features in the context of our sample application.

AWS Systems Manager is a powerful service that streamlines the management of your infrastructure, both on AWS and in hybrid environments. You can think of this service as the *Swiss Army knife* of an SRE. This may be the most important service you will master as an SRE on AWS, yet in my experience I have seen so many organizations not consistently using this or even understanding how this can help with SRE tasks. When they understand what this offers, they quickly see how this can save hours of time for the cloud operations and SRE teams. As this book primarily focuses on cloud workloads, we will not explore the hybrid scenarios in depth. Before we begin to look at the features, let us understand a little bit about the component of AWS Systems Manager that enables most of these features. This is called the AWS **Systems Manager Agent (SSM Agent)**.

AWS Systems Manager Agent

Managing a large network of servers across your AWS infrastructure and on-premises environments can be daunting. Manually configuring each server, deploying updates individually, and establishing individual remote access connections takes a toll on your operations team. The SSM Agent steps in as a lightweight software component that unlocks centralized management and automation without consuming significant resources on your instances.

Traditionally, managing servers involved complex processes. You may have relied on scripts, individual SSH connections, and manual configuration changes. This approach is not only time-consuming but also prone to errors and inconsistencies. The SSM Agent eliminates this complexity by acting as a bridge between your managed instances (both EC2 instances in the cloud and on-premises servers) and the AWS Systems Manager service. This two-way communication empowers a centralized approach, allowing you to manage your entire infrastructure centrally. SSM Agent is designed with minimal resource consumption in mind. This means it will not bog down your servers or impact their performance. However, while being simple, it is also very powerful.

Figure 5.2, shows how operations team and SREs can manage their AWS infrastructure using the features of Systems Manager, with the help of the SSM Agent.

The following figure shows how Systems Manager functionalities can make use of SSM Agents on your EC2 instances to perform a range of maintenance tasks:

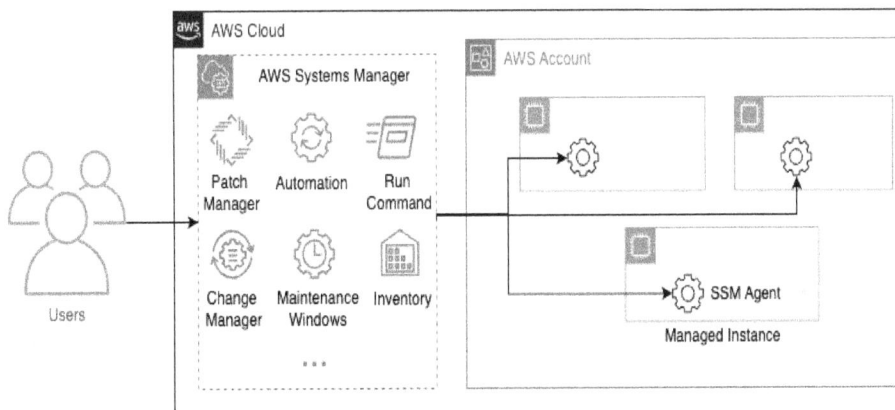

Figure 5.2: Systems Manager features using SSM Agent

SSM Agent is available for different versions of Linux, macOS, and Windows. When EC2 instances created from some of the AMIs offered by AWS are launched, you may find that the SSM Agent is already installed. The AWS documentation provides commands for checking if the SSM Agent is installed and running. If it is not installed, you can also install it using instructions specific to your operating system. We do not cover installation in this chapter, as installation instructions are likely to be frequently updated in the AWS documentation.

Following are some features that the SSM Agent unlocks for you:

- **Simplified remote access**: Juggling multiple SSH connections can be cumbersome. SSM Agent empowers features like Session Manager and Fleet Manager, which allows you to initiate **Secure Shell (SSH)** sessions directly from your web browser. This eliminates the need for dedicated terminal applications and simplifies remote access for troubleshooting, configuration changes, or software installations.

- **Automated configuration management**: Tired of manually configuring each server? The agent paves the way for the State Manager. This powerful feature allows you to define desired configurations as code (IaC). The agent on each instance ensures the configuration state matches your defined parameters, automatically applying updates and maintaining consistency across your infrastructure.

- **Streamlined Patch management**: Patching vulnerabilities across numerous instances on a well-defined schedule can be overwhelming for the operations team. Patch Manager leverages the agent for efficient patch deployment. The agent facilitates communication, allowing you to scan for missing patches, create patch baselines (defining the patches to apply), and schedule automated patching across your instances.

- **Centralized command execution**: You will often find yourself with a need to execute scripts or commands on multiple instances simultaneously. The agent also powers the Run Command feature of Systems Manager. This feature allows you to target specific instances or groups and execute shell scripts or PowerShell commands directly from the Systems Manager console. The agent on each instance receives the command and executes it, providing real-time status updates and detailed logs for monitoring purposes.

- **Security and scalability**: The SSM Agent leverages IAM roles to define access permissions, ensuring only authorized users or groups can interact with your managed instances. Additionally, its lightweight design allows it to scale seamlessly across your growing infrastructure.

Overall, the SSM Agent acts as a powerful yet resource-friendly facilitator. It empowers you to move away from manual processes and fragmented management tools, replacing them with efficient workflows, automation, and ultimately, a more secure and centralized approach to governing your IT landscape. As mentioned before, an SSM Agent can be installed on both your AWS resources and your on-premises resources, but our focus here will be mostly on the AWS portion of your IT landscape.

Let us now look at how the features of AWS Systems Manager correlate with the categories of maintenance concerns that we saw in the following sections, such as *Operations management, Node management, Change management, and Application management*.

Operations management

Operations management within AWS Systems Manager is about gaining visibility and control over your infrastructure, ensuring it runs smoothly and efficiently. It offers a suite of features designed to centralize monitoring, automate tasks, and streamline troubleshooting. Systems Manager Explorer acts as your mission control centre. It empowers you to take a proactive approach to managing your infrastructure. You can identify and address issues before they become critical, automate repetitive tasks, and streamline incident response workflows. This contributes to a more efficient and reliable cloud environment.

Let us now explore the features of Systems Manager that addresses these concerns. After learning about the features, we will look at how we can apply some of these features to our sample application:

- **Systems Manager Explorer:** Explorer is a powerful tool that helps you visualize and analyze the health and performance of your AWS resources. It brings together everything you need to see how your infrastructure is performing, in one place. Explorer enables you to not jump between accounts and regions, as it offers a consolidated dashboard showing the health, compliance, and configuration of your resources from your different accounts across various regions. You can spot trends and potential issues in your operational data before they turn into problems. You can design your dashboards to focus on the metrics that matter most to you and your team. Explorer works hand-in-hand with OpsCenter, a tool for managing operational tasks. From the high-level view that you see in Explorer, you can drill down and investigate specific issues and take action in OpsCenter.

  Explorer is accessible through the AWS Management Console. Navigate to the Systems Manager service and select **Explorer** from the navigation pane. By default, Explorer aggregates data from various AWS services like EC2, S3, CloudWatch, and more. You can further customize data sources using Resource Data Sync, allowing you to integrate data from on-premises environments or other cloud providers. The Explorer interface consists of customizable widgets that display KPIs and operational data in various formats like charts, graphs, and tables. You can arrange these widgets to create informative dashboards tailored to your specific requirements. You can refine your view of the data by applying filters based on accounts, regions, resources, or custom tags. Related data points can be grouped together for easier analysis and identification of trends.

  You can configure alerts within Explorer to receive notifications when specific metrics exceed predefined thresholds. This allows you to stay informed about potential issues and take timely action. You must ensure you have the necessary IAM permissions to access Explorer and view data from relevant services. The timeframe for which Explorer retains historical data depends on the underlying service generating the OpsData. By effectively utilizing Systems Manager Explorer, you can gain a deeper understanding of your infrastructure's health and performance, identify potential issues proactively, and ensure a well-functioning and optimized AWS environment.

> Note: **Systems Manager Explorer cannot be directly configured using IaC tools like Terraform or CloudFormation at this time. However, you can leverage IaC to configure resource tagging, which can then be used for filtering and categorization within Explorer.**

- **OpsCenter:** OpsCenter is a central hub which gives you a real-time view into potential operational issues in your AWS environment. It acts as a single pane of glass for issues affecting your AWS resources. This includes issues such as failing instances, security alerts, and configuration drifts. Alongside showing the problem, OpsCenter also helps you understand it. It provides you contextual information about each OpsItem, including related events, affected resources, and historical data. This big picture view allows you to diagnose issues faster and pinpoint the root cause. It facilitates collaboration by allowing you to assign OpsItems to specific team members, share notes and updates, and track the resolution process. This ensures everyone is on the same page and working together to resolve issues efficiently. It can also help you identify trends and patterns in your OpsData. This allows you to proactively address potential issues before they cause major disruptions. It integrates with tools like Amazon CloudWatch and AWS Config, allowing you to pull in additional data for a more comprehensive view of your infrastructure health. This streamlined approach saves you time and eliminates the need to jump between different consoles.

Configuring OpsCenter is mainly done using the AWS Management Console. In the AWS Management Console, navigate to the Systems Manager service and select OpsCenter in the left navigation pane. Next, click on the **Create workspace** button and provide a descriptive **Name** for your workspace. You may optionally, define **Tags** to categorize your workspace for easier organization within your environment. Lastly, click **Create** to establish your workspace.

OpsCenter aggregates data from various AWS services by default. However, you can further customize data sources. OpsCenter offers predefined dashboards for various purposes. You can customize these views or create new ones. You can drag and drop widgets from the available options to visualize the data relevant to your needs. OpsCenter integrates seamlessly with other AWS services for enhanced functionality OpsCenter can visualize and analyse CloudWatch logs and metrics alongside operational data for a holistic view. You can define AWS Config Rules that trigger OpsItems within OpsCenter when configuration changes deviate from your established compliance standards. You must ensure IAM roles associated with OpsCenter have the necessary permissions to access resources, Run Commands, and manage configurations. You can set up alerts and notifications within OpsCenter based on specific metrics or OpsItem creation to stay informed about potential issues. You can explore the AWS documentation for detailed information on advanced functionalities offered by OpsCenter and its integration with other AWS services.

- **Incident Manager:** Incident Manager is a console for incident management which allows you to create pre-configured response plans that outline the steps to take when an issue arises. These plans can include things like who to notify, what resources need to be investigated, and even automated actions to take to isolate the problem. With a plan in place, your team can react quickly and efficiently, minimizing downtime and impact on your users. Incident Manager understands that clear communication is crucial during a crisis. It allows you to define different notification methods, like email, SMS or phone calls, to ensure the right people are alerted right away. Incident Manager acts as a central hub for your team to collaborate and resolve the issue. You can assign tasks, share notes, and track the progress of the incident in real-time. This shared workspace ensures everyone is on the same page and working towards the common goal of getting your infrastructure back online as fast as possible. Even the best teams experience incidents. But with Incident Manager, you can learn from them and improve your response for the next time. The service provides insights into the incident, such as the timeline of events and the resources involved. This allows you to identify areas for improvement and refine your response plans to be even more effective in the future.

Application management

This is a set of capabilities which simplifies application deployment and management of applications running in AWS. You want to manage your cloud resources on AWS in the context of business applications, so that you can make informed decisions about the health of your applications and plan for remedial actions.

The features outlined empower you to achieve this in simplified manner:

- **Application Manager:** When you want to manage the growing list of interconnected applications running on AWS, Systems Manager Application Manager becomes your essential tool. It offers a granular view and a comprehensive set of features to navigate the complexities of your application landscape. With this, you can avoid manually tracking down every application in your environment. Application Manager employs automated discovery mechanisms. It can identify applications built using various deployment tools like AWS CloudFormation stacks, Amazon ECS clusters, or even custom deployments on EC2 instances. It creates a comprehensive map of your application ecosystem. Further, it allows you to define hierarchies within your applications. This is particularly beneficial for complex applications with multiple components. You can group related components together for a more organized view and streamlined management. Application Manager offers customizable dashboards that display key metrics related to your applications. These can include health status, resource utilization, performance indicators, and even custom metrics specific to your application's needs. Application Manager empowers you with various options for deploying configurations to your applications. The deployment process itself can be triggered manually or automated using Systems Manager Automation. Application Manager allows you to maintain different versions of your configurations and easily roll back to a previous version if needed. This ensures you can quickly rectify any configuration-related problems.

Application Manager integrates with services like Amazon CloudWatch, which provides detailed insights into your application's performance metrics, such as resource utilization, error rates, latency, and API call durations. This allows you to anticipate potential issues before they become major problems. Application Manager allows you to define custom alerts based on specific performance thresholds. These alerts can be triggered via email, SMS, or SNS notifications, ensuring you are promptly informed of any potential performance bottlenecks. Application Manager allows you to create automated runbooks using Systems Manager Automation. These runbooks can be designed to address common application issues, such as restarting a stalled service or scaling resources during a traffic spike. This empowers you to resolve problems quickly and minimize downtime.

Application Manager works together with AWS Systems Manager OpsCenter. OpsItems created within Application Manager can trigger workflows and alerts in OpsCenter, facilitating a centralized approach to incident management and remediation. It also can integrate with various third-party monitoring and logging tools, allowing you to consolidate performance data from various sources into a single pane of glass. This provides a more holistic view of your application's health and performance. Application data and dashboards can be shared with relevant personnel, ensuring everyone has access to the same information for informed decision-making. Teams can collaborate by leaving comments, sharing insights, and tracking the progress of changes or ongoing issues. This open communication fosters a more efficient and streamlined application management process.

Application Manager adheres to the principle of least privilege. Granular access controls through IAM policies ensure only authorized users can access and modify application configurations or perform actions within the service. This safeguards your application environment from unauthorized access and potential security breaches. Application Manager leverages AWS **Key Management Service** (**KMS**) to encrypt application configurations stored within Parameter Store. This ensures sensitive data remains protected even at rest within AWS infrastructure. By leveraging the comprehensive features of AWS Systems Manager Application Manager, you can effectively navigate the complexities of your application landscape.

- **AppConfig:** AWS Systems Manager AppConfig allows you to make software component changes and configuration updates seamlessly and with minimal disruption to the performance. AppConfig is not limited to one type of configuration data. It supports various formats like JSON, YAML, INI, or even custom formats defined by your application. This flexibility allows you to manage a wide range of application settings from environment variables to API keys and feature flags. It integrates seamlessly with AWS Systems Manager Parameter Store, allowing you to leverage its secure storage capabilities. AppConfig allows you to define different configurations for various environments (for example, dev, test, prod). This ensures you are deploying the appropriate settings for each stage of the application lifecycle.

AppConfig allows you to implement blue/green deployments for updates. This involves creating a new application version (**green**) with the updated configuration alongside the existing one (**blue**). Traffic is then gradually shifted to the green version, allowing you to roll back seamlessly if any issues arise. For less disruptive updates, AppConfig supports rolling deployments. This involves incrementally updating individual instances of your application with the new configuration. You can define the update batch size and health checks to ensure a smooth transition and minimize downtime. AppConfig does not require you to update your entire application fleet at once. You can target specific application instances, groups of instances based on tags, or even individual AWS accounts and Regions. This granular control allows you to stage deployments and minimize risk. Imagine selectively updating costumes for specific characters or scenes during rehearsals.

These rules can be based on schemas, syntax checks, or even custom validation logic. This ensures only valid configurations are deployed to your application, preventing potential errors. AppConfig keeps a detailed history of all your deployments. This allows you to track changes, identify successful deployments, and easily roll back to a previous configuration if needed. AppConfig allows you to leverage feature flags. These are essentially on/off switches for specific functionalities within your application. You can control the rollout of new features to a limited audience or disable buggy features instantly without redeploying the entire application. For particularly risky updates, AppConfig allows you to perform canary deployments. This involves deploying the new configuration to a small subset of your application instances and monitoring its impact before rolling it out to the entire fleet. Overall, AWS AppConfig, empowers you to manage configurations effectively, orchestrate deployments with minimal disruption, validate changes for correctness, and even experiment with features on the fly.

- **Parameter Store:** AWS Systems Manager Parameter Store acts as your secure vault, storing all the critical properties, secrets and configurations that keeps your infrastructure running smoothly. It takes the security of your sensitive data seriously. It offers a secure central repository for storing secrets like API keys, database credentials, access tokens, and other bits of information that should never be exposed in plain text. Think of it as a locked vault backstage, holding all the confidential documents and keys needed for the production. Parameter Store encrypts all data at rest using AWS

KMS. This ensures even if someone gains unauthorized access to the vault, they cannot decrypt the secrets. Data is also encrypted in transit using HTTPS, adding another layer of protection during transfers. Parameter Store allows you to define granular access controls through IAM policies. You can specify which users or roles can view, modify, or delete specific parameters. This ensures only authorized personnel can access sensitive information, minimizing the risk of exposure. Parameter Store allows you to define hierarchies within your parameters. You can group related parameters together based on application, environment, or functionality. This makes it easier to find specific settings and ensures the vault remains organized as the number of parameters grows.

Parameter Store allows you to maintain different versions of your parameters, providing a way to easily roll back to a previous version. It works seamlessly with AppConfig, as it can leverage Parameter Store as its secure storage backend for application configurations. This eliminates the need to manage configurations in multiple locations and ensures a centralized source of truth for your application settings. You can interact with it programmatically using the AWS SDK or the AWS CLI. This allows you to integrate parameter management within your development and deployment pipelines for a more streamlined workflow. By leveraging the comprehensive features of AWS Systems Manager Parameter Store, you can ensure the security and integrity of your sensitive data and configurations.

To create a parameter in Parameter Store, you can use the AWS CLI command shown:

```
aws ssm put-parameter \
--name <parameter-name> \
--type SecureString \
--value <parameter-value> \
--description "<optional-description>" \
--region <region>
```

Use <parameter-name> to provide the desired name for your parameter. Alphanumeric characters, hyphens, and underscores are allowed. In <parameter-value>, provide the actual value you want to store (up to 4 KB in size). You can include a brief description of the parameter's purpose using the **description** parameter and **region** is with the AWS Region where you want to store the parameter. The type we have specified here is SecureString. Other options are String and StringList. SecureString is designed specifically for storing sensitive data like passwords, API keys, or other credentials. It utilizes AWS KMS to encrypt the data at rest within the Parameter Store. String stores data in plain text and is suitable for non-sensitive information like environment variables. With StringList, you can specify multiple values separated by commas.

Once you have created a parameter, you can retrieve its value using the `get-parameter` command:

```
aws ssm get-parameter --name <parameter-name> --region <region>
```

For SecureString type parameters, the value returned is not in plain text. To retrieve the actual parameter value, you need to further decrypt the encrypted value using AWS KMS decryption.

Change management

This is a set of features that help you make changes to your AWS resources in a controlled and auditable manner. Changes to your infrastructure can come in many forms, and Systems Manager has you covered by providing functionalities to simplify applying changes across your AWS environment:

- **Automation:** AWS Systems Manager Automation is your control centre, which allows you to orchestrate tasks with the help of AWS **Systems Manager document (SSM documents)**. These documents are more than just text files, they are the blueprints for your automated actions. An automation document is not a simple script. It is a structured document written in either YAML or JSON that defines a series of steps for your automation to execute. These documents are ideal for managing individual EC2 instances or on-premises servers. They leverage shell commands, the familiar tools used by system administrators, to perform tasks like installing software, restarting services, or applying configuration changes. There are more than 100 pre-configured SSM documents available, which are categorized by the type of tasks they perform. You can also customize the actions and steps in a document by creating your own. Automation documents can be designed in a modular fashion. You can create reusable building blocks that define common tasks and reference them within other documents. This modularity simplifies document creation and reduces redundancy. Your documents can be public or shared with specific AWS accounts in a region. You can trigger documents manually on-demand for a single execution or schedule them to run automatically at predefined intervals. You can also configure them to respond to events in real-time through integration with Amazon EventBridge. This allows you to define workflows that are triggered by specific events within your AWS environment. This event-driven approach empowers proactive automation for incident response or preventative maintenance. Routine tasks like patching servers, applying security updates, or backing up data can all be automated, freeing up your team to focus on more strategic initiatives.

  You can automate complex multi-step processes, like deploying new application versions, responding to incidents, or scaling resources based on demand. This leads to a more efficient and reliable infrastructure that requires less manual intervention, ensuring your applications run smoothly and efficiently. Automation documents follow a defined execution pipeline, including checking pre-requisites to ensure the target instances meet necessary conditions for successful execution. This is followed by the step-by-step execution of the defined tasks within the document. Automation provides real-time status updates for each execution of a document. You can track the progress of each step, identify any errors or failures, and monitor the overall health of your automated workflows. It generates detailed logs for each document execution, capturing the output of each step, any errors encountered, and the overall execution status. This allows you to troubleshoot issues, analyse successes, and maintain a record of your automated actions.

Automation documents leverage IAM roles to define access permissions. You can configure specific roles for users or groups, granting them the necessary permissions to create, edit, and execute automation documents. This ensures only authorized personnel can manage these automated workflows within your infrastructure. With AWS Systems Manager Automation, you can move beyond manual processes and scripted tasks. It empowers you to define, codify, and automate complex workflows, ensuring consistent configurations, efficient incident response, and ultimately, a more streamlined and well-managed IT infrastructure.

Let us look at a simple automation example. The examples in this chapter can also be created using CloudFormation, but we will instead see how to use SSM with AWS CLI. There is no preferred option for this, and you may choose to use whatever you find convenient. Another option is to write programs with your preferred AWS SDK, such as boto3, to accomplish the same things. Our infrastructure is deployed using AWS CloudFormation in *Chapter 4, Infrastructure as Code*. This would have created 2 EC2 instances in private subnets of the VPC. Let us assume you want to restart these EC2 instances for maintenance purposes. Normally, with **ClickOps** you, would navigate to the AWS EC2 console, find each instance, and restart them with mouse clicks.

Note: **As your EC2 instances are part of an auto scaling group (ASG), when you try to restart them using the automation example that follows, the ASG may respond to your instances temporarily, reporting as unhealthy, and start new instances.**

To prevent this, you can temporarily pause autoscaling by running this command:

```
aws autoscaling suspend-processes --auto-scaling-group-name <<asg-name>>
```

You can retrieve the name of your ASG from the list of resources that your CloudFormation template has created by viewing it in the AWS Console.

When you have completed the following example, you can resume autoscaling by running the command:

```
aws autoscaling resume-processes --auto-scaling-group-name <<asg-name>>
```

However, you can achieve the same result by using an automation document. Here is how you would execute this automation from the AWS CLI. These CLI commands can be executed from any terminal that is configured for AWS access. Alternatively, you may use AWS CloudShell to obtain a preconfigured terminal within your AWS Console, as follows:

```
aws ssm start-automation-execution \
--document-name "AWS-RestartEC2Instance" \
--targets "Key=tag:Env,Values=Prod"  \
--target-parameter-name "InstanceId"
--region us-west-2
```

Let us understand the parameters for the command aforementioned:

- **--targets** parameter specifies which resources to target based on tags

- **--target-parameter-name** tells Systems Manager which parameter in the automation document should receive the instance IDs

- **--document-name** parameter specifies the name of the automation document we are executing. Here, the name of our document is **AWS-RestartEC2Instance**.

The automation will create a child automation for each instance that matches the specified tags. You will also need to use the same region that you used to create your infrastructure. When you run the CLI command aforementioned, you will get back an **AutomationExecutionId**.

You can use this to check the status of the automation execution:

aws ssm get-automation-execution --automation-execution-id <<execution-id>>

This command will give you the overall execution status for the automation. Additionally, it will also show you the status for each step within the automation. For example, if you inspect the automation document for **AWS-RestartEC2Instance**, you will notice that it has two steps, one that stops the instances and the other that starts the instances.

You can run this command to see the contents of the automation document:

aws ssm get-document --name "AWS-RestartEC2Instance"

In the output of this command, you will see the following section, which shows the two steps that make up this automation:

```
"mainSteps": [
    {
      "name": "stopInstances",
      "action": "aws:changeInstanceState",
      "inputs": {
        "InstanceIds": "{{ InstanceId }}",
        "DesiredState": "stopped"
      }
    },
```

```
{
    "name": "startInstances",
    "action": "aws:changeInstanceState",
    "inputs": {
        "InstanceIds": "{{ InstanceId }}",
        "DesiredState": "running"
    }
  }
}
]
```

You may have noticed, this automation is quite simple. However, you can build very powerful multi-step automations with the help of automation documents. These documents are usually referred to as runbooks, as they are intended to provide a standardized, documented process to achieve specific outcomes in a systematic manner. The example targeted instances to execute automations using tag key and the tag value, but you could also have used instance IDs, or the name of a resource group. You can also run your automations across multiple accounts and regions at once. This is very powerful, as it allows you to execute automations centrally from a designated automation account or an SRE/operations account.

Lastly, you can also specify maximum concurrency and maximum errors your automation can tolerate. This can be specified as either a percentage of the targets or an absolute number. With concurrency, you can control the scale of your automation across your fleet. You can configure this to achieve the right scale and parallelism for your needs, without overburdening the service or risking being throttled. With errors, you decide how many or what percentage of errors you are willing to tolerate before you decide to stop sending more automation requests to your resources and troubleshoot.

The following is a canonical example of an intricate automation that makes use of some of these options:

```
aws ssm start-automation-execution \
--document-name <<runbook name>> \
--parameters AutomationAssumeRole=arn:aws:iam::management account ID:role/AWS-SystemsManager-AutomationAdministrationRole \
--target-parameter-name parameter <<param_name>> \
--targets Key=tag key,Values=value \
--target-locations Accounts=account ID A,account ID B,Regions=Region X,Region Y, ExecutionRoleName=AWS-SystemsManager-AutomationExecutionRole \
--max-concurrency 10 \
--max-errors 25%
```

In this example, we are running the automation across multiple accounts and regions using a service IAM role that exists in the management account of your AWS Organization in the parameters. This IAM role gives automation the permission it needs to perform the actions you have specified. Further, you are targeting resources using tags by specifying the tag key and tag value in the targets parameter. The `target-parameter-name` in this command specifies the type of resource on which you are running your automation. For example, this could be InstanceId for EC2 instances, VolumeId if you are targeting EBS volumes, etc. To learn more about the command parameters, refer to the AWS documentation, as follows:

- **Change Manager:** AWS Systems Manager Change Manager offers a suite of features to streamline the planning, execution, and review of changes within your environment. It eliminates the need for scattered change requests across various tools or emails. It provides a central repository for submitting, reviewing, and approving all change requests related to your AWS infrastructure. This fosters transparency and ensures all changes are documented and tracked in a single location. You can adapt the change approval process to your specific needs. Change Manager allows you to define custom workflows that route requests to the appropriate reviewers based on pre-determined criteria. This could involve routing network configuration changes to a dedicated networking team or security updates to the security operations centre.

  Change Manager integrates with services like AWS Config to assess the potential impact of a proposed change on your existing infrastructure. This allows you to identify potential conflicts or areas of risk early on in the process, enabling informed decision-making before approving the change. It enables planning for approved changes, outlining the specific steps involved, the resources required, and the rollback strategy in case of unforeseen issues. This detailed roadmap ensures everyone involved understands the change process and can anticipate potential challenges. You can reduce manual effort and improve consistency by leveraging Automation workflows within Change Manager execution plans. Change Manager allows you to define phased rollouts, where the change is applied to a limited set of resources first. This allows for testing and validation before a wider rollout, minimizing the potential impact on your production environment. Using IAM, Change Manager allows you to define granular access controls. This ensures that only individuals with the appropriate permissions can submit or approve changes, mitigating the risk of unauthorized modifications to your environment.

  Change Manager provides a real-time view of the execution status of your changes. You can track the progress of each step within the execution plan, identify any errors, and make adjustments as needed. It maintains a detailed history of all change requests, approvals, and executions, using which you can identify trends, troubleshoot issues, and continuously improve. This positively evolves your change management processes over time while breaking down silos and enabling collaboration between teams. With a secure, efficient, and well-documented change management process you can navigate changes with confidence and minimize disruption to your critical applications.

- **Maintenance Windows:** When performing actions on your resources like patching operating systems, updating software, or installing new applications, it is important to it in a manner that does not disrupt your business. AWS Systems Manager Maintenance Windows offer granular control over scheduling these potentially disruptive changes. You can define recurring windows that run daily, weekly, monthly, or even on specific days of the week. This flexibility allows you to schedule maintenance activities during periods of low traffic or outside of business hours to minimize disruption to your users. It allows you to specify the duration of the window, ensuring your maintenance activities are completed within a defined timeframe. This helps minimize the window of vulnerability introduced by applying updates. Maintenance Windows allow you to specify the time zone in which the window applies. This ensures consistency regardless of the geographical location of your resources or users.

You do not need to target your entire infrastructure at once with Maintenance Windows. You can specify individual EC2 instances, groups of instances based on tags, or even resources across other AWS services like Amazon S3 buckets or Amazon SNS topics. This granular targeting ensures you only update the resources that require maintenance within the defined window. It also allows you to gradually roll out changes to a subset of resources first, and then to the entire fleet if successful by integrating with services like AWS CodeDeploy, which we will learn about in future chapters. It can also integrate with both System Run Command and automation documents. These documents use the SSM Agent to receive communication from the Systems Manager control plane to the target instances for executing commands or workflows during the maintenance window.

You can configure notifications to be sent via Amazon SNS topics before, during, and after the maintenance window. You can use this to alert relevant personnel about upcoming maintenance activities, the status of ongoing tasks, or any unexpected issues encountered during the window. Maintenance Windows integrates with Amazon CloudWatch, which provides detailed logs and metrics related to the tasks executed within the window. This allows you to monitor the success or failure of individual commands or workflows and troubleshoot any issues that may arise. By leveraging the features of AWS Systems Manager Maintenance Windows, you can establish a structured and controlled approach to performing maintenance activities on your AWS resources. This ensures your infrastructure remains up-to-date, secure, and functioning optimally with minimal disruption to your applications and users.

Let us look at an example of how you create a maintenance window using the AWS CLI:

```
aws ssm create-maintenance-window \
    --name "Sample-App-Maintenance-Window" \
    --allow-unassociated-targets \
    --duration 3 \
    --cutoff 1 \
```

```
--start-date 2024-06-01T00:00:00-08:00 \
--schedule-timezone "America/Chicago" \
--schedule "rate(7 days)"
--tags "Key"="Task","Value"="Patching"
```

Let us examine the parameters of this command. **Sample-App-Maintenance-Window** is the name of the maintenance window you are creating. **--allow-unassociated-targets** parameter allows you to run maintenance window tasks on resources that are not associated with the maintenance window. By default, maintenance window tasks can only run on resources that are registered with the maintenance window. **--duration 3** sets the duration of the maintenance to be open for three hours, and **--cutoff 1** specifies that stops scheduling new tasks. Here we have set it to one hour before the end of the maintenance window. **-start-date 2024-06-01T00:00:00-08:00** and **--schedule-timezone America/Chicago** parameters sets the start date of the maintenance window to 1st June, 2024 at 8 AM in the Chicago (Central) time zone in the United States. Make sure that you update the start date of your maintenance window to a future timestamp, as this timestamp represents a time when this book is being authored. **--schedule rate(7 days)** parameter specifies that the maintenance window will recur every seven days. You can also associate tags with the maintenance window to describe its intended purpose.

Running this command returns an identifier for the maintenance window. You will use this identifier when you associate targets and tasks with the maintenance window. For example, you can associate a target with a maintenance window, as shown. In this case, we are using tags to associate the maintenance window with the target nodes. You can also use instance IDs or resource groups to register your targets:

```
aws ssm register-target-with-maintenance-window \
--window-id "mw-0a1234567bcdefgh" \
--resource-type "INSTANCE" \
--target "Key=tag:Env,Values=Prod"
```

You need to associate tasks with your maintenance windows to perform actions when the maintenance window runs. There are four types of tasks you can associate with a maintenance window:

- AWS Systems Manager Run Command
- Systems Manager Automation workflows
- AWS Step Functions tasks
- AWS Lambda functions

Registering targets with the maintenance window is optional for Step Functions tasks and Lambda Functions. However, for Run Command and Automation workflows, you must associate targets with your maintenance windows before you associate tasks with them. The tasks are performed on the associated targets when the maintenance window runs.

The following is an example of associating a task with the maintenance window using AWS CLI:

```
aws ssm register-task-with-maintenance-window \
--window-id "mw-0a1234567bcdefgh"  \
--task-arn "AWS-RestartEC2Instance" \
--task-type "AUTOMATION"  \
--targets "Key=WindowTargetIds,Values=4c756389-1a69-
4bd0-a7db-dc07920fbdf6"    --task-invocation-parameters
"Automation={DocumentVersion=5,Parameters={InstanceId='{{RESOURCE_ID}}'}}"\
--name "RestartEC2Task" \
--priority 1 \
--max-concurrency "1" \
--max-errors "1"
--description "Automation task to restart EC2 instances"
```

The command registers an automation task with an AWS Systems Manager Maintenance Window. The **--window-id** parameter specifies the ID of the Maintenance Window with which you want to register the task. The **task-arn** parameter identifies the resource on which the task operates. For a Run Command or Automation workflow task, this can either be the full **Amazon Resource Name (ARN)** or just the name of the SSM document. For a Lambda function or a Step Function, it is going to be the ARN of the Lambda function or the Step Function state machine. This example uses the **AWS-RestartEC2Instance** SSM document to restart EC2 instances. For some tasks, you may need to specify the **service-role-arn** parameter. This would be the ARN of the service role that the Systems Manager service assumes to run a maintenance window task. It provides the permissions necessary for the Maintenance Window to run the registered task.

The **task-type** parameter specifies the type of task. In this example, we have used an **AUTOMATION** task. Other options are **RUN_COMMAND**, **LAMBDA**, and **STEP_FUNCTIONS**. **--task-invocation-parameters** specifies additional parameters to the task when it runs. This command provides the automation document version number and the parameter name, which specifies the instance IDs for the automation. For other types of tasks, this would have invocation parameters specific to that task type. You may have noticed the {{**RESOURCE_ID**}} placeholder in the command. This is a pseudo parameter. At runtime, these pseudo parameters are replaced with the actual values. In this case, it will have the instance IDs of the targets registered with the maintenance window. There are other pseudo parameters you can use as well, depending on the type of input you want to provide to the task and the task that you want to perform. You can learn about the other options available in the AWS documentation. The **priority** parameter specifies the priority of the task within the maintenance window. The lower the number, the higher the priority it indicates. This is useful when you have multiple tasks assigned to the same maintenance window and you want to prioritize among them.

If two tasks have the same priority, they are scheduled in parallel. You can also optionally provide a name and a description to the task using parameters for them.

Node management

This is a set of features to perform operations on a Systems Manager-managed node. A managed node is a host on AWS or on-premises that has the SSM Agent installed and is configured to work with the Systems Manager. As we mentioned in the SSM Agent overview, it unlocks a range of features for managing nodes, which we will explore now.

Session Manager

Traditional methods of managing a network of servers often involve juggling SSH keys, managing bastion hosts, and establishing individual connections. AWS Systems Manager Session Manager offers a secure and streamlined approach to remotely accessing and managing your EC2 instances, on-premises servers, and virtual machines. It relies on the SSM Agent to facilitate secure communication between your management console and the target server, eliminating the need for complex manual configuration. AWS Session Manager leverages IAM roles to define access permissions. You can configure specific IAM roles for users or groups, granting them the necessary permissions to initiate remote sessions to authorized instances. This ensures only authorized personnel can access your servers. It allows you to initiate and manage remote sessions directly from your web browser within the AWS Management Console or from the command line on a terminal configured for AWS access.

Once a session is established, the Session Manager provides an SSH connection to the target instance. This allows you to execute commands, manage files, troubleshoot issues, and perform administrative tasks directly on the server as if you were physically logged in. You can open and manage multiple sessions concurrently within the same browser window. This can significantly improve efficiency when working across several servers at once. Session Manager offers optional session recording functionality. This can be valuable for auditing purposes, documenting troubleshooting steps, or training new team members on server administration tasks. Session Manager removes the need for bastion hosts, a traditional approach that often introduces additional security vulnerabilities. By establishing direct, secure connections, Session Manager reduces the attack surface and strengthens your overall security posture. Traditional SSH connections require open inbound ports on your servers, which is a potential security risk. Session Manager utilizes existing outbound connections to the AWS cloud, eliminating the need to expose inbound ports on your instances.

While Session Manager primarily focuses on interactive sessions, it can also be used for executing one-off commands on target instances. This can be useful for automating simple tasks like restarting services or deploying configuration changes. Session Manager can integrate with various third-party tools and platforms. This allows you to leverage existing workflows and integrate remote access with your preferred development or IT operations tools. By leveraging the secure, centralized, and user-friendly approach offered by Session

Manager, you can streamline remote access management for your EC2 instances, on-premises servers, and virtual machines. It eliminates the complexities of traditional methods, improves security posture, and empowers authorized personnel to efficiently manage your server infrastructure from a central location.

Following is an example of how you can start a terminal session on your managed nodes using AWS Session Manager:

```
aws ssm start-session --target i-0123456789xxxxxx
```

You can try the command aforementioned by using one of the EC2 instance IDs that have been created for you as part of the CloudFormation stack. This will start a terminal session on the instance you have specified as the target. You can achieve this without the instance requiring a public IP address assigned to it, and your instance can be in a private subnet. The security group assigned to the instance does not need to allow traffic on port 22 for inbound SSH connections. The instance also does not need to be associated with an SSH key pair. What this means is that you can connect to your instance safely and securely without a bastion host in your public subnet. This is enabled through a combination of the SSM Agent on the instance and permissions provided by the IAM role associated with the instance profile. This is because our sample app makes use of Amazon Linux 2 AMI, it should already come with the SSM Agent installed. Additionally, the IAM role attached to the instance profile associated with the launch template that creates the EC2 instances for the sample app already has the required permissions to allow Session Manager connections.

Fleet Manager

Closely related to the features offered by Session Manager is AWS Systems Manager Fleet Manager. Fleet Manager acts as your central hub for managing your entire server fleet, regardless of location or operating system (Windows, Linux, macOS) on AWS EC2 or on-premises. This eliminates the need for separate management tools, simplifying your workflow. Granular IAM access controls ensure only authorized personnel interact with your servers. It automatically discovers and aggregates information about your managed instances, eliminating the need to switch between different consoles or tools to monitor the health and status of your servers. Fleet Manager allows you to view detailed information about each server in your fleet, like operating system version, instance type, installed software, and configuration settings. It provides real-time status information for each server in your fleet. This includes details like CPU utilization, memory usage, and any running processes or services. This allows you to proactively identify potential performance bottlenecks or resource constraints before they impact your applications.

Fleet Manager integrates with Session Manager for secure remote access to individual servers. You can troubleshoot issues, make configuration changes, or install software directly from the console, eliminating the need for manual connections. It also integrates with Run Command and automation documents for script execution and complex workflows. Fleet Manager can integrate with AWS Systems Manager Patch Manager, allowing you to define automated patching schedules for your servers, ensuring they remain up-to-date with the latest security updates and bug fixes.

By leveraging the granular control and centralized visibility offered by AWS Systems Manager Fleet Manager, you can streamline the management of your server fleet, regardless of their location or operating system. It empowers you to gain a comprehensive understanding of your server health, perform remote actions efficiently, and automate routine tasks, ultimately saving you time and effort in managing your ever-growing server infrastructure.

Inventory

AWS Systems Manager Inventory helps you automatically collect and aggregate metadata from your managed instances, providing a comprehensive inventory of your environment. It can collect data from a variety of platforms, including EC2 instances, on-premises servers, virtual machines, and even containers running on Amazon ECS. This gives you a holistic view of your entire infrastructure, regardless of where it resides. Inventory comes pre-configured to collect essential data points about your instances. This includes details like operating system information, installed software (applications and packages), hardware specifications, network configuration, and running processes. Inventory allows you to define custom data types specific to your needs. This could involve collecting information about specific applications, configuration files, or security settings on your instances. This customization allows you to tailor the inventory to your unique environment.

You can configure inventory to collect data on a recurring basis (hourly, daily, weekly) or on demand as needed. This allows you to balance the need for up-to-date information with minimizing resource consumption on your instances. Collected metadata is securely stored in a designated Amazon S3 bucket within your account. This allows for centralized storage, easy access for analysis, and integration with other AWS services for further processing. For example, you can leverage Amazon Athena to query the inventory data stored in S3, enabling you to generate reports, identify trends, and analyse the configuration state of your infrastructure. Inventory data can also be valuable for security and compliance purposes. You can use it to identify unauthorized software installations, outdated configurations, or potential security vulnerabilities on your instances. This proactive approach helps you maintain a secure and compliant infrastructure.

Inventory data can be used to trigger automated actions within AWS Systems Manager Automation. For example, you could configure Automation to automatically remediate instances with missing security patches or outdated software versions identified by inventory data. For complex environments, inventory aggregates allow you to group similar instances for data collection and reporting. This can simplify analysis and identify patterns or inconsistencies across specific types of instances within your infrastructure. Inventory can assist in application discovery. By analysing installed software and processes on instances, it can help you identify applications running in your environment, even if they have not been formally documented. This can be helpful for gaining a complete picture of your software landscape.

By leveraging the comprehensive data collection, flexible targeting, and integration capabilities of AWS Systems Manager Inventory, you gain a deeper understanding of your infrastructure. This empowers you to make informed decisions about resource management, improve security posture, and automate routine tasks for a more efficient and well-managed AWS environment.

Run Command

AWS Systems Manager Run Command offers a centralized platform to execute shell scripts or PowerShell commands on your EC2 instances, on-premises servers, or even virtual machines in your hybrid environment. Run Command can target specific instances for command execution. This can be done by selecting individual instances, using tags assigned to your instances, or leveraging filters based on instance ID, operating system, or security groups. This targeted approach ensures commands are only executed on the intended resources. For large-scale deployments, Run Command integrates with AWS Systems Manager Fleet Manager. This allows you to target entire fleets of servers managed by Fleet Manager for command execution. This streamlines large-scale deployments of configuration changes or software updates across your server infrastructure.

Run Command offers broad compatibility. It allows you to execute shell scripts for Linux and macOS instances or PowerShell commands for Windows instances. It allows you to pass parameters along with your scripts or commands. This enables dynamic execution based on specific criteria, making your commands more versatile and adaptable to different scenarios. Run Command allows you to define the working directory on the target instance where the command will be executed. This ensures your commands have access to the necessary files and configurations for successful execution. Run Command provides real-time status updates for each instance targeted for command execution. This allows you to monitor progress, identify any errors or failures, and take corrective actions as needed. Gain insights into execution details. Run Command generates detailed logs for each command execution on each targeted instance. These logs capture the command output, any errors encountered, and the overall execution status. This allows you to troubleshoot issues, analyse successes, and maintain a record of actions performed on your servers.

Run Command retrieves the output of the executed commands from each targeted instance. This output can be crucial for analysing the success or failure of the commands and identifying potential issues on your servers. It integrates with AWS Systems Manager Parameter Store where commonly used scripts or commands as can be stored as parameters referenced within your Run executions. This promotes code reuse, reduces errors, and ensures consistency across your infrastructure. Run Command integrates with AWS Systems Manager Automation documents, allowing you to define multi-step workflows that include Run Command executions along with other actions. This empowers you to automate complex configuration management tasks or incident response procedures across your server fleet. It adheres to strict security protocols. It leverages IAM roles to define access permissions for users or groups authorized to execute commands on your instances. This ensures only authorized personnel can initiate actions within your infrastructure.

By leveraging the granular targeting, execution control, and monitoring capabilities of AWS Systems Manager Run Command, you gain a centralized and efficient way to execute scripts and commands across your hybrid infrastructure. This streamlines routine tasks, automates complex workflows, and empowers you to manage your server fleet with greater control and efficiency.

Let us look at how you can use Run Command to determine the disk space usage on our instances. The command **df -dh** gives you information about the disk usage on an instance. Run Command makes use of command SSM documents. In this case, we are using the **AWS-RunShellScript** command document to run the **df -dh** command on two instances that we are identifying by their instance IDs. You can also select the instances by tags or resource groups.

The CLI command that you want to run is specified as parameters to the **AWS-RunShellScript** SSM document:

```
aws ssm send-command \
    --document-name "AWS-RunShellScript" \
    --parameters '{"commands":["df -h"]}' \
    --targets "Key=InstanceIds,Values= i-0123456789xxxxxx,
i-xxxxxx9876543210" \
    --query "Command.CommandId" \
    --output text \
    --region us-west-2
```

You must replace the example instance Ids above with the ones in your account. When you run this command, it does not immediately return the results of the shell command that you are executing. Instead, it returns a **CommandId** as an identifier. As commands can take some time to execute, you can use the **CommandId** to poll the result of the command execution. You can do this as shown, using the get-command-invocation command.

Here, you will need to specify the instance ID for each instance you want to view the command execution result for:

```
aws ssm get-command-invocation \
    --command-id "0510585d-a029-41e6-a14c-a9359cf85986" \
    --instance-id "i-0123456789xxxxxx" \
    --query "StandardOutputContent" \
    --output text \
    --region us-west-2
```

Like AWS-RunShellScript, you will also find other command documents for actions like executing PowerShell commands, applying Ansible playbooks, applying Chef recipes and such. You can pick the right one based on the operating system of your managed instances, your configuration management needs etc. Each of these documents also needs specific parameters that are applicable to that document.

You can learn more about the parameters applicable for a specific document by executing the describe-document command as shown in the following:

```
aws ssm describe-document \
  --name "AWS-RunShellScript"
```

State Manager

AWS Systems Manager State Manager helps you automate the process of ensuring your managed instances adhere to a desired configuration state you define. You define the desired configuration state of your instances using SSM documents. These documents specify configuration details like software packages to install, user accounts to create, or security settings to apply. A state manager association links a specific SSM document to a set of targeted instances based on tags, instance IDs, or resource groups. This association defines how the desired configuration state specified in the SSM document will be applied to the targeted instances. You can use Systems Manager Automation documents to trigger State Manager associations during deployment or configuration changes. This allows for orchestration of multi-step workflows that involve not only configuration management but also other actions. State Manager follows a defined execution process. It first performs a pre-requisite check to ensure the target instances meet any conditions necessary for successful configuration application. Then, it executes the steps defined in the SSM document to configure the instances. The SSM Agent installed on a managed instance communicates with the State Manager service and executes the configuration steps defined in the associated document.

State Manager operations are idempotent, meaning they produce the same outcome regardless of how many times they are executed. This ensures your desired configuration state is achieved and avoids unintended modifications. It allows you to define rollback configurations within your SSM document. This enables you to revert to a previous configuration state if necessary, minimizing the impact of potential errors during configuration application. State Manager provides detailed reports on the compliance state of your managed instances. These reports identify any deviations from the desired configuration state, allowing you to take corrective actions and maintain consistency across your infrastructure. It can be integrated with AWS Systems Manager Automation to define automated remediation workflows. These workflows can be triggered when compliance reports identify configuration drift, automatically bringing instances back to the desired state.

By leveraging the comprehensive configuration management capabilities of AWS Systems Manager State Manager, you can ensure consistent configurations across your hybrid infrastructure. This reduces manual effort, minimizes configuration drift, and empowers you to maintain a secure, well-managed and compliant environment.

Let us now look at an example of how you can create a State Manager association. Previously, we had learned about Systems Manager Inventory. Following is how you can create a State Manager association to gather software inventory from your managed instances:

```
aws ssm create-association \
--name AWS-GatherSoftwareInventory \
--targets "Key=tag:Env,Values=Prod" \
--schedule-expression "rate(1 day)" \
--region us-west-2 \
--parameters applications=Enabled,awsComponents=Enabled
,customInventory=Enabled,instanceDetailedInformation=Enabled,
networkConfig=Enabled,services=Enabled,windowsRoles=Enabled
```

This association will gather software inventory from the instances associated with the tags you have specified on a daily basis based on the rate you have specified in the scheduling expression. In the parameters, we have also specified what types of inventory we want to gather. Here, we have turned on information about applications, AWS components, detailed instance information, any custom inventory, information about services, and network configuration. There are also other metadata you can collect from your instances, such as file information, process information, patch summary, etc. For the complete list of all inventory options, refer to the latest AWS documentation.

After the association is created, as shown above, you can check the status of the association in this manner for a particular instance:

```
aws ssm describe-instance-associations-status \
        --instance-id i-0123456789xxxxxx \
--region us-west-2
```

This will show you the status of the association, and you can see if it was successful. For the inventory use case, you can view the details of a specific inventory metadata type using the **list-inventory-entries** command. Following, you can see how we can view application-related inventory metadata for a particular instance.

```
aws ssm list-inventory-entries \
--instance-id i-0123456789xxxxxx \
--type-name AWS:Application \
--region us-west-2
```

Let us look at another example of how you can keep your SSM Agent updated automatically with the help of State Manager association:

```
aws ssm create-association \
  --name "AWS-UpdateSSMAgent" \
  --association-name "UpdateSSMAgent" \
```

```
--targets Key="instanceIds,Values=*" \
--schedule-expression "rate(7 days)" \
--output text --region us-west-2
```

Here, we are making use of a document **AWS-UpdateSSMAgent** and targeting all managed instances using the wildcard *. This will automatically try to update the SSM Agent on all your managed instances every 7 days.

Overall, you can use State Manager to ensure your managed instances maintain a state that you desire and check the compliance.

Patch Manager

AWS Systems Manager Patch Manager helps you automate the process of patching both security-related updates and other types of updates across your managed instances. Patch Manager caters to a variety of operating systems commonly used in AWS environments. This includes popular options like Amazon Linux, Ubuntu, **Red Hat Enterprise Linux (RHEL)**, and Microsoft Windows Server. Patch Manager allows you to leverage multiple sources for software updates. These include the official repositories maintained by the operating system vendors as well as curated patch repositories offered by AWS itself.

With Patch Manager you can choose to perform a scan first, identifying missing patches applicable to your defined baseline, without automatically installing them. This allows you to review the findings and prioritize patches before deployment. Patch Manager allows you to schedule automated patching for your managed instances based on pre-defined schedules, ensuring your instances receive critical security updates promptly without requiring manual intervention. You can define a list of specific patches (regardless of their inclusion in your baseline) to be installed on selected instances, providing targeted patching capabilities for critical situations. You can track the history of the status of each patch deployment across your instances, including successful installations, failures, and any errors encountered. This allows you to identify instances requiring attention and ensure successful patching completion. It generates reports that indicate the percentage of instances that are compliant with your defined patch baselines. This allows you to track progress and identify areas where patching efforts might need to be focused. For deeper analysis, Patch Manager integrates with Amazon CloudWatch. You can leverage CloudWatch to monitor patching metrics, set alarms for unexpected patching failures, and gain further insights into the health and security posture of your infrastructure. Patch Manager leverages IAM roles to define access permissions. You can configure specific roles for users or groups, granting them the necessary permissions to manage patch baselines, initiate patching actions, and view compliance reports.

AWS Systems Manager Patch Manager empowers you to take control of your infrastructure's security posture. By providing a centralized platform for defining patch baselines, automating deployment schedules, and offering detailed reporting, it simplifies the entire patching process. This translates to a more secure environment with reduced vulnerability windows, streamlined IT operations, and ultimately, peace of mind knowing your infrastructure is protected against evolving threats. Let us now take a moment to understand how Patch Manager works. Patch Manager empowers you to define custom patch baselines. These baselines act as blueprints, specifying which patches (based on severity, product, classification, etc.) should be applied to your managed instances. This allows you to tailor your patching strategy based on your specific security requirements and risk tolerance. Additionally, there are standard patch baselines that AWS provides for different operating supported. A patch group is a way to organize instances for patching in AWS Systems Manager. It helps you organize and control the patching process across different sets of instances using tags. AWS Systems Manager uses a coordinated approach between Patch Baselines, Patch Groups, and Maintenance Windows to manage instance patching. Patch Baselines define the rules for patch approval and which patches should be installed on instances, while Patch Groups help organize instances into logical sets for patching purposes, and these groups are then associated with specific patch baselines. Maintenance Windows tie everything together by providing scheduled time slots during which the patching operations can occur. They define when patches should be applied, which instances (identified by their patch groups) should be patched, and what specific patching actions should be taken using the AWS-RunPatchBaseline document. When a maintenance window starts, Systems Manager checks the patch baseline associated with each instance's patch group, determines which patches need to be applied according to the baseline rules, and then executes the patching operation on the targeted instances within the defined maintenance window period, ensuring that patching occurs in a controlled, predictable manner while adhering to the organization's patch compliance requirements. This is shown in the following figure:

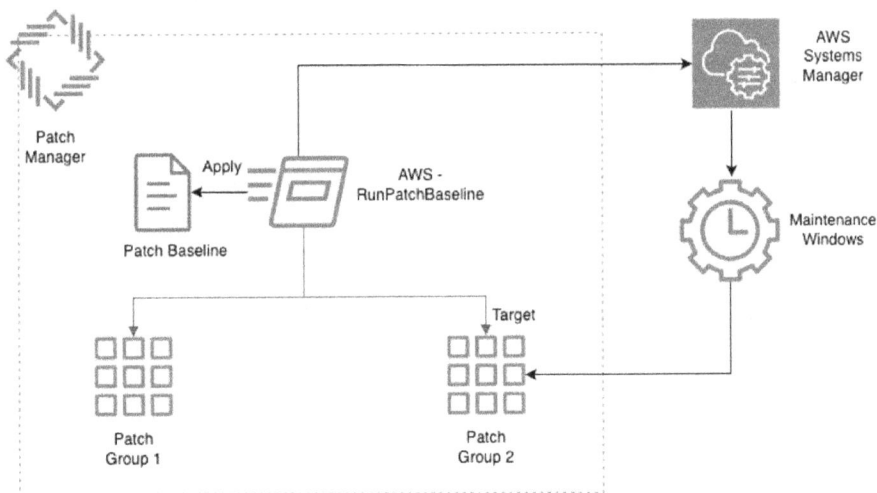

Figure 5.3: *Systems Manager Patch Manager in action*

Let us now look at how we can create a patch baseline for our managed instances in the sample app and set up automatic patch management. For most operating systems, AWS provides predefined patch baselines with an auto-approval delay of seven days. However, when you want more control over when your patches are installed, you can create custom patch baselines. Let us look at an example of how to set this up.

Following is the CLI command we can use to define a custom patch baseline:

```
aws ssm create-patch-baseline \
  --name "AutoApprovePatches-AL2" \
  --operating-system "AMAZON_LINUX_2" \
  --approval-rules "PatchRules=[{PatchFilterGroup={PatchFilters=
[{Key=SEVERITY,Values=[Important,Criti
cal]},{Key=CLASSIFICATION,Values=[Security,Bugfix, Enhancement,
 Recommended]},{Key=PRODUCT,Values=AmazonLinux2}]},
ApproveAfterDays=5}]" \
  --region us-west-2
```

This command is defining a custom patch baseline, where it is going to auto-approve all important and critical severity patches for the Amazon Linux 2 operating system after five days. Among the patches, it is going to pick the ones classified as security-related patches, bug fixes, enhancements, and any other recommended patches. You have the ability to pick the patches that you want to auto-approve. For operating system types based on Linux with a reported severity level for patches, Patch Manager uses the level reported by the publisher for the individual patch or update notice. For Amazon Linux 2, the patch baseline uses repositories preconfigured on the managed node. The options you specify in the command can differ for other operating systems. For example, for Windows Server patching, the filter for severity is called MSRC_SEVERITY, and the values of the classification also differ slightly. You can obtain the right values from the documentation. A detailed Windows Server patching discussion is beyond the scope of this book.

For Linux, the patch rules are evaluated on each node, and Patch Manager uses the native package manager to install the patches approved by the patch baseline. It retrieves the list of updates and patches from the repositories that are configured on each managed node. For Amazon Linux 2, it uses the YUM library and checks the updateinfo.xml. Amongst the different attributes configured in the update notice, it matches the filters with **type** for the classification patch filter and **severity** for the severity patch filter. It uses an **update date** in combination with an approval after days and compares it with the current timestamp to see if the patch is ready to be approved for installation.

Next, let us create a maintenance window for our patches to be installed:

```
aws ssm create-maintenance-window \
    --name "Production" \
    --tags "Key=Environment,Value=Production" \
    --schedule "cron(0 0 14 ? * SUN *)" \
```

```
--duration 2 \
--cutoff 0 \
--no-allow-unassociated-targets \
--region us-west-2
```

This maintenance window has a two-hour duration, and we have set the cutoff time to zero, as we do not have too many instances and we do not expect our patching operations to run very long. You may adjust your maintenance window duration and cutoff as needed. We only want to allow targets associated with the maintenance window to be patched. The maintenance window is scheduled to run every Sunday at 2 PM UTC. This will return you a maintenance window ID, which you can use to register your targets:

```
aws ssm register-target-with-maintenance-window \
    --window-id mw-0c012345b01abcedfg \
    --targets "Key=tag:PatchGroup,Values=Application Servers" \
    --owner-information "Application Servers" \
    --resource-type "INSTANCE" \
    --region us-west-2
```

In this case, we are selecting our instances to be registered as targets using tags. In our CloudFormation template, in the LaunchTemplate definition, we tagged our instances with the key **PatchGroup** and the value **Application Servers**. This allows us to select all instances that are tagged with this key and value combination, and if our autoscaling group spins up more instances due to increased load, they can also be patched in the same maintenance window. Running this command returns a WindowTargetId, which we can use when we associate the patching task with the maintenance window.

Lastly, we will associate a Run Command task with our maintenance window to perform the patching. AWS provides an SSM document called **AWS-RunPatchBaseline** for this purpose:

```
aws ssm register-task-with-maintenance-window \
    --window-id "mw-0123456789abcdef0" \
    --task-arn "AWS-RunPatchBaseline" \
    --service-role-arn "arn:aws:iam::123456789012:role/
MaintenanceWindowRole" \
    --task-type "RUN_COMMAND" \
    --task-invocation-parameters "{
        \"RunCommand\": {
            \"Parameters\": {
                \"Operation\": [\"Install\"],
                \"RebootOption\": [\"RebootIfNeeded\"]
            }
```

```
        }
    }" \
    --name "PatchingTask" \
    --priority 1 \
    --max-concurrency 2 \
    --max-errors 1 \
    --targets "Key=WindowTargetIds,Values=d3696b4f-e267-4388-
99fc-dfe63b99e909"
```

We have already discussed this command and the parameters in the Maintenance Windows section of this chapter. What is different here is that we are now using this maintenance window with a Run Command task to perform patching on our instances. For the maintenance window targets, we are using WindowTargetId we got from the previous step where we associated targets with the maintenance window. Lastly, in the task invocation parameters, we are specifying the patching operation as **Install**. The other option for this is Scan. When you choose **Install**, `AWS-RunPatchBaseline` attempts to install the approved patches that may be missing from your managed node. When you choose **Scan**, no attempt is made to install any patches. Instead, it checks for the patch compliance state on the managed node and reports on it.

Distributor

Let us understand about the Distributor.

The Systems Manager Distributor helps in streamlining software distribution across your EC2 instances, on-premises servers, and even virtual machines in your hybrid environment. Distributing software traditionally involves manual processes or third-party tools. You might upload software packages to an S3 bucket and then rely on scripts or configuration management tools to install them on target instances. This approach can be cumbersome and error-prone. Distributor simplifies software distribution by providing a centralized console for creating, managing, and deploying software packages. It eliminates the need for complex scripts and streamlines the entire delivery process. You can create packages for various software types, including agent software provided by AWS (like AmazonCloudWatchAgent) or third-party software packages you obtain from vendors.

With Distributor, you can create simple packages by uploading the software directly, or leverage the advanced mode for more granular control. The advanced mode allows you to specify installation and uninstallation scripts, define dependencies, and tailor the package to your specific needs. Distributor does not blast software everywhere at once. You can target specific instances for deployment based on various criteria. This could involve targeting instances by tags, operating system type, or security groups. This targeted approach ensures that software is only deployed to the intended recipients. It offers two deployment modes. You can leverage AWS Systems Manager Run Command for one-time deployments, ideal for installing critical software updates or new tools. Alternatively, you can integrate Distributor with AWS Systems Manager State Manager for automated deployments based on pre-defined configurations. This allows you to schedule recurring software updates or ensure consistent software versions across your infrastructure.

Distributor leverages IAM roles to define access permissions. You can configure specific IAM roles for users or groups, granting them the necessary permissions to create, manage, and deploy software packages. This ensures only authorized personnel can distribute software within your environment. This ensures that even if someone gains unauthorized access to the Distributor console, they cannot decrypt sensitive software packages. By creating pre-configured software packages, you can ensure consistent software versions and configurations across your entire infrastructure, reducing the risk of errors or inconsistencies. It eliminates the need for manual processes or complex scripts. You can easily create and manage packages for third-party software, streamlining the deployment process.

Distributor automates software distribution tasks, freeing up valuable IT resources. You can focus on strategic initiatives while Distributor handles the routine software deployments and updates. You gain a powerful tool to streamline software distribution across your hybrid environment. It empowers you to deliver software efficiently, maintain consistent configurations, and reduce the burden of manual software management tasks.

Conclusion

AWS Systems Manager empowers you to take control of your infrastructure management. With its comprehensive feature set, you can automate tasks, ensure consistent and compliant infrastructure states, and take actions on anomalies and non-compliant states. In this chapter, we learned about the different categories of infrastructure management tasks and how the functionalities offered by AWS Systems Manager map to these tasks. AWS Systems Manager provides a unified platform for automating operational tasks, maintaining system reliability, and reducing manual intervention across cloud infrastructure. It enables SREs to implement key reliability principles through features like automated patching, configuration management, and operational insights, which directly contribute to reducing toil and maintaining SLOs. The service's ability to manage instances at scale, automate routine maintenance through maintenance windows, handle incident response with automation runbooks, and provide centralized operational control helps SREs maintain consistency across environments while reducing MTTR. Through its integration with other AWS services, Systems Manager allows SREs to implement IaC, maintain security compliance, and gather detailed operational metrics, which are essential for making data-driven decisions about system reliability and performance.

In the next chapter, you will learn how you can automate the release process for your applications on AWS.

Points to remember

- AWS Systems Manager is a comprehensive service that provides a range of features to simplify infrastructure maintenance and management in the cloud.

- The SSM Agent is a lightweight software component installed on managed instances that enables centralized management and automation through Systems Manager.

- Systems Manager offers capabilities for operations management, node management, change management, and application management, helping streamline various maintenance tasks.

- Systems Manager allows you to securely perform operations tasks by making use of AWS IAM permissions.

- Systems Manager integrates with other AWS services like CloudWatch and Config to provide a holistic view of infrastructure health and compliance.

- Automating infrastructure maintenance tasks through Systems Manager can significantly improve efficiency, consistency, and security compared to manual processes.

Multiple choice questions

1. What is the primary purpose of the AWS SSM Agent?

    a. To provide secure remote access to instances

    b. To enable centralized management and automation of instances

    c. To collect detailed inventory data about instances

    d. All of the above

2. Which Systems Manager feature allows you to execute shell scripts or PowerShell commands on your managed instances?

    a. Session Manager

    b. Run Command

    c. State Manager

    d. Patch Manager

3. What is the main benefit of using AWS Systems Manager Automation documents?

    a. They allow you to define and execute complex multi-step workflows

    b. They provide a graphical user interface for managing infrastructure

    c. They automatically generate detailed logs for all actions performed

    d. They enable real-time monitoring of instance performance metrics

4. **Which Systems Manager feature helps ensure your managed instances adhere to a desired configuration state?**

    a. OpsCenter

    b. Application Manager

    c. State Manager

    d. Distributor

5. **What is the primary purpose of AWS Systems Manager Patch Manager?**

    a. To automate the patching of managed instances

    b. To provide a centralized dashboard for infrastructure health

    c. To distribute custom software packages to instances

    d. To enable secure remote access to instances

6. **Which Systems Manager feature allows you to create, manage, and deploy software packages across your infrastructure?**

    a. Session Manager

    b. Run Command

    c. Distributor

    d. Parameter Store

7. **What is the main advantage of using AWS Systems Manager Parameter Store?**

    a. It provides a secure central repository for storing sensitive data

    b. It allows you to define custom data types for inventory collection

    c. It integrates with Amazon CloudWatch for advanced monitoring

    d. It enables the execution of shell scripts on managed instances

8. **Which Systems Manager feature provides a consolidated view of the health and performance of your AWS resources?**

    a. OpsCenter

    b. Application Manager

    c. Explorer

    d. Fleet Manager

9. **What is the primary benefit of using AWS Systems Manager Change Manager?**

    a. It automates the patching of managed instances

    b. It streamlines the planning, execution, and review of infrastructure changes

    c. It enables secure remote access to instances for troubleshooting

    d. It provides a centralized dashboard for monitoring application performance

10. **Which Systems Manager feature allows you to define recurring maintenance windows for performing potentially disruptive actions on your resources?**

    a. Run Command

    b. Maintenance Windows

    c. State Manager

    d. Patch Manager

Answers

1.	d
2.	b
3.	a
4.	c
5.	a
6.	c
7.	a
8.	c
9.	b
10.	b

Join our Discord space

Join our Discord workspace for latest updates, offers, tech happenings around the world, new releases, and sessions with the authors:

https://discord.bpbonline.com

CHAPTER 6
Release Automation

Introduction

This chapter introduces you to release automation. Release automation refers to the process of automating your software release process, which includes building, testing, packaging, and deploying applications to various environments (such as development, staging, and production). It is a key component of modern software delivery practices like **continuous integration/continuous delivery (CI/CD),** which has become synonymous with the term, DevOps. We will explore these concepts in the context of AWS services and look at options available to you to achieve automation for different stages of your software release process.

Structure

The chapter covers the following topics:

- Release automation tasks
- Introduction to AWS release automation tools
- Release pipeline for our sample workload
- DevSecOps on AWS

Objectives

By the end of this chapter, you will become familiar with your options for release automation on AWS. You will get a quick recap of the various tasks involved in the release process. We touched upon this in *Chapter 2, SRE versus DevOps,* where we compared DevOps and site reliability engineering. You will understand the services you can use on AWS to automate your release process. You will also understand the concept of DevSecOps and how you may implement it on AWS.

Release automation tasks

Release engineering on **Amazon Web Services (AWS)** involves solving for various concerns and considerations to ensure a smooth and reliable deployment process for applications and services.

Following are the various release engineering concerns on AWS:

- **Infrastructure as code (IaC):** AWS provides tools like AWS CloudFormation and AWS **Cloud Development Kit (CDK)** to define and manage infrastructure resources using code. Release engineers should leverage IaC to ensure consistent and repeatable deployments across different environments (development, staging, production). IaC enables version control, automated provisioning, and easy rollbacks if needed. While this is something we already covered in a previous chapter, this is an important aspect that release engineering is concerned with. Deploying applications using automated pipelines is more effective when the infrastructure creation is also automated. The SRE team must understand the infrastructure the application code will be deployed to. When infrastructure is defined as code with IaC, it provides a consistent, well-established configuration for the code to be deployed to.

- **Continuous integration/continuous deployment:** AWS offers services that allow you to define your continuous delivery pipeline, test and build your code, and deploy your code to your targets. AWS provides services like AWS CodePipeline, AWS CodeBuild, and AWS CodeDeploy to implement CI/CD pipelines. Release engineers should set up automated build, test, and deployment processes to streamline the release cycle. CI/CD pipelines help catch issues early, ensure code quality, and enable faster and more frequent deployments. In this chapter, we will be diving deep into understanding these services and setting up a deployment pipeline for our sample application.

- **Monitoring and logging:** AWS provides monitoring and logging services like Amazon CloudWatch, AWS X-Ray, and AWS CloudTrail. Release engineers should implement comprehensive monitoring and logging strategies to track application performance, identify issues, and troubleshoot problems during and after deployments. Monitoring and logging help ensure application availability, reliability, and security. We will be covering observability in a subsequent chapter and understanding these services in more detail.

- **Security and Compliance:** AWS offers various security services and features, such as AWS **Identity and Access Management (IAM)**. Release engineers should follow best practices for secure deployments, including role-based access control, encryption, and compliance with industry standards and regulations (for example, **Health Insurance Portability and Accountability Act (HIPAA)**, **Payment Card Industry Data Security Standard (PCI-DSS)**). The idea of integrating security into your release pipeline is called DevSecOps. We will be looking into DevSecOps through the course of this chapter.

- **Scalability and high availability:** AWS offers auto-scaling capabilities and load-balancing services like **Elastic Load Balancing (ELB)** and Amazon Route 53. SRE should design and implement architectures that can scale automatically based on demand and ensure high availability of applications and services across multiple Availability Zones or Regions. We have already implemented load balancing and auto-scaling groups in our architecture. In this chapter, we will discuss how we can implement canary or blue-green deployments to reduce downtime during deployments.

In this chapter, we will focus more on the CI/CD aspect of the release process. There are several ways in which you can go about designing a release pipeline. This is going to be highly dependent on your application, but common pipeline stages are depicted in the following:

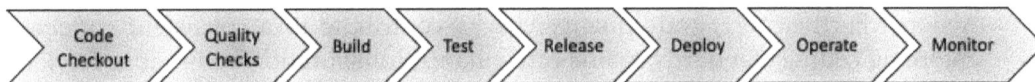

Figure 6.1: Sample application architecture with release pipeline

Let us understand each of these stages in a little more detail:

- **Code checkout**: Software development starts with writing code. Once the code is finished, it needs to be stored safely. This is where a **Source Code Management (SCM)** system comes in. Popular SCM systems include Git and Apache Subversion SVN. When programmers finish writing a part of the code, they push it to this code library, making it available to other members of the team and for the release process. Before the software can be built and used, the code needs to be copied from the SCM system to a computer where it can be turned into a program. This is called **checking out** the code. The code checkout step of a release pipeline begins by retrieving the necessary code from the SCM. This step involves fetching the specific version or branch required for the build. Some engineering teams may also implement a pre-commit hook to check for certain things before the code is committed to the SCM. This is like a gatekeeper that checks the code before it is saved to the SCM system. It acts as a preventative approach to ensure the release pipeline is not even executed for code that is not compliant with quality checks that the engineering team determines to be unsuitable for release. This helps to keep the code clean and makes it easier to build the software later on.

- **Quality checks:** An important stage of a robust release pipeline is a stage dedicated to assessing code quality. This checks that your code adheres to the code hygiene standards established for the programming language it has been developed in. Code quality checks are essential for maintaining code readability, maintainability, and reliability. By integrating these checks into the pipeline, teams can proactively identify potential issues early in the development process. This prevents defects from propagating to later stages, such as testing or production, where they can be more costly and time-consuming to rectify. Common code quality metrics include code complexity, code duplication, code readability, and adherence to coding style guides. Static code analyzers can automatically examine the code for potential errors, security vulnerabilities, and performance bottlenecks. Popular static code analyzers include pycodestyle, Pylint, Flake8, and Bandit for Python; SonarQube, PMD, and FindBugs for Java; ESLint, JSHint, and SonarJS for JavaScript; StyleCop and FxCop for C#; and RuboCop for Ruby. These tools provide valuable insights into code health and help developers improve their coding practices by identifying issues such as unused variables, method complexity, potential null pointer exceptions, and security vulnerabilities like SQL injection or **cross-site scripting** (**XSS**). Many of these analyzers can be configured with custom rules to match specific project requirements and can be integrated with popular IDEs and CI/CD platforms like Jenkins, GitLab CI, or GitHub Actions. Furthermore, code quality checks contribute to a consistent codebase. By enforcing coding standards, teams can enhance collaboration and reduce the learning curve for new developers. This ultimately leads to more efficient development and maintenance efforts, while also helping teams maintain high-quality standards throughout the software development lifecycle.

- **Build:** The build stage of a release pipeline is an important juncture in the release pipeline where raw code is transformed into a deployable package or artifact. This process involves several steps, depending on the nature of the application and the chosen programming language. For compiled languages like C++, Java, or Go, the build process typically includes:

  o **Dependency management**: Acquiring the necessary libraries, frameworks, or packages required for the application to function. These dependencies are often downloaded from repositories like Maven Central or npm.

  o **Compilation**: Translating human-readable source code into machine-readable code (binary format) that the computer can execute directly.

  o **Linking**: Combining compiled code modules and libraries into a single executable file or shared library.

o **Packaging**: Bundling the compiled code and its dependencies into a deployable artifact, such as an executable **Java Archive (JAR)** file or a **Dynamic Link Library (DLL)**.

In contrast, interpreted languages like Python, Ruby, or JavaScript often require less complex build processes. They might involve:

o **Dependency management**: It is similar to compiled languages, but the dependencies are often included in the final package.

o **Packaging**: Creating a deployable artifact, such as a ZIP file or a virtual environment containing the code and its dependencies.

For applications designed to run in containerized environments, the build stage takes on additional responsibilities:

o **Container image creation**: Constructing an **Open Container Initiative (OCI)** compliant container image based on a base operating system image. This involves installing necessary runtime dependencies, copying the application code, and configuring the container environment.

o **Image optimization**: Reducing image size and improving startup time through techniques like layer optimization and dependency minimization.

o **Image pushing**: Uploading the container image to a container registry for distribution and deployment.

By successfully completing the build stage, the release pipeline progresses to the next phase, where the generated artifact is prepared for deployment to various environments.

• **Test**: The test stage of the release pipeline is used to perform different types of tests on your application code. It is dedicated to ensuring the quality and reliability of the application. This phase involves executing a comprehensive suite of tests designed to uncover defects, vulnerabilities, and performance issues. Types of tests in a typical release pipeline include:

o **Unit tests**: These tests focus on individual code components to verify their correct functionality in isolation. They are typically written by developers and executed automatically as part of the build process.

o **Integration tests**: These tests examine how different components of the application interact with each other. They ensure that the integration between modules is seamless and that data flows correctly.

o **Functional tests**: These tests validate that the application behaves as expected from a user's perspective. They cover various user scenarios and interactions.

o **Performance tests**: These tests evaluate the application's performance under different load conditions to identify bottlenecks and optimize response times.

o **Security tests**: These tests identify vulnerabilities in the application to protect against security threats. This can include penetration testing, vulnerability scanning, and security audits.

o **Usability tests**: These tests assess the user experience to ensure the application is easy to use and understand.

o **Regression tests**: These tests verify that recent code changes have not introduced new defects or broken existing functionality.

By systematically executing these tests, development teams can identify and address issues early in the development process, reducing the risk of defects reaching production. While manual testing has its place, the test stage in a modern release pipeline heavily relies on automation to achieve efficiency and thoroughness. Test automation involves using specialized tools and frameworks to execute test cases repeatedly and consistently. Automated tests can be executed much faster than manual tests, accelerating the release process. They eliminate human error, improving test reliability. Tests can be run consistently across different environments and configurations. Automated tests can be used to verify that new code changes have not introduced unintended side effects. Test cases can be run simultaneously across multiple machines, reducing test execution time.

Following are some common test automation frameworks:

o **Unit testing**: JUnit, NUnit, pytest

o **Integration testing**: Mockito, WireMock

o **UI testing**: Selenium, Cypress

o **Performance testing**: JMeter, Gatling

- **Release:** The release stage of a pipeline is where your packaged code is prepared for release. Here, the focus shifts from development and testing to preparation for deployment. While it might seem redundant to have a **release** stage within a **release pipeline**, this phase encompasses the crucial activities necessary to ensure a smooth and successful deployment. During the release stage, several key tasks are performed:

    o **Artifact validation**: The build artifact produced in the previous stage is meticulously examined to verify its integrity, completeness, and compliance with release criteria. This includes checking for correct versioning, dependencies, and security vulnerabilities.

    o **Configuration management**: Necessary configuration files, database scripts, and environment-specific settings are prepared and packaged for deployment. This ensures that the application functions correctly in the target environment.

o **Deployment package creation**: The final deployment package is assembled, incorporating the application code, configuration files, and any required dependencies. This package is optimized for deployment to the target environment.

o **Release planning:** The release process is planned, including defining deployment timelines, resource allocation, and communication strategies. This ensures a coordinated and efficient release execution.

o **Approval and authorization**: Release approvals are obtained from relevant stakeholders, such as product owners, quality assurance teams, and security personnel. This step ensures that the release aligns with business objectives and meets quality standards.

By effectively managing these activities, the release stage minimizes the risk of deployment-related issues. Release management is the cornerstone of successful software delivery. It encompasses the planning, scheduling, and control of software releases throughout the entire lifecycle, from development to deployment. Effective release management ensures that software is delivered on time, within budget, and with minimal disruption to business operations. By following a structured release process, organizations can identify and mitigate potential issues before they impact production. Streamlined release processes optimize resource utilization and reduce cycle times. It fosters collaboration between development, testing, operations, and business teams, leading to customer satisfaction and loyalty. Release management helps organizations comply with industry regulations and standards.

- **Deploy:** The deployment stage in a release pipeline is where the validated software artifact is moved to a production environment. This stage involves a series of steps to ensure a smooth and successful transition. The target environment is configured and prepared to receive the new application version. This includes setting up databases, network configurations, and other required resources. You transfer the validated build artifact to the deployment environment, and the deployment process is initiated. This involves installing or updating the application, configuring settings, and starting necessary services. Any required configuration changes are applied to the deployed application. A rollback plan can be put in place to revert to the previous version if issues arise. The deployed application is tested in the production environment to ensure it functions as expected. This may include smoke tests, functional tests, and performance checks.

Deployment strategies can vary depending on the application and organizational requirements. Common strategies include blue-green deployments, canary deployments, and rolling deployments. Successful deployment requires careful planning, coordination, and automation to minimize downtime and risks. Production environments can often differ significantly from testing environments in terms of hardware, software, network configurations, and load. These discrepancies can lead to unexpected issues. Incorrect configurations can cause the application to fail or behave unexpectedly. Implementing a smooth rollback process in case of deployment failures can be difficult, especially in complex environments. To address these challenges, you can employ strategies such as thorough testing, configuration management tools, deployment automation, and incident response plans.

- **Operate:** The operate stage is the ongoing process of managing and maintaining an application in a production environment. It encompasses a wide range of activities that ensure the application continues to deliver value to users. Key activities in the operate stage include:

  o **Monitoring**: Continuously tracking the application's performance, availability, and user experience.

  o **Incident management**: Responding to and resolving issues that arise in production.

  o **Capacity planning**: Ensuring the application has sufficient resources to handle varying workloads. This includes forecasting user demand, identifying potential bottlenecks, and scaling infrastructure accordingly. Effective capacity planning ensures optimal performance, prevents system failures, and supports the application's ability to handle increasing user loads.

  o **Performance optimization**: Involves identifying and addressing performance bottlenecks. This includes profiling code, optimizing database queries, fine-tuning server configurations, and load-testing to simulate real-world conditions. By continuously monitoring performance metrics and implementing targeted improvements, teams can enhance user experience, reduce costs, and ensure the application scales effectively under increasing load.

  o **Security management**: This protects the application and its data from threats. We will look at the security aspect of the release pipeline in more detail later in this chapter.

  o **Change management**: This is managing changes to the production environment, including updates, patches, and configuration changes. his includes evaluating change requests, assessing their impact, planning and scheduling changes, executing the changes, and verifying their successful implementation. Effective change management minimizes disruptions, reduces risks, and ensures that changes align with overall business objectives.

The operate stage emphasizes collaboration between development and operations teams. By focusing on these activities, organizations can maintain high levels of service quality and customer satisfaction.

- **Monitor:** While monitoring is called out as an important activity of the operate stage, you may also look at monitoring as its own defined stage in a release pipeline. The monitor stage is the ongoing observation and analysis of your workload in production. It is about gathering data, identifying trends, and uncovering potential issues to ensure the system functions optimally. Key activities in a typical monitor stage include:

- o **Log management**: Collecting, analyzing, and storing logs for troubleshooting and performance analysis. This includes logs from build, test, deployment, and production environments. By effectively managing logs, teams can gain valuable insights into system behavior, troubleshoot issues, identify performance bottlenecks, and ensure application health, ultimately improving the overall release process.

- o **Performance monitoring**: Tracking response times, error rates, and resource utilization to identify performance bottlenecks.

- o **User behavior analysis**: Understanding how users interact with the system to identify areas for improvement. By collecting and analyzing data on user actions, you can gain insights into user preferences, motivations, and pain points. This information is essential for improving user experience, optimizing product features, and making data-driven decisions to drive growth and success.

- o **Infrastructure monitoring**: This is keeping track of the health and performance of underlying infrastructure components.

- o **Alerting**: Setting up notifications for critical events or thresholds.

The goal of the monitor stage is to provide insights into the system's behavior, enabling teams to make informed decisions about improvements, optimizations, and incident response. Data collected in this stage is often fed back into the earlier stages of the pipeline to inform development and testing efforts. By continuously monitoring the system, you can proactively address issues, improve user experience, and optimize resource utilization.

Not all release pipelines you create will require all the stages we have discussed. Your pipeline can have as many or as few stages based on the needs of your application.

Introduction to AWS release automation tools

AWS provides several services that focus on releasing and updating code to production environments. These services are designed to streamline the software deployment process, ensuring efficient and reliable code delivery.

Following are some of the key AWS services focused on releasing and updating code to production:

- **AWS CodeBuild:** AWS CodeBuild is a fully managed CI service provided by AWS. Essentially, it automates the process of compiling source code, running tests, and producing deployable software packages. This eliminates the need for organizations to provision and manage their own build servers. CodeBuild offers a high degree of scalability, allowing it to handle multiple builds concurrently without compromising performance.

The **buildspec.yml** file is a key component of AWS CodeBuild, which is a fully managed CI and continuous delivery service. This file is a YAML-formatted text file that defines the build commands and related settings for your software project. The **buildspec.yml** file allows you to specify the sequence of commands that CodeBuild should run during the build process. It typically includes sections for installing dependencies, pre-build steps, the actual build commands, and post-build actions. You can also define environment variables, build artifacts to be generated, and cache behavior for dependencies. The **buildspec.yml** file provides flexibility to customize the build process according to your project's requirements, whether it is a simple script or a complex multi-stage build involving multiple programming languages and tools. By storing the **buildspec.yml** file in your source code repository, it becomes part of your project's version control, ensuring consistent and repeatable builds across different environments.

The service supports various programming languages and build environments, providing flexibility for different project requirements. AWS CodeBuild leverages container-based runtimes to provide isolated and consistent build environments. When a build project is initiated, CodeBuild provisions a Docker container based on the specified image. This container serves as the execution environment for the build process. The use of containers offers several advantages:

o **Isolation**: Each build operates within its own container, preventing interference from other builds and ensuring reproducibility.

o **Consistency**: Preconfigured container images provide a standardized build environment, reducing inconsistencies between development and production.

o **Scalability**: CodeBuild can rapidly create and destroy containers to accommodate fluctuating build workloads.

o **Security**: Containers provide an additional layer of isolation, helping to protect build environments from vulnerabilities.

By employing container-based runtimes, CodeBuild delivers a reliable, efficient, and secure build service for various programming languages and frameworks. CodeBuild integrates seamlessly with other AWS services, such as CodePipeline, for continuous delivery. By using pre-configured build environments or creating custom ones, organizations can tailor the build process to their specific needs. Within a release pipeline, CodeBuild typically occupies a central role. It is triggered by code changes pushed to a source code repository. Once activated, CodeBuild executes the build process, which includes compiling code, running quality checks and tests, and generating artifacts. These artifacts, which can be software packages, container images, or other deployable assets, are then passed to the subsequent stages of the pipeline, such as testing and deployment.

CodeBuild's ability to scale automatically, combined with its integration capabilities, makes it a valuable tool for accelerating software delivery and improving overall build efficiency.

- **AWS CodeDeploy**: AWS CodeDeploy is a deployment service offered by AWS that automates the deployment of applications to various compute services. Essentially, it handles the process of taking your application code or configuration files and delivering them to your instances, eliminating the need for manual deployment procedures. CodeDeploy supports several deployment strategies, allowing you to choose the method that best suits your application's requirements.

The AWS CodeDeploy agent is a software component that runs on target EC2 instances or on-premises servers, facilitating the deployment process by coordinating with the CodeDeploy service. It handles tasks such as downloading application revisions, executing deployment hooks (scripts or commands), monitoring application health, supporting rollbacks in case of failures, providing detailed deployment logs and status updates, and automatically updating itself to the latest version. The CodeDeploy agent acts as the bridge between the CodeDeploy service and the target deployment environments, enabling automated and consistent application deployments across various platforms while reducing manual effort and providing centralized deployment management and monitoring.

The **appspec.yml** file, also known as the **application specification file**, is an important component in AWS CodeDeploy. It is a YAML-formatted file that provides instructions to CodeDeploy on how to deploy your application to the target compute platform, such as Amazon EC2 instances, AWS Lambda functions, or Amazon ECS services. The **appspec.yml** file typically includes sections for specifying the source files to be deployed, the destination locations on the target instances, and any scripts or hooks that need to be executed during the deployment lifecycle. For EC2/On-Premises deployments, the file maps source files to their destinations, specifies custom permissions, and includes scripts to run at various stages of the deployment process. For AWS Lambda and Amazon ECS deployments, the file determines the function or task definition to deploy, as well as any validation tests. The **appspec.yml** file also allows you to define deployment hooks, which are scripts that run at specific points during the deployment process, enabling you to perform custom actions like application stop/start or validation tests. By providing a declarative way to define the deployment process, the **appspec.yml** file ensures consistent and repeatable deployments across different environments.

CodeDeploy integrates with other AWS services, particularly CodePipeline. In a typical continuous deployment pipeline, CodePipeline orchestrates the build, test, and deployment process. When it is time to deploy the application, CodePipeline invokes CodeDeploy, specifying the deployment configuration. CodeDeploy then manages the deployment to the target environment, such as Amazon EC2 instances, AWS Lambda functions, or on-premises servers.

CodeDeploy offers several deployment strategies to accommodate different application types and deployment preferences. The in-place deployment strategy updates applications on individual instances without stopping them. The rolling deployment strategy gradually updates instances in batches, minimizing downtime. The blue or green deployment strategy creates a separate environment for the new version of the application, allowing for testing before switching traffic. For Amazon **Elastic Container Service** (**ECS**) and AWS Lambda, you can use deployment configuration to shift traffic to targets using a canary, linear or all-at-once. Canary deployments are useful when you do not want all your application users to see the new version of the application at the same time. This lets you test the application version with a smaller subset of users and react to any feedback from the users.

To ensure successful deployments, CodeDeploy provides detailed deployment information and status updates. You can monitor the progress of deployments, view deployment history, and troubleshoot issues using the CodeDeploy console or AWS CLI. Additionally, CodeDeploy supports application revisions, allowing you to roll back to previous versions if necessary. By leveraging CodeDeploy, you can significantly improve your deployment process, reducing deployment time, and minimizing the risk of errors.

- **AWS CodePipeline**: AWS CodePipeline is a CI/CD service offered by AWS. Essentially, it is a platform that automates the build, test, and deployment processes for your software applications. By modelling, visualizing, and automating these steps, CodePipeline helps streamline software delivery and improve efficiency. At the core of CodePipeline is the concept of a pipeline. A pipeline is composed of stages, which represent distinct phases of the software delivery process. Each stage contains one or more actions, which are specific tasks such as building code, running tests, or deploying to different environments. CodePipeline supports various action types, including source, build, test, deploy, approval, and invoke, offering flexibility in configuring the pipeline to match specific requirements. Each action can be serviced by one or more other services. For example, the source stage could be AWS CodeCommit (refer to the note), Amazon S3, or third-party integrations like GitHub, GitLab or Bitbucket. Build stage can be AWS CodeBuild, Amazon **Elastic Container Registry** (**ECR**) or a Jenkins server. While build stage can perform unit tests, you can optionally add a separate test stage, serviced by CodeBuild, AWS Device Farm or specialized integrations like Ghost Inspector for browser based testing, Micro Focus StormRunner for load testing, RunScope API monitoring for API performance testing etc.

The power of CodePipeline lies in its integration with other AWS services. For instance, it can pull source code from GitHub, or other supported repositories. The build process can be handled by AWS CodeBuild, which compiles the code and runs tests. Deployment can be automated using AWS CodeDeploy, AWS Elastic Beanstalk, or other deployment targets. This interconnectedness creates a seamless workflow, accelerating software delivery. To ensure quality and control, CodePipeline allows for manual approval stages. This means you can incorporate human decision points into the pipeline, such as requiring approval before deploying to production. Additionally, the service provides detailed visibility into the pipeline's execution, making it easy to monitor progress, troubleshoot issues, and identify bottlenecks.

By leveraging CodePipeline, you can significantly reduce the time it takes to deliver software updates, improve software quality through automated testing, and increase overall developer productivity.

Note: **This book had originally planned to cover AWS CodeCommit, a managed service for scalable private Git repositories. Through the development of this book, this service is not accepting new customers. Existing customers of AWS CodeCommmit can continue to use it. As a result, we will use S3 for the code checkout stage of the sample CI/CD pipeline that we will build for our application.**

Release pipeline for our sample workload

The infrastructure we defined for our application in *Chapter 4, Infrastructure as Code*, did not include a release pipeline. In the following, you can see the revised architecture diagram with the services for the release pipeline depicted. The developer commits code to the source control, and this event can be used to trigger AWS CodePipeline, which begins our release process. Within this, we will include AWS CodeBuild and AWS CodeDeploy to test and package the code and deploy it to our EC2 targets.

Following is the revised architecture figure with the release pipeline-related services included. We have used an S3 bucket as the source control here. CodePipeline can also integrate other source control systems like Bitbucket and Gitlab:

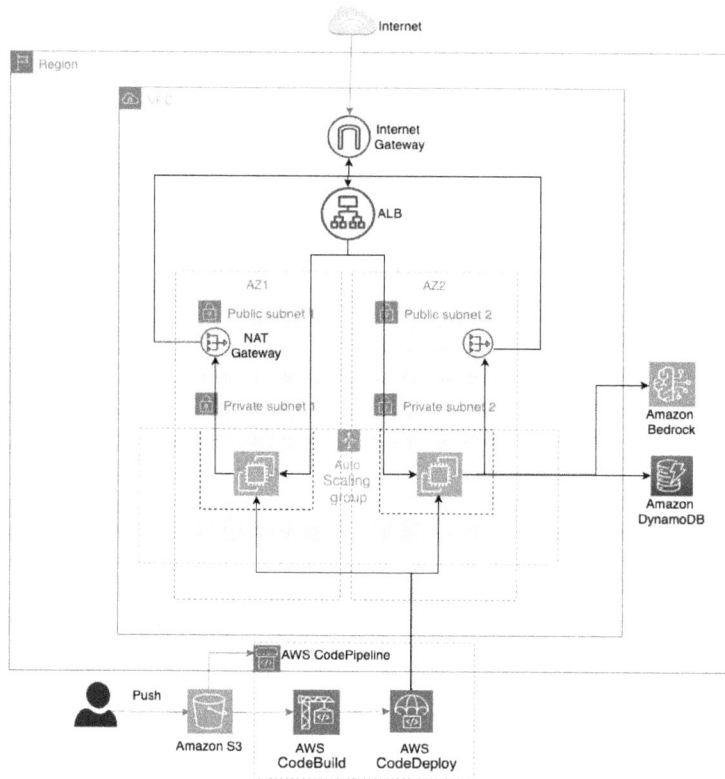

Figure 6.2: *Sample application architecture with release pipeline*

Let us create another CloudFormation template, which defines the resources required for your release pipeline setup. We avoid adding these resources to our existing CloudFormation template from *Chapter 4, Infrastructure as Code.* It is considered a good practice to define logically separate resources in a CloudFormation template. This can be related back to your main application stack by either creating the template as a nested stack or another standalone stack which uses cross-stack references to reference values from the application stack. We have chosen the latter approach and you will find that we reference the names of the AutoScaling Group and the Load Balancer Target Group names from the Application CloudFormation stack by using `Fn::ImportValue` in the following template. We have shown resource definitions of the key resources for your release pipeline.

Some other required resources such as IAM role definitions have been excluded for brevityas follows:

You will be able to find them in the full version of this template that will be shared with this book.

```
AWSTemplateFormatVersion: 2010-09-09

Description: CI CD Pipeline for the Sample App
```

```
Resources:
  AppPipelineArtifactStoreBucket:
    Type: "AWS::S3::Bucket"
...
  SourceBucket:
    Type: "AWS::S3::Bucket"
    Properties:
      VersioningConfiguration:
        Status: Enabled
      NotificationConfiguration:
        EventBridgeConfiguration:
          EventBridgeEnabled: true
      BucketEncryption:
        ServerSideEncryptionConfiguration:
          - ServerSideEncryptionByDefault:
              SSEAlgorithm: AES256
  S3EventRule:
    Type: AWS::Events::Rule
    Properties:
      Description: "Rule to trigger pipeline when source.zip is uploaded to S3"
      EventPattern:
        source:
          - aws.s3
        detail-type:
          - "Object Created"
        detail:
          bucket:
            name:
              - !Ref SourceBucket
          object:
            key:
              - "source.zip"
      State: ENABLED
      Targets:
```

```
    - Arn: !Sub arn:aws:codepipeline:${AWS::Region}:${AWS::AccountId}:${AppPipeline}
        Id: TriggerPipeline
        RoleArn: !GetAtt AppPipelineCloudWatchEventRole.Arn
  AppPipeline:
    Type: "AWS::CodePipeline::Pipeline"
    Properties:
      Name: SampleApp-Pipeline
      RoleArn: !GetAtt
        - AppPipelineServiceRole
        - Arn
      Stages:
        - Name: Source
          Actions:
            - Name: SourceAction
              ActionTypeId:
                Category: Source
                Owner: AWS
                Provider: S3
                Version: "1"
              OutputArtifacts:
                - Name: SourceArtifact
              Configuration:
                S3Bucket: !Ref SourceBucket
                S3ObjectKey: "source.zip" # Source code zip file name
                PollForSourceChanges: false
              RunOrder: 1
        - Name: Build
          Actions:
            - Name: Build
              ActionTypeId:
                Category: Build
                Owner: AWS
                Provider: CodeBuild
                Version: 1
```

```
            Configuration:
              ProjectName: !Ref AppCodeBuildProject
            InputArtifacts:
              - Name: SourceArtifact
            OutputArtifacts:
              - Name: BuildOutput
    - Name: Release
      Actions:
        - Name: ReleaseAction
          ActionTypeId:
            Category: Deploy
            Owner: AWS
            Version: 1
            Provider: CodeDeploy
          Configuration:
            ApplicationName: SampleApp-CodeDeploy
            DeploymentGroupName: SampleAppDeploy
          OutputArtifacts: []
          InputArtifacts:
            - Name: BuildOutput
          RunOrder: 1
  ArtifactStore:
    Type: S3
    Location: !Ref AppPipelineArtifactStoreBucket
CodeDeployDeploymentGroup:
  Type: AWS::CodeDeploy::DeploymentGroup
  Properties:
    DeploymentGroupName: SampleAppDeploy
    ApplicationName: !Ref CodeDeployApplication
    ServiceRoleArn: !GetAtt CodeDeployServiceRole.Arn
    AutoScalingGroups:
      - !ImportValue ASG-Name
    DeploymentStyle:
      DeploymentOption: WITH_TRAFFIC_CONTROL
```

```yaml
        DeploymentType: IN_PLACE
      DeploymentConfigName: CodeDeployDefault.OneAtATime
      LoadBalancerInfo:
        TargetGroupInfoList:
          - Name: !ImportValue TG-Name
  CodeDeployApplication:
    Type: AWS::CodeDeploy::Application
    Properties:
      ApplicationName: SampleApp-CodeDeploy
      ComputePlatform: Server
  AppCodeBuildProject:
    Type: AWS::CodeBuild::Project
    Properties:
      Name: SampleApp-Build-Package
      Source:
        Type: CODEPIPELINE
        BuildSpec: buildspec.yaml
      Artifacts:
        Type: CODEPIPELINE
      Cache:
        Type: LOCAL
        Modes:
          - LOCAL_CUSTOM_CACHE
          - LOCAL_SOURCE_CACHE
      ServiceRole: !GetAtt AppCodeBuildServiceRole.Arn
      Environment:
        Type: LINUX_CONTAINER
        ComputeType: BUILD_GENERAL1_MEDIUM
        Image: aws/codebuild/amazonlinux2-x86_64-standard:5.0
        PrivilegedMode: true
        EnvironmentVariables:
          - Name: S3_BUCKET
            Value: !Ref AppPipelineArtifactStoreBucket
          - Name: AWS_ACCOUNT_ID
```

```
        Value: !Sub ${AWS::AccountId}
      - Name: AWS_DEFAULT_REGION
        Value: !Sub ${AWS::Region}
```

This CloudFormation template sets up a CI/CD pipeline with the following key components:

- An S3 bucket to store pipeline artifacts and another S3 bucket as the source for deployments.

- A CodePipeline with three stages:

  1. **Source stage**: Pulls source code from S3 (triggered when source.zip is uploaded)

  2. **Build stage**: Uses CodeBuild to build the application

  3. **Release stage**: Uses CodeDeploy to deploy the application

- A CodeBuild project that builds the application using Amazon Linux 2 container.

- A CodeDeploy application and deployment group that handles deployments to an existing auto scaling group with:

  o In-place deployment strategy

  o One-at-a-time deployment configuration

  o Integration with an existing target group for load balancing

To test this pipeline, you can download the code from the GitHub project accompanying this book as a zip file. Once you have the zip file, you can upload it to the S3 bucket created by the CloudFormation template aforementioned. This will kick off the pipeline execution. The pipeline is automatically triggered when a file named **source.zip** is uploaded to the source S3 bucket, and the deployment uses traffic control to safely deploy to the target instances. The source code for our sample Streamlit based Python application will be made available with this book. You can exercise this release pipeline by creating a **.zip** archive of the source code with the name **source.zip** and dropping it in the source S3 bucket that is created as part of this CloudFormation stack. This file drop will automatically trigger the CodePipeline based release pipeline though an Amazon EventBridge integration. This will kick in the Source action of the pipeline, where source code from the S3 bucket will be made available to the subsequent stages of the pipeline.

The pipeline will run through the CodeBuild action next. Here you will see the dependencies for the Python application being installed using **pip**. Static source code analysis being performed using **pycodestyle** and unit tests executed using the Python **unittest** library.

Let us look at the build specification or **buildspec.yaml** file which is used in the CodeBuild stage of your release pipeline:

```
version: 0.2
phases:
  pre_build:
    commands:
      - pwd
      - ls -l
  build:
    commands:
      - echo Build started on `date`
      - yum install -y pip
      - pip install -r requirements.txt
      - pwd
      - pycodestyle .
      - python3 -m unittest test.test_app
  post_build:
    commands:
      - if [ $CODEBUILD_BUILD_SUCCEEDING = 1 ]; then echo Build completed on
`date`; echo Starting deployment;else echo Build failed ignoring deployment; fi
artifacts:
  files:
    - '**/*'
  name: myapp-$CODEBUILD_BUILD_NUMBER-$(date +%Y-%m-%d-%H-%M-%S)
```

Our **buildspec.yaml** consists of these sections:

- **Pre-build**: The pre-build stage is executed before the actual build process begins. It can be used for tasks like code linting, static code analysis, or any other pre-build checks or validations.

- **Build**: This is the main stage where the actual compilation or building of your application code takes place. It typically involves running build commands specific to your programming language or framework, such as npm run build for Node.js applications or mvn package for Java applications.

- **Post-build**: The post-build stage is executed after the build stage and can be used for tasks like running unit tests, code coverage reports, or any other post-build activities.

- **Artifacts**: This stage is used to specify the files or directories that should be treated as build artifacts and uploaded to the specified output location (for example, Amazon S3 bucket). These artifacts can be used for subsequent deployment or testing stages.

In addition to these, you can also include other sections such as env, install, proxy, reports, and cache as required for your application testing, code quality checks, and build.

The last stage of this pipeline is the CodeDeploy action. Here our application code will be deployed to the targets, which are the autoscaled EC2 instances attached to the target group of a load balancer. We have chosen a one-at-a-time deployment configuration, so the deployment will happen on one EC2 instance at a time.

Following are the **appspec.yaml** file for the CodeDeploy stage of our release pipeline:

```
version: 0.0
os: linux
files:
 - source: /app
   destination: /usr/local/webapp
 - source: requirements.txt
   destination: /usr/local/webapp
file_exists_behavior: OVERWRITE
permissions:
   - object: /usr/local/webapp/app.py
     owner: root
     mode: 644
     type:
        - file
   - object: /usr/local/webapp/requirements.txt
     owner: root
     mode: 644
     type:
        - file
hooks:
   AfterInstall:
      - location: scripts/install_dependencies
        timeout: 300
        runas: root
      - location: scripts/start_server
        timeout: 300
        runas: root
```

```
ApplicationStop:
  - location: scripts/stop_server
    timeout: 300
    runas: root
```

Our **appspec.yaml** file consists of the following sections:

- **OS**: You can use this section to specify the operating system of the instances you deploy to. We have used Linux as the value, but you can also specify Windows.

- **Files**: This stage specifies the source files that need to be copied from the deployment package to the destination instances. You can specify individual files or entire directories to be copied. In our example, we are copying the directory with the application source and the requirements.txt dependency manifest for Python applications.

- **Permissions**: In this stage, you can specify any file or directory permissions that need to be set on the destination instances after the files have been copied.

- **Hooks**: This is one of the most important stages in the AppSpec file. Hooks allow you to run scripts at specific points during the deployment process. There are several hook points available:

  ○ **AfterInstall**: These are scripts you can run after the application is installed. In our case, we are using this to install dependencies associated with our application.

  ○ **ApplicationStart**: You can define scripts here that use this deployment lifecycle event to start services that make up your application.

  ○ **ApplicationStop** : The scripts in this section can be used to stop your running applications. This can involve actions you may take to gracefully terminate the application and perform any cleanup.

  Other options available for this stage are:

  ○ **BeforeInstall**: These scripts are run before your application is installed.

  ○ **ValidateService**: If you want to validate your deployment, you can define scripts in this section for it.

  ○ **BeforeBlockTraffic**: When your application runs on instances behind a load balancer, this lifecycle event can be used to run tasks on instances before they are deregistered.

  ○ **AfterBlockTraffic**: This lifecycle event can be used to run tasks on instances after they are deregistered from a load balancer.

  ○ **BeforeAllowTraffic**: You can use this event to perform actions on an instance before it is registered with a load balancer.

- o **AfterAllowTraffic**: This event can perform actions on an instance after it is registered with a load balancer.

- **Resources**: This stage allows you to define and manage additional resources that your application might need, such as AWS Lambda functions, Amazon DynamoDB tables, or Amazon SNS topics.

The AppSpec file allows you to customize the deployment process according to your application's specific requirements. By defining the appropriate actions in each stage, you can ensure that your application is deployed correctly and consistently across different environments.

If your pipeline executes as expected, you should see it appear as shown in your AWS Console:

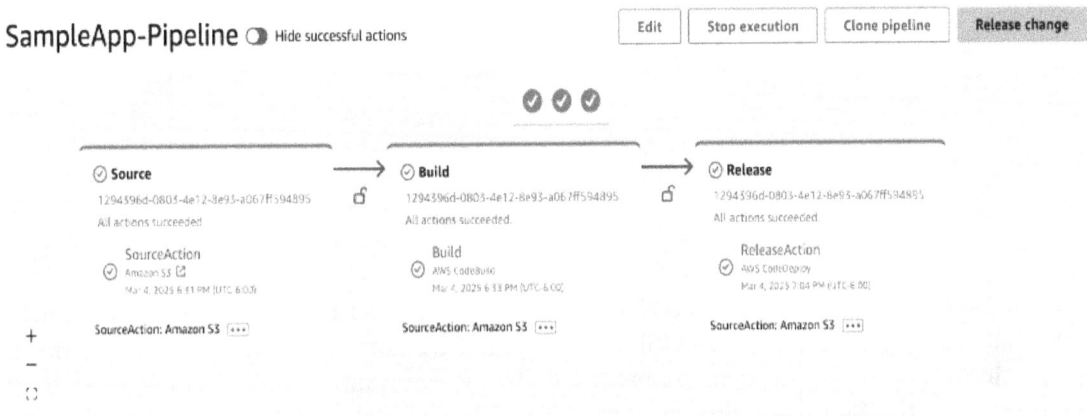

Figure 6.3: Successful execution of the release pipeline

Note: When we created our initial infrastructure with CloudFormation in *Chapter 4, Infrastructure as Code*, we only showed a placeholder content in the browser window when you accessed the load balancer DNS name.

However, after a successful execution of the release pipeline, you will see the Streamlit application frontend appear in your browser window when you access the load balancer DNS name, as follows:

Review Sentiment Analyzer

Add New Review

Product Name

Reviewer Name

Review

Submit Review

Figure 6.4: Streamlit application in your browser

This simple application allows to collect reviews about products and analyzes the review sentiment using generative AI capabilities provided by Amazon Bedrock. Before you test the application, you will need to enable access to the Foundation Model being used by the application. In the Bedrock Console, you can use the Model Access page to enable access to either all available models or specific models. There is no charge for enabling access to models. You are only billed for your actual interactions with the models for sentiment analysis, where the billing is by the number of tokens exchanged with the model. Each token normally measures as approximately 4 characters. For our application, we will be using the Claude Haiku 3.5 model.

DevSecOps on AWS

DevSecOps is a practice that integrates security practices into the DevOps workflow, ensuring that security is addressed throughout the entire software development lifecycle, from planning and coding to deployment and operations. By incorporating security early and continuously, DevSecOps aims to deliver secure applications and infrastructure more efficiently and with fewer vulnerabilities. DevSecOps prescribes shifting security left. Shifting security left refers to the practice of integrating security measures and considerations early in the **software development life cycle (SDLC)**, rather than treating security as an afterthought or a separate phase at the end of the development process. Traditionally, security testing and validation were often performed towards the end of the SDLC, after the application or system had been developed and deployed. However, this approach made it more difficult and costly to address security issues, as they were discovered late in the process, potentially requiring significant rework or redesign. By shifting security left, organizations aim to incorporate security practices and controls from the earliest stages of the SDLC, such as requirements gathering, design, and coding.

AWS provides various services and tools that can be leveraged to implement DevSecOps practices during the continuous delivery process. You can implement DevSecOps using AWS services, as follows:

- **Code Analysis and Static Application Security Testing (SAST)**: SAST is a technique used to analyze the source code, bytecode, or application binaries to identify potential security vulnerabilities without executing the application. SAST tools examine the code structure, data flows, control flows, and other code patterns to detect security flaws and weaknesses.

  o **AWS CodeBuild**: Use CodeBuild to integrate static code analysis tools like SonarQube, Checkmarx, or Fortify into your build process. As CodeBuild offers a just-in-time compute environment for your builds, you can integrate the security tooling of your choice in the build phase of your application. These tools can scan your code for vulnerabilities, coding errors, and compliance violations. This allows you to detect security issues early in the release cycle.

  o **Amazon CodeGuru**: Amazon CodeGuru Security is a fully managed, machine learning-powered service that helps identify security vulnerabilities and provide recommendations for remediation in your application code. It performs deep semantic analysis of your code to detect a wide range of security issues, such as log injection, hardcoded credentials, and resource leaks, with a low rate of false positives. CodeGuru Security is designed to integrate seamlessly into your development workflow, allowing you to scan your code at different stages, including code repositories, CI/CD pipelines, and container registries. The service provides contextually relevant remediation suggestions, including in-context code patches for certain classes of vulnerabilities, helping you fix security issues more efficiently. CodeGuru Security supports applications written in Python, Java, and JavaScript, and its rules are developed in partnership with Amazon's application security teams, leveraging years of security best practices.

- **Dependency scanning and Software Composition Analysis (SCA)**: Dependency scanning and SCA are security practices that focus on identifying and mitigating risks associated with the use of third-party components or open-source libraries in software applications:

  o **AWS CodeArtifact**: Amazon CodeArtifact stores and manages application dependencies securely by providing private repositories within your AWS account or organization, with access controlled through IAM policies and roles. All packages and metadata are encrypted at rest using KMS, and communication is encrypted in transit. CodeArtifact supports package signatures for verifying integrity, upstream repository connections for fetching approved open-source dependencies, versioning and immutability to prevent unauthorized modifications, audit logging and monitoring through CloudTrail integration, and package group configurations to control how packages are updated. These features ensure that your application dependencies are isolated, secured, and protected from supply chain attacks, while maintaining a controlled and auditable environment for managing your software development process.

○ **Amazon Elastic Container Registry (ECR)**: For your containers-based applications, Amazon ECR provides several security features to store and manage container images securely. It integrates with AWS IAM for access control, encrypts images at rest using AWS **Key Management Service (KMS)**, and supports encryption in transit using HTTPS. ECR offers image scanning capabilities to identify software vulnerabilities in container images. Images can be scanned automatically on push or on demand using Amazon Inspector or the open-source Clair scanner. Scan findings are logged to Amazon EventBridge for monitoring and automated actions. ECR also supports immutable tags to prevent overwriting images, repository policies for fine-grained access control, and AWS PrivateLink for secure communication over the AWS network. Additionally, ECR integrates with CI/CD tools like AWS CodePipeline, allowing security scans and policy checks to be performed as part of the release pipeline, ensuring only compliant and secure images are deployed to production environments.

○ **AWS CodeBuild**: You can integrate open-source tools like OWASP Dependency-Check or commercial tools like Snyk into your CodeBuild projects to scan your application dependencies for known vulnerabilities as part of your release pipeline.

• **Dynamic Application Security Testing (DAST):** DAST is a type of security testing technique that analyzes an application's behavior and interactions during runtime to identify potential security vulnerabilities. Unlike SAST, which examines the source code, DAST tests the running application from the outside, simulating real-world attacks and exploits:

○ **AWS CodeBuild**: You can CodeBuild to run DAST tools like OWASP ZAP or Burp Suite against your deployed applications to identify runtime vulnerabilities.

• **Infrastructure as code (IaC) Security:** IaC security in AWS involves implementing best practices and security controls to ensure that your infrastructure definitions and deployments are secure and compliant with your organization's policies and industry standards:

○ **AWS CloudFormation Guard**: Use CloudFormation Guard to validate your CloudFormation templates against security rules and best practices before deploying them. We learned about CloudFormation Guard in *Chapter 4, Infrastructure as Code.*

- o **AWS Config**: Use Config to continuously monitor and assess the configuration of your AWS resources against security best practices and compliance requirements. We will look at AWS Config in more detail in future chapters.

- **Secrets management:** Secrets management in AWS refers to the secure storage, retrieval, and rotation of sensitive data, such as passwords, **application programming interface** (**API**) keys, and other credentials, used by applications and services. Secrets management is a secure coding practice that prevents leaking sensitive information in your application code and configuration:

  - o **AWS Secrets Manager**: This is a dedicated service for storing and managing secrets, such as database credentials, API keys, and other sensitive information. Secrets Manager encrypts secrets using AWS KMS and provides features like automatic rotation, auditing, and fine-grained access control through IAM policies.

  - o **AWS Systems Manager Parameter Store**: Parameter Store is a component of AWS Systems Manager that allows you to store and retrieve configuration data, including encrypted secrets. It supports the hierarchical organization of parameters and integrates with AWS KMS for encryption. We learned about AWS Systems Manager Parameter Store in *Chapter 5, Automating Infrastructure Maintenance.*

To implement DevSecOps using these AWS services, you can integrate them into your continuous delivery pipelines using services like AWS CodePipeline, AWS CodeBuild, and AWS CodeDeploy. For example, you can configure CodeBuild to run static code analysis, dependency scanning, and DAST tests as part of your build and deployment stages. You can also use AWS Lambda functions or AWS Step Functions to orchestrate and automate security checks and remediation actions throughout the delivery process.

By incorporating these AWS services and practices into your continuous delivery workflows, you can shift security left, identify and address security issues early, and continuously monitor and improve the security posture of your applications and infrastructure. By shifting security left and incorporating it throughout the software development lifecycle, you can proactively address vulnerabilities and reduce the risk of security breaches.

Conclusion

In conclusion, release automation is a critical component of modern software development practices, enabling organizations to streamline their software delivery processes, improve quality, and reduce time-to-market. Throughout this chapter, we have explored the various aspects of release automation, including the key tasks involved, the stages of a release pipeline, and the tools provided by AWS to facilitate this process. We have seen how services like AWS CodeBuild, CodeDeploy, and CodePipeline work together to create a seamless, automated release workflow. The integration of these services allows for CI, testing, and deployment, ensuring that code changes are thoroughly vetted before reaching production environments. We have also discussed the importance of DevSecOps, highlighting how security can be integrated into every stage of the release process using AWS services like Amazon CodeGuru, AWS CodeArtifact, and AWS Secrets Manager. The sample application architecture and CloudFormation template provided in this chapter serve as practical examples of how to implement a release pipeline using AWS services. By leveraging these tools and best practices, teams can achieve greater efficiency, reliability, and security in their software delivery processes. As the field of release engineering continues to evolve, embracing automation and integrating security will remain crucial for organizations aiming to stay competitive in the fast-paced world of software development.

In the next chapter, you will learn how to configure observability for your AWS environment to assess how your workload is performing.

Points to remember

- Release automation refers to the process of automating software release tasks, including building, testing, packaging, and deploying applications.

- A typical release pipeline includes stages such as code checkout, quality checks, build, test, release, deploy, operate, and monitor.

- AWS provides several services for release automation, including AWS CodeBuild, AWS CodeDeploy, and AWS CodePipeline.

- AWS CodeBuild is a fully managed CI service that compiles source code, runs tests, and produces deployable software packages.

- AWS CodeDeploy is a deployment service that automates application deployments to various compute services.

- AWS CodePipeline is a CI/CD service that automates the build, test, and deployment processes.

- The buildspec.yml file is a key component of AWS CodeBuild, defining build commands and settings for software projects.

- The appspec.yml file is crucial for AWS CodeDeploy, providing instructions on how to deploy applications to target compute platforms.

- DevSecOps integrates security practices into the DevOps workflow, ensuring security is addressed throughout the entire software development lifecycle.

- AWS offers various services for implementing DevSecOps, including Amazon CodeGuru for code analysis, AWS CodeArtifact for dependency management, and AWS Secrets Manager for secrets management.

Multiple choice questions

1. **What is release automation?**

    a. The process of manually deploying software

    b. The process of automating software release tasks, including building, testing, packaging, and deploying applications

    c. The process of writing code

    d. The process of designing user interfaces

2. **Which of the following is NOT a typical stage in a release pipeline?**

    a. Code checkout

    b. Quality checks

    c. User acceptance testing

    d. Deploy

3. **Which AWS service is used for compiling source code, running tests, and producing deployable software packages?**

    a. AWS CodeDeploy

    b. AWS CodePipeline

    c. AWS CodeBuild

    d. AWS CodeCommit

4. **Which AWS service is primarily used for automating application deployments to various compute services?**

    a. AWS CodeBuild

    b. AWS CodeDeploy

    c. AWS CodePipeline

    d. AWS CloudFormation

5. **Which file provides the instructions on how to deploy applications using AWS CodeDeploy?**

    a. buildspec.yml

    b. appspec.yml

    c. deployspec.yml

    d. configspec.yml

6. **What is DevSecOps?**

    a. A type of deployment strategy

    b. A coding language

    c. The integration of security practices into the DevOps workflow

    d. A monitoring tool

7. **Which AWS service is used for code analysis in DevSecOps practices?**

    a. Amazon CodeGuru

    b. AWS CodeArtifact

    c. AWS Secrets Manager

    d. AWS Config

8. **What is the purpose of AWS Secrets Manager in a DevSecOps context?**

    a. To analyze code for vulnerabilities

    b. To manage and store secrets securely

    c. To automate deployments

    d. To scan dependencies for vulnerabilities

9. **What is the purpose of the buildspec.yml file in AWS CodeBuild?**

    a. To define the deployment instructions

    b. To specify the source code repository

    c. To define build commands and settings for software projects

    d. To configure the AWS environment

10. **What is the main purpose of AWS CodePipeline?**

    a. To compile source code

    b. To deploy applications

    c. To automate the build, test, and deployment processes

    d. To manage infrastructure as code

Answers

1.	b
2.	c
3.	c
4.	b
5.	b
6.	c
7.	a
8.	b
9.	c
10.	c

Join our Discord space

Join our Discord workspace for latest updates, offers, tech happenings around the world, new releases, and sessions with the authors:

https://discord.bpbonline.com

CHAPTER 7
Observability for Reliable Operations

Introduction

Observability and monitoring are two critical aspects of managing large-scale cloud applications. They provide essential insights into the health, performance, and behavior of your systems, enabling you to detect and address issues proactively. This chapter will dive into the fundamental concepts, tools, and best practices for implementing observability and monitoring on AWS. We will begin by discovering the core principles of observability, including its relationship to monitoring and its importance in modern cloud environments. You will learn about AWS services that help with monitoring and how they can be effectively utilized to gather and analyze data. You will learn about designing and implementing observability strategies, including metrics, logs, and distributed tracing. By the end of this chapter, you will have a solid understanding of the concepts, tools, and strategies necessary to build robust and observable applications on AWS.

Structure

This chapter will cover the following topics:

- Observability, monitoring, and distributed tracing on AWS
- Amazon CloudWatch

- CloudWatch metrics
- Using metrics to determine workload health
- Anomaly detection
- AWS X-Ray

Objectives

By the end of this chapter, you will understand how to define observability and explain its relationship to monitoring. You will identify the key components of an observability strategy. You will understand the core features and functions of AWS monitoring tools like CloudWatch and X-Ray. Further, you will learn to implement effective metrics, logs, and distributed tracing within AWS applications. You will understand how to utilize advanced techniques such as anomaly detection, root cause analysis, and alerting to enhance observability. This chapter will demonstrate the ability to troubleshoot and optimize AWS applications using observability data.

Observability, monitoring, and distributed tracing on AWS

Observability is the science of understanding the internal state of a system based on its external properties. In the AWS context, it means having the ability to gain insights into the health, performance, and behavior of your cloud applications. Effective observability provides the foundation for all system measurement and improvement. *If you can't measure it, you can't improve it.* This quote from British mathematician *Lord Kelvin* perfectly captures why metrics are at the heart of site reliability engineering. To make systems more reliable, SREs must first be able to measure their performance. This involves collecting and analyzing data like metrics, logs and traces from various sources to gain a comprehensive understanding of how your system is functioning.

Let us take a closer look at each of these sources and how they can help with observability.

Logs

These are text-based records of events that occur within your AWS resources. They can provide valuable insights into the actions performed, errors encountered, and system configurations. For example, logs from your web server can reveal information about HTTP requests, response times, and any exceptions that occurred. Logs are essential for observability in AWS, providing a rich source of information about the events and actions that occur within your cloud applications. They can help you understand system behavior, identify errors, and troubleshoot issues. AWS offers various logging services, including Amazon CloudWatch Logs, Amazon Elasticsearch Service, and AWS X-Ray. Each service has its own strengths and use cases. CloudWatch Logs is a good starting point for most applications, as it provides a simple way to collect, store, and analyze logs.

To effectively use logs for observability, you need to understand the different types of logs that AWS generates. Some common types include application logs, system logs, and custom logs. Application logs are generated by your own applications, while system logs are generated by AWS services. Custom logs can be created to capture specific events or data points. Once you have collected your logs, you can use them to perform various tasks, such as identifying errors and exceptions. Logs can help you pinpoint the root cause of errors and exceptions in your applications. By examining the error messages and stack traces, you can determine the exact location and nature of the problem. Logs can provide insights into performance bottlenecks and slowdowns. By analyzing the timing of events and the resource usage of your application, you can identify areas where optimization is needed. Logs can help you detect security threats and anomalies. By monitoring for suspicious activity, such as unauthorized access or data breaches, you can take proactive steps to protect your systems. Logs can provide information about how users interact with your applications. By examining user behavior patterns, you can identify areas for improvement and personalize the user experience.

To make the most of your logs, consider using log aggregation and analysis tools. These tools can help you centralize your logs, search for specific patterns, and create visualizations to better understand your data. AWS offers several log aggregation and analysis tools, including Amazon CloudWatch, Amazon Elasticsearch Service, and AWS Athena.

Metrics

Metrics are numerical measurements that track the performance of your AWS resources over time. Examples include CPU utilization, memory usage, network traffic, and response times. Metrics can help you identify performance bottlenecks and trends in your application's behavior. Metrics are a fundamental component of observability in AWS, providing quantitative data about the performance and health of your cloud applications. By collecting and analyzing metrics, you can gain insights into resource utilization, response times, error rates, and other key performance indicators.

AWS offers a variety of metrics services, including Amazon CloudWatch, AWS X-Ray, and AWS Lambda Insights. Each service has its own strengths and use cases. CloudWatch is a general-purpose monitoring service that provides metrics for a wide range of AWS resources. X-Ray is specifically designed for monitoring distributed applications, while Lambda Insights provides metrics for Lambda functions. To effectively use metrics for observability, you need to understand the different types of metrics that AWS generates. Some common types include system metrics, application metrics, and custom metrics. System metrics are generated by AWS services, while application metrics are generated by your own applications. Custom metrics can be created to track specific data points that are important to your business. Once you have collected your metrics, you can use them to perform various tasks, such as identifying areas of your application that are consuming excessive resources or causing delays. By examining metrics like CPU utilization, memory usage, and network traffic, you can pinpoint the root causes of performance issues. Metrics can help you track the utilization of your AWS resources, such as EC2 instances, S3 buckets, and RDS databases. By understanding how your resources are being used, you can optimize your infrastructure and avoid unnecessary costs. Metrics can be used to detect anomalies in your application's behavior. By setting up alerts for unusual spikes or drops in metrics, you can be notified of potential problems early. You can use metrics to identify trends over time. By examining historical data, you can understand how your application's performance is evolving and make informed decisions about scaling, optimization, and other strategies. To make the most of your metrics, consider using visualization tools and dashboards. These tools can help you present your data in a clear and understandable way. AWS offers several visualization tools, including Amazon CloudWatch Dashboards and Amazon QuickSight.

Traces

A collection of data points that represent a single request or transaction flowing through your application. Traces can help you understand how requests are processed, identify latency bottlenecks, and pinpoint the root causes of performance issues. Traces are a powerful tool for observability in AWS, providing a detailed view of how requests flow through your distributed applications. By analyzing traces, you can understand the performance of individual components, identify latency bottlenecks, and diagnose complex issues. AWS X-Ray is the primary tool for collecting and analyzing traces in AWS. X-Ray automatically instruments your applications to capture information about incoming requests, outgoing calls, and internal processing. This data is then used to create a visual representation of your application's architecture and the flow of requests. To effectively use traces for observability, you need to understand the different components of a trace. A trace consists of segments, which represent individual functions or services, and subsegments, which represent smaller units of work within a segment. By examining the relationships between segments and subsegments, you can understand how requests are processed and identify areas where performance can be improved.

Once you have collected your traces, you can use them to perform various tasks. Traces can help you pinpoint the specific components of your application that are causing delays. By examining the timing of segments and subsegments, you can identify areas where optimization is needed. Traces can be invaluable for debugging complex distributed systems. By visualizing the flow of requests and identifying error points, you can isolate and resolve issues more efficiently. Traces can help you understand the architecture of your application and how different components interact. This information can be useful for troubleshooting, optimization, and refactoring.

Traces can provide insights into how users interact with your application. By examining the sequence of calls made by users, you can identify common patterns and areas for improvement. To maximize the value of your data, consider utilizing visualization tools and analytical techniques. AWS X-Ray provides built-in visualization capabilities, but you can also use third-party tools to analyze your traces in more detail. By effectively using traces, you can gain a deep understanding of your application's performance and behavior.

AWS services helping observability

By combining these data sources, you can gain a comprehensive understanding of how your AWS applications are performing. By understanding how your application is using resources, you can make informed decisions about scaling, caching, and other optimization strategies. Observability can help you reduce your AWS costs by identifying underutilized resources and optimizing your infrastructure. By understanding how your applications are using resources, you can right-size your instances and avoid unnecessary expenses. Observability can help you remain compliant with industry regulations and company policies. By monitoring your AWS resources, you can collect the data needed to demonstrate compliance and audit your systems. Here are some AWS services that help you with observability.

The following are some of the AWS services that help you with observability:

- **Amazon CloudWatch:** A monitoring service that provides metrics, logs, and alarms for AWS resources. With CloudWatch, you can create custom dashboards, set alarms, and analyze trends to identify issues and optimize your workloads. It's a valuable tool for gaining visibility into your AWS environment and ensuring the reliability and performance of your applications. We will look at the features of CloudWatch in detail in this chapter.

- **AWS X-Ray:** A service that helps you analyze and debug distributed applications. It gives you a visual representation of your application's requests and how they flow through your microservices architecture. It enhances observability by providing insights into the performance and behavior of your distributed applications. X-Ray captures and analyzes data from your applications and AWS services, allowing you to identify bottlenecks, errors, and latency issues. This information can be used to optimize your application's performance and improve experience for end users.

- **AWS CloudTrail:** A service that provides a record of API calls made to AWS services. It helps with observability by providing a detailed audit log of all actions performed on your AWS resources. This information can be used to monitor and track changes, identify security threats, and comply with regulatory requirements. CloudTrail records can be integrated with other AWS services like CloudWatch and S3 for further analysis and storage.

- **AWS Lambda Insights:** This provides deep visibility into your Lambda functions. It automatically collects and analyses metrics, logs, and traces to help you understand the performance and behavior of your functions. With Lambda Insights, you can easily identify issues, troubleshoot problems, and optimize your Lambda applications. It's a valuable tool for developers who want to ensure the reliability and efficiency of their serverless workloads.

- **Amazon OpenSearch service:** A fully managed OpenSearch service that can be used for log analysis and search. OpenSearch is an open-source fork of ElasticSearch which allows to ingest and search log records at scale. With a fully managed OpenSearch

Service, you can focus on your applications without worrying about the underlying infrastructure.

- **Amazon Managed Prometheus:** This is a fully managed Prometheus monitoring service that provides a scalable, reliable, and cost-effective way to collect, store, and query metrics. Prometheus is an open-source monitoring system that is widely used for time series data. By using **Amazon Managed Prometheus (AMP)**, you can easily deploy and manage Prometheus in AWS without the need for complex infrastructure setup or maintenance.

- **Amazon Managed Grafana:** This is a fully managed Grafana service that provides a powerful and flexible way to visualize and analyze metrics. Grafana is an open-source analytics platform that allows you to create custom dashboards, alerts, and visualizations. By using **Amazon Managed Grafana (AMG)**, you can easily connect to your AMP metrics and create beautiful and informative dashboards to monitor the performance and health of your AWS applications.

Monitoring is a subset of observability that focuses on collecting and analyzing data to track the performance and health of a system over time. It typically focuses on predefined metrics and thresholds, alerting users when specific conditions are met. It relies on alerts to notify users of potential issues.

While monitoring provides valuable information about system performance, it may not always provide the deep insights needed to understand the root causes of issues or predict future problems. Observability is the ability to understand the internal state of a system based on its outputs. It involves collecting and analyzing a wide range of data, including metrics, logs, traces, and distributed context. It enables teams to anticipate and prevent problems before they occur. It relies on data analysis to identify trends, patterns, and anomalies.

Amazon CloudWatch

Amazon CloudWatch is a monitoring service that provides you with a comprehensive view of your AWS resources and applications. It enables you to collect, analyze, and act on metrics from your AWS resources and applications. It allows you to gain insights into performance, optimize resource utilization, and proactively address issues.

Let us look at the key components and features of CloudWatch:

- **CloudWatch agent:** This is a software component that runs on your EC2 instances, on-premises servers, and containers across operating systems. It collects metrics, logs, and custom data from your applications and sends them to CloudWatch for analysis and monitoring. This allows you to gain visibility into the performance and health of your resources, even if they are not running on AWS. It aids with system-level metrics collection from EC2 instances, system-level metrics from on-premises servers, and custom metrics from applications and services. It can collect logs from EC2 instances or servers running on-premises, and it can also collect traces from **OpenTelemetry** (**OTEL**) collectors or X-Ray clients and send them to the AWS X-Ray service.

Amazon Linux 2 AMIs do not come pre-installed with CloudWatch agent. You can use Systems Manager Run Command with the AWS-ConfigureAWSPackage command document to install and ensure that the agent is started correctly.

Here are the commands you would need to execute:

```
aws ssm send-command  \
  --document-name "AWS-ConfigureAWSPackage" \
  --targets "Key=tag:Env,Values=Prod"  \
  --parameters '{
        "action": ["Install"],
        "installationType": ["Uninstall and reinstall"],
        "name": ["AmazonCloudWatchAgent"],
        "version": [""]
    }' \
  --region us-west-2
```

To check if the CloudWatch agent is running successfully, we can use the Systems Manager Run Command again, this time with AWS-RunShellScript document. If the CloudWatch agent is running, the output of the command will show a running status as follows:

```
aws ssm send-command  \
   --document-name "AWS-RunShellScript" \
   --targets "Key=tag:Env,Values=Prod" \
   --parameters 'commands=["sudo /opt/aws/amazon-cloudwatch-agent/bin/amazon-cloudwatch-agent-ctl -m ec2 -a status"]'
```

Let us now create a Systems Manager Parameter to represent the configuration for the CloudWatch agent. This will be utilized later when we start to send custom metrics and application logs to CloudWatch:

```
aws ssm put-parameter \
    --name "AmazonCloudWatch-Config" \
    --type "String" \
    --value ' {
       "agent": {
            "metrics_collection_interval": 60,
            "logfile": "/opt/aws/amazon-cloudwatch-agent/logs/amazon-cloudwatch-agent.log"
       },
```

```
    "metrics": {
        "namespace": "review-analyzer",
        "metrics_collected": {
            "mem": {
                "measurement": [
                    "mem_used_percent",
                    «mem_available»
                ]
            }
        },
        «append_dimensions»: {
            «InstanceId»: «${aws:InstanceId}»,
            «Environment»: «Production»
        }
    },
    "logs": {
        "logs_collected": {
            "files": {
                "collect_list": [
                    {
                        "file_path": "/var/log/application.log",
                        "log_group_name": "review-analyzer-logs",
                        "log_stream_name": "{instance_id}-application",
                        "timestamp_format": "%Y-%m-%d %H:%M:%S",
                        "timezone": "Local"
                    }
                ]
            }
        }
    }
}'
```

If the CloudWatch agent is stopped, you can start it using the **AmazonCloudWatch-ManageAgent** command document, again using SSM Run Command. This references the parameter that we created in the previous step to configure the CloudWatch agent with the configuration when it starts, as shown:

```
aws ssm send-command  \
```

```
    --document-name "AmazonCloudWatch-ManageAgent" \
    --targets "Key=tag:Env,Values=Prod"   \
    --parameters '{
        "action": ["start"],
        "mode": ["ec2"],
        "optionalConfigurationSource": ["ssm"],
        "optionalConfigurationLocation": ["AmazonCloudWatch-Config"],
        "optionalRestart": ["yes"]
    }'
```

If the CloudWatch agent is already started and running, you can configure it using the **AmazonCloudWatch-ManageAgent** command document. The key difference here is that you use the action **configure** instead of **start**:

```
aws ssm send-command   \
    --document-name "AmazonCloudWatch-ManageAgent" \
    --targets "Key=tag:Env,Values=Prod"   \
    --parameters '{
        "action": ["configure"],
        "mode": ["ec2"],
        "optionalConfigurationSource": ["ssm"],
        "optionalConfigurationLocation": ["AmazonCloudWatch-Config"],
        "optionalRestart": ["yes"]
    }'
```

The advantage of using Systems Manager Run Command for these operations is that you can install CloudWatch agent on multiple instances at the same time. This is possible, as we are targeting instances by the **Env** tag, with the **Prod** value. All managed instances that have this tag, will be configured with CloudWatch agent.

- **Metrics**: Metrics are numerical values that represent the performance of your AWS resources or applications. CloudWatch provides a wide range of metrics, including CPU utilization, network traffic, disk I/O, and custom metrics. Metrics can be collected automatically from various AWS services or can be emitted by your applications using the CloudWatch API. Given the fundamental role of metrics in SRE, we'll explore them in greater detail in the next section.

- **Alarms**: Alarms are configured to monitor metrics and trigger actions when conditions are met or exceeded. They enable you to set thresholds for metrics and trigger actions when those thresholds are met or exceeded. When an alarm is triggered, it can perform actions like sending notifications, executing scripts, or scaling EC2 instances. Alarms can be simple (based on a single metric) or composite (based on multiple metrics).

To create an alarm, you select the metric you want to monitor. Next, you specify the threshold value for the metric. After this, you determine the period over which the metric will be evaluated. With this, you also need to specify the number of data points that must exceed or fall below the threshold for the alarm to trigger. Alarms are useful when you take an action in response to the alarm state. This could involve sending a notification, scaling your compute, shutting down a resource, or anything that makes sense for the situation. You can use other AWS services such as Amazon SNS, AWS Lambda, AWS Auto Scaling, etc., to perform these actions. This allows you to proactively identify and address potential issues before they impact your users.

- **Logs**: Amazon CloudWatch Logs is a centralized service that provides a scalable and reliable way to store and access log files from various AWS services and applications. Logs are text data that capture information about the events and activities of your applications. CloudWatch Logs supports various log types, including application logs, system logs, and custom logs. Logs can be ingested into CloudWatch Logs from various sources, including EC2 instances, Lambda functions, and custom applications.

  Log groups and log streams are used to organize log data. While retention policies help manage storage costs. Log groups are containers for log streams. They represent a logical grouping of logs, such as logs from a specific application or service. Log streams are sequences of log events within a log group. Each log stream represents a different instance of an application or service. You can set a retention period for your log groups to specify how long logs will be retained. You can pick a retention time between one day and 10 years or choose to retain the logs indefinitely. Log events that exceed the retention period will be automatically deleted. Retention policies can help you manage storage costs. Logs can be streamed to Kinesis Data Firehose, triggered Lambda functions, stored in S3 buckets, or subscribed to SNS topics.

  CloudWatch Logs Insights is a powerful log analytics feature provided by Amazon CloudWatch. It allows you to interactively search, analyze, and visualize log data from various AWS services and applications. You can use it to gain insights and visibility into log data and troubleshoot operational issues and application errors. It is helpful in analyzing and visualizing log patterns and trends. Log Insights includes an interactive Query Editor, providing a user-friendly interface for writing and running queries on log data. It supports a powerful query syntax with commands like filter, parse, stats, and more. You can filter log data based on specific patterns and conditions. It can perform statistical aggregations like sum, count, max, min, etc. Log insights also allow you to use regular expressions to search for specific patterns in log data.

Let us look at an example of a log insight query. This query shows you the 25 most recent log messages with their timestamps. It is commonly used for quick troubleshooting to see the latest activity in your logs.

```
fields @timestamp, @message
| sort @timestamp desc
| limit 25
```

Let us break down the anatomy of this query:

- **Fields selection**: `fields @timestamp, @message`. Specifies which fields to include in the result set.
  - ○ **@timestamp**: The timestamp of the log entry.
  - ○ **@message:** The full content of the log message.
- **Sorting**: `| sort timestamp desc`

Orders the results based on the timestamp field. `desc` indicates descending order (latest to oldest).

- **Limiting results**: `| limit 25`

Restricts the output to the top 25 results.

Key components:

- Each line starts with a command (e.g., fields, sort, limit).
- Lines are separated by pipe (|) characters, indicating sequential operations.
- Built-in fields, such as **@timestamp** and **@message**, are prefixed with an '@' symbol.

The example aforementioned is a very basic example of a log insights query. Log insights queries support various operations: selection, filtering, parsing, aggregation, sorting, and limiting. Using a combination of these, you can build very sophisticated queries. It can automatically detect and suggest fields from structured log data (e.g., JSON). It offers pre-built sample queries for various AWS services and common use cases. You can generate visualizations, such as bar charts, pie charts, and time-series graphs, from query results. You can also save and share frequently used queries.

Additional features include log search, metric filters, subscriptions, cross-account logging, and CloudTrail integration, enabling you to gain valuable insights into your system behavior and troubleshoot issues effectively, as follows:

- **Dashboards**: Dashboards provide a customizable interface for visualizing metrics and alarms. You can create custom dashboards to monitor specific aspects of your AWS resources and applications. Dashboards use widgets to display metrics, alarms, and other information. They offer a single pane of glass to determine your workload health. Dashboards can consolidate and visualize multiple metrics and alarms from different AWS services and resources across one or more regions onto a single view. This gives you a comprehensive picture of your operational health. You can create custom dashboards tailored to your specific monitoring needs. This includes selecting the metrics, alarms, and layout that are most relevant to your use case. Dashboards help you quickly identify issues, correlate metrics across services, and track performance trends over time. This enables faster troubleshooting and proactive issue resolution.

  You can share your dashboards across teams or stakeholders to facilitate better communication and coordinated response during operational events. With

CloudWatch dashboards, you can populate your dashboard with different widget types like line graphs, stacked area charts, numbers, and more to visualize your chosen metrics. Configure alarms on metrics to get notified when thresholds are breached. Overall, CloudWatch dashboards offer a powerful way to gain operational visibility, optimize resource utilization, and facilitate effective collaboration for monitoring AWS environments.

The following figure is a sample dashboard that shows the default metrics for your EC2 instances:

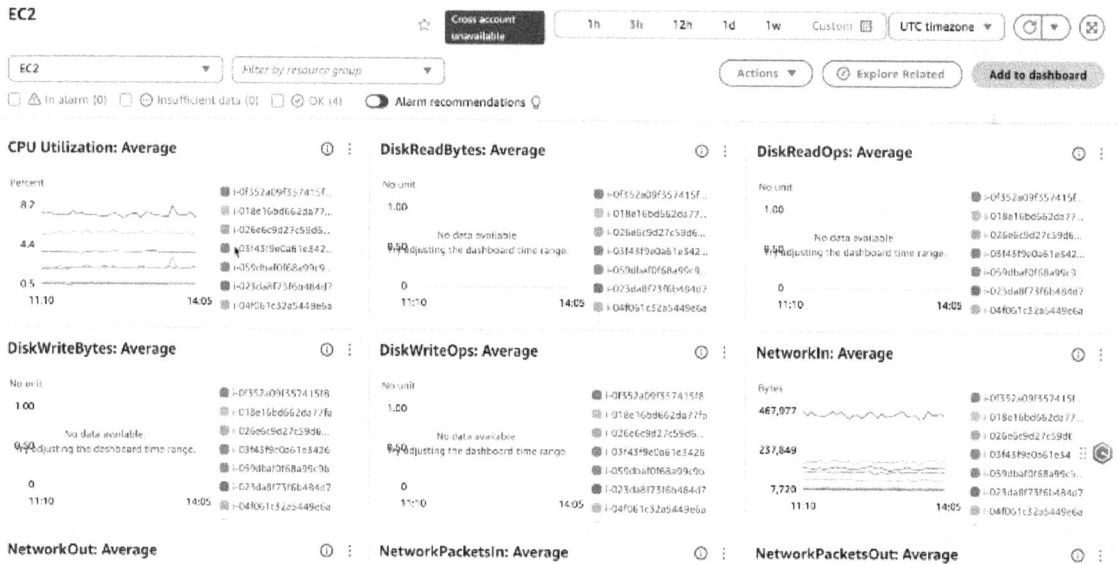

Figure 7.1: Sample CloudWatch dashboard with EC2 metrics

- **Synthetics**: CloudWatch Synthetics is a service that allows you to monitor the availability and performance of your web applications from around the world. It enables you to create synthetic transactions that simulate real user interactions with your applications, helping you identify and address potential issues before they impact your users. They can be made using JavaScript or Python. Synthetics captures performance metrics, including response times, error rates, and content availability. Canaries are scripts that run periodically to monitor the availability and performance of your applications. If a canary fails a health check, it can trigger alarms or notifications through its integration with CloudWatch. You can schedule the canary to run periodically. This can be a valuable tool in the SRE toolbelt, enabling continuous and proactive monitoring of the health and performance of your APIs and applications.

- **Amazon CloudWatch Real User Monitoring (RUM):** CloudWatch RUM provides insights into the performance of your web applications from the perspective of your end users. It collects client-side data about user interactions, including page load times, client-side errors, and user behaviors in real time to identify performance issues promptly. It tracks metrics like page load times, client-side errors, and user interactions and automatically detects anomalies in performance metrics. It integrates with other AWS services, such as CloudWatch Synthetics and X-Ray, to help you identify and debug performance issues. To configure CloudWatch RUM, you first register your web application with CloudWatch RUM. Next, you add a JavaScript snippet to your web application's header. The snippet collects data from user sessions and sends it to CloudWatch RUM, which can be viewed and analyzed in the CloudWatch console. You can use CloudWatch RUM to understand end-user behavior and optimize the user experience. You can gain valuable insights into the performance of your web applications from the perspective of your end users, helping you deliver a better user experience.

CloudWatch integrates with other AWS services, such as AWS Lambda, AWS Auto Scaling, and AWS Systems Manager. By effectively using CloudWatch, you can gain valuable insights into the performance and health of your AWS resources and applications, enabling you to identify and address issues proactively.

CloudWatch metrics

CloudWatch metrics are numerical values that represent the performance of your AWS resources and applications. They are ordered by time and represent values at different intervals. Each data point in a metric is associated with a timestamp and an optional unit of measure. You can statistically retrieve metrics data points as time-series data. AWS services publish different metrics to CloudWatch. Default metrics do not have a cost associated with them. However, if you choose to enable detailed monitoring for eligible services, an additional cost will be incurred. You can also publish your custom metrics from your workload to CloudWatch. You can pick the intervals at which you publish your custom metrics. There is also a cost associated with custom metrics.

Each metric has a namespace, name, and an associated dimension. Metrics cannot be deleted; however, data points will expire after 15 months as new data points are added.

There are different retention periods for metrics based on the period of the data points as follows:

- Data points period < 60 seconds, retained as such for 3 hours, and aggregated to 1-minute resolution after 3 hours.

- The 60-second data point period was retained for 15 days. Aggregated to 5-minute resolution after 15 days.

- The 300-second data point period was retained for 63 days and then aggregated to a 1-hour resolution after 63 days.

- Data points period of 3600 seconds, retained as such for 15 months. Data points expire after 15 months.

Metrics provide valuable insights into the health and behavior of your systems, allowing you to monitor and troubleshoot issues proactively.

Let us now explore more concepts related to CloudWatch metrics as follows:

- **Namespaces**: Namespaces in CloudWatch metrics serve as organizational categories for different types of metrics. They provide a hierarchical structure to help you group related metrics together and make them easier to manage and analyze. Each namespace represents a distinct category of metrics, and metrics within a namespace are logically related.

  Common namespaces include:
  - **AWS/EC2**: Metrics related to EC2 instances.
  - **AWS/Lambda**: Metrics related to Lambda functions.
  - **AWS/RDS**: Metrics related to RDS databases.
  - **Custom**: Custom metrics you create.

  Namespace is a mandatory property of a metric, and there is no default for it.

- **Dimensions**: Dimensions in CloudWatch metrics provide additional context and granularity to your data, allowing you to filter and analyze metrics more effectively. You associate zero or more (up to 30) dimensions as key-value pairs to each CloudWatch metric. By using dimensions, you can break down metrics into more specific categories, such as by instance ID, region, or application name. Dimensions uniquely identify a metric and can be used and treated as a variant of the metric. For example, if you are monitoring the CPU utilization of multiple EC2 instances, you can use the InstanceId dimension to filter the data for a specific instance. This allows you to analyze the performance of individual instances separately rather than looking at the overall average for all instances. Dimensions are essential for understanding the nuances of your metrics and making informed decisions about your AWS resources.

When retrieving metrics from CloudWatch to generate aggregation statistics, you must specify parameters to uniquely identify them. The parameters include the namespace, name, dimension, and start and end timestamp markers.

Refer to the following example:

```
aws cloudwatch get-metric-statistics --metric-name CPUUtilization --namespace AWS/EC2 --start-time 2024-09-13T00:00:00 --end-time 2024-09-14T00:00:00 --period 300 --statistics Average --region us-east-1 --dimensions Name=InstanceId,Value=i-01245abcefghi
```

In the example aforementioned, we retrieve the metric **CPUUtilization** from the namespace AWS/EC2 and filter by the dimension InstanceId with the value corresponding to the instance ID for which we want to retrieve the statistics. The statistic that we have chosen is Average. You can also select other statistics such as Minimum, Maximum, Sum, or SampleCount. We have also specified a period of 300 seconds (5 minutes) and a start and end timestamp for the duration we want the statistics for, as shown:

- **Resolution**: The resolution of a metric specifies the granularity with which the metric is published to CloudWatch. The standard resolution is 60 seconds of granularity. AWS services produce standard resolution metrics by default. If you need a metric with a granularity of less than 60 seconds, you will need to publish a high-resolution metric. High-resolution metrics have a granularity of 1 second. High-resolution metrics can be retrieved within a period of 1, 5, 10, 30, or 60 seconds. Publishing high-resolution metrics can incur higher costs than publishing standard-resolution metrics. It is essential to select the right metrics to publish at high resolution, ensuring you are not overspending. Additionally, alarmingly high-resolution metrics can also incur more costs.

- **Statistics**: CloudWatch statistics are aggregations of metric data collected over specific periods. These summaries are calculated based on the data points you provide or those collected from other AWS services. The aggregation process takes into account factors such as the metric's namespace, name, dimensions, and unit of measurement for the specified period of time.

- **Units**: CloudWatch statistics are based on metric data points, and each metric has a unit of measurement. Common units include Bytes, Seconds, Count, and Percent. When creating custom metrics, you can specify a unit. If one is not specified, CloudWatch defaults the unit to *None*. Units offer logical meaning to your data. While CloudWatch does not interpret units any differently, other applications can interpret them semantically. Metric data points with specified units are aggregated separately. If you retrieve statistics without specifying a unit, CloudWatch combines data points of the same unit. For metrics with different units, CloudWatch returns separate data streams, ensuring data integrity.

- **Periods**: A period in CloudWatch represents the time interval used to aggregate metric data. Each statistic is calculated based on data points collected within a specified period. Periods are measured in seconds, with valid values being 1, 5, 10, 30, or a multiple of 60. Adjusting the period length affects data aggregation. The default period is 60 seconds, but you can choose shorter durations (down to one second for certain metrics) or longer durations (multiples of 60 seconds). The choice of period aligns with how the metric is stored, as sub-minute periods are supported only for custom metrics with a 1-second storage resolution.

When retrieving statistics, you can specify a period, start, and end time to define the overall time frame. The default values provide the last hour's statistics. The specified values determine the number of periods returned. For example, using default values returns statistics for each minute of the previous hour. To aggregate data in ten-minute blocks, use a period of 600, and for hourly aggregation, you would use 3600. Statistics are timestamped at the beginning of the period they represent. Data aggregated from 1:00 PM to 2:00 PM is stamped as 2:00 PM. Periods are important for defining

CloudWatch alarms. When creating alarms, you specify a period for comparing the metric against the threshold. This allows you to control the sensitivity of the alarm based on the number of data points evaluated.

- **Aggregation**: CloudWatch aggregates metric data based on the specified period length. You can submit numerous data points with similar timestamps, and CloudWatch will group them according to the period. While CloudWatch doesn't automatically aggregate data across regions, you can use metric math to combine metrics from different locations.

  Data points with identical timestamps, namespaces, and dimensions are treated as a single metric. CloudWatch aggregates these points, allowing you to analyze the overall trend. You can also submit multiple data points for the same or different metrics, regardless of timestamps. For large datasets, statistical sets offer efficiency. By pre-aggregating data into Min, Max, Sum, and SampleCount, you can reduce the volume of data sent to CloudWatch. This is particularly useful for frequently collected metrics, such as webpage request latency.

  CloudWatch does not distinguish between metric sources. Metrics with the same namespace, dimensions, and unit of measure are treated as a single metric, regardless of the source. This is beneficial for distributed systems where multiple hosts publish identical metrics. It allows you to analyze the overall performance and trends across the entire application.

- **Alarms**: CloudWatch alarms automate actions based on metric values. An alarm monitors a metric over a specified period and triggers actions when the metric exceeds or falls below a threshold. These actions can be notifications sent to SNS topics or scaling policies for Auto Scaling groups. Alarms can also be added to dashboards for visualization.

  Alarms only trigger for sustained state changes. The alarm must remain in a particular state (above or below the threshold) for a defined number of periods before actions are invoked. When creating an alarm, the monitoring period should be at least as long as the metric's resolution. For basic monitoring (5-minute resolution), set the alarm period to 300 seconds or more. For detailed monitoring (1-minute resolution), set the period to 60 seconds or more.

  High-resolution alarms, which support 10-second or 30-second periods, incur additional charges. For more details, refer to the documentation on custom metrics and CloudWatch alarms.

Using metrics to determine workload health

Now that we understand CloudWatch metrics, let us examine how CloudWatch metrics can be used to determine the health of your workload and respond to situations where the metrics indicate a drop in performance or a failure.

Each metric data point represents a snapshot of the value of the metric you are tracking over a specific time interval. For CPU Utilization of an EC2 instance, each data point typically represents the average CPU Utilization of that EC2 instance over the previous 5-minute period (or 1-minute period if detailed monitoring is enabled) when the metric is reported to Amazon CloudWatch. When you set up CloudWatch alarms, you set them up to react when the metric exceeds or falls below a certain threshold. However, you do not want CloudWatch to alarm as soon as the threshold is breached for the first time. This can cause your setup to be overly reactive and lead to more noise than genuine signals. Transient spikes or brief fluctuations in a metric can occur without indicating a real problem. An alarm triggered immediately on a single breach could lead to many false positives. This can lead to alert fatigue, where important alerts might be overlooked due to the frequency of less critical notifications. This can lead to alert fatigue, where important alerts might be overlooked due to the frequency of less critical notifications. CloudWatch allows you to configure how many evaluation periods a threshold must be breached before an alarm is triggered. This is typically done using the *Evaluation Periods* and *Datapoints to Alarm* settings.

To implement this approach, you would do this:

- **Set an appropriate threshold for your metric**: This is the marker for the metric you are observing. Either an increase or a decrease from this level could be a trigger for you to take action.

- **Define an evaluation period** (e.g., 5 minutes): The evaluation period is determined by the period for the metric being emitted to CloudWatch.

- Specify how many consecutive periods the threshold must be breached before the alarm triggers (e.g., 3 out of 3 periods, or 2 out of 3 periods).

This setup allows you to balance between responsiveness to real issues and resistance to false alarms. The exact settings would depend on the specific metric and your operational requirements. Let us look at this visually to understand it better. Let us use average CPU utilization for your EC2 instances for this example. Assuming we have set the Alarm threshold at 60% and the periods to alarm as 2.

Consider a scenario where the CPU utilization metric value exceeds the threshold of 60%. This is likely to happen on occasions. However, we do not want to react to this unless the threshold is breached consistently. In this case, we are awaiting two successive periods of 5 minutes before we alarm. If we do not have two successive periods of 5 minutes where the datapoint breaches the alarm threshold, the Alarm state does not flip to *In Alarm*. This indicates that the process running on the instance, which was causing high CPU utilization, has remediated itself, and no further action is required.

In the following figure, you see that metric data points do not breach the 60% threshold for two successive 5-minute periods:

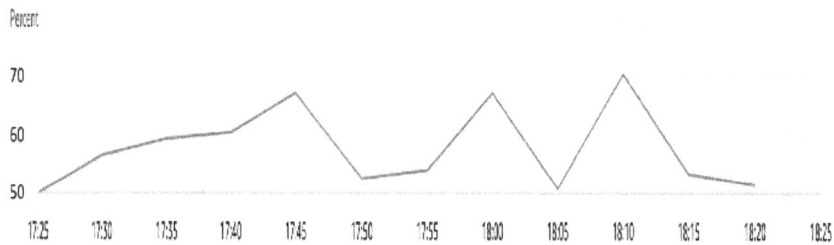

Figure 7.2: *Metric breaching threshold for non-continuous intervals*

Let us look at another example for the same metric. Here you will see that the metric datapoints again breach the 60% threshold. However, this time, the datapoints are breached for two or more continuous 5-minute periods. This indicates that the CPU utilization was consistently high for a period of time that was long enough that we want to take action in response. The action could be a notification to your SRE team to review the CPU usage on the instance and what could be causing it. Another common action is triggering an autoscaling action, which will scale the number of instances in your autoscaling group to ensure that the load is balanced across available compute instances. The action you take depends on your workload and what action is appropriate for the metric behavior observed.

The following figure shows how the metric is breaching the 60% threshold more than 2 successive 5-minute periods:

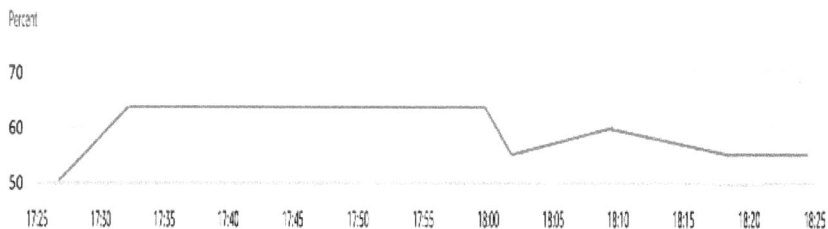

Figure 7.3: *Metric breaching threshold for continuous intervals*

The key to determining the health of your workload using CloudWatch metrics is understanding how to collect, analyze, and interpret the data effectively. Metrics provide valuable insights into your AWS resources and applications' performance, utilization, and behavior. By effectively leveraging CloudWatch metrics, you can comprehensively understand your workload's health and identify potential issues before they impact your users.

Let us now look at some key aspects of CloudWatch metrics:

- **Metric math**: When individual metrics may be insufficient to draw a conclusion about your workload health, you can consider employing metric math. CloudWatch Metric Math allows you to combine and transform existing metrics to create new, derived metrics. This feature provides flexibility in analyzing your data and gaining deeper insights into your application's performance. Metric math uses expressions to combine and transform metrics. Arithmetic operators (e.g., +, -, *, /) and logical operators (e.g., AND, OR) are used in expressions. CloudWatch provides built-in functions for common mathematical operations (e.g., AVG, SUM, MIN, MAX).

Let us consider the example of calculating average CPUUtilization across multiple instances. You have multiple EC2 instances and want to calculate the average CPU utilization across all instances.

Here are the steps you would need to take:

- **Identify the Metric**: The `CPUUtilization` metric from the AWS/EC2 namespace provides the CPU utilization for each instance.

- **Create a Metric Filter**: Use a metric filter to extract the `CPUUtilization` metric for each instance you want to include in the calculation.

- **Define the Metric Math Expression**: Create a metric math expression that calculates the average of the filtered `CPUUtilization` metrics.

  Example expression:
  ```
  AVG({
    "MetricName": "CPUUtilization",
    "Namespace": "AWS/EC2",
    "Dimensions": {
      "Name": "InstanceId",
      "Value": "i-1234567890"
    }
  })
  ```

  This expression calculates the average CPU utilization for the EC2 instance with the ID i-1234567890. You can modify the dimensions to include multiple instances or use a wildcard to match all instances. The metrics you are combining have the same evaluation period and time alignment. You can create custom metrics using metric math to derive new values from existing metrics.

Let us look at a more complex example. Consider a scenario where you are monitoring a web application running on EC2 instances behind an **Application Load Balancer** (**ALB**). We want to create a complex metric that combines information from the ALB, EC2 instances, and the application itself.

Here is an example of a complex metric math expression:

- Calculate the error rate as a percentage:

  *error_rate = 100 * (m1 / m2)*

Where:

m1 = Sum of HTTP 5XX errors from the ALB

m2 = Total number of requests to the ALB

- Calculate the average CPU utilization across all EC2 instances:

avg_cpu = AVG(m3)

Where:

m3 = CPUUtilization metric for EC2 instances

- Calculate the average response time from the application:

avg_response_time = AVG(m4)

Where:

m4 = Custom metric for application response time

Let us now create a composite health score using these metrics:

```
health_score = 100 - (error_rate * 0.5 + IF(avg_cpu > 80, 30, avg_cpu * 0.375)
+ IF(avg_response_time > 1, 20, avg_response_time * 20))
```

This health score decreases based on error rate, high CPU utilization, and high response times.

To implement this in CloudWatch, you would use a series of metric math expressions.

Here is how you might set this up using the AWS CLI:

```
aws cloudwatch get-metric-data \
  --start-time 2023-06-01T00:00:00Z \
  --end-time 2023-06-02T00:00:00Z \
  --metric-data-queries '[
    {
      "Id": "m1",
      "MetricStat": {
        "Metric": {
          "Namespace": "AWS/ApplicationELB",
          "MetricName": "HTTPCode_ELB_5XX_Count",
          "Dimensions": [{"Name": "LoadBalancer", "Value": "my-load-balancer"}]
        },
        "Period": 300,
        "Stat": "Sum"
      }
    },
    {
      "Id": "m2",
```

```
    "MetricStat": {
      "Metric": {
        "Namespace": "AWS/ApplicationELB",
        "MetricName": "RequestCount",
        "Dimensions": [{"Name": "LoadBalancer", "Value": "my-load-balancer"}]
      },
      "Period": 300,
      "Stat": "Sum"
    }
  },
  {
    "Id": "m3",
    "MetricStat": {
      "Metric": {
        "Namespace": "AWS/EC2",
        "MetricName": "CPUUtilization",
        "Dimensions": [{"Name": "AutoScalingGroupName", "Value": "my-asg"}]
      },
      "Period": 300,
      "Stat": "Average"
    }
  },
  {
    "Id": "m4",
    "MetricStat": {
      "Metric": {
        "Namespace": "MyApplication",
        "MetricName": "ResponseTime",
        "Dimensions": [{"Name": "AppName", "Value": "MyWebApp"}]
      },
      "Period": 300,
      "Stat": "Average"
    }
  },
  {
    "Id": "error_rate",
    "Expression": "100 * (m1 / m2)",
    "Label": "Error Rate (%)"
```

```
    },
    {
      "Id": "avg_cpu",
      "Expression": "AVG(m3)",
      "Label": "Average CPU Utilization"
    },
    {
      "Id": "avg_response_time",
      "Expression": "AVG(m4)",
      "Label": "Average Response Time"
    },
    {
      "Id": "health_score",
      "Expression": "100 - (error_rate * 0.5 + IF(avg_cpu > 80, 30, avg_cpu *
0.375) + IF(avg_response_time > 1, 20, avg_response_time * 20))",
      "Label": "Application Health Score"
    }
  ]'
```

This complex metric math expression combines multiple metrics to create a holistic view of application health. It takes into account error rates from the load balancer, CPU utilization from EC2 instances, and custom application response time metrics. The example is not intended to be tried with our sample application. The conditions expressed in the math above is hard to simulate with a sample workload. As a reader you can think of more practical scenarios where an expression like this with metric math could be useful.

You can use this composite health score to create alarms, add to dashboards, or trigger automated actions based on your application's overall health. Remember to adjust the weights and thresholds in the health score calculation to best suit your specific application's needs and characteristics.

By effectively using CloudWatch Metric Math, you can create custom metrics that provide valuable insights into your application's performance and help you make data-driven decisions.

Custom Metrics and Logs

CloudWatch agent is capable of collecting system metrics from Linux or Windows based EC2 instances or on-premises servers. The CloudWatch agent configuration file is a JSON file that specifies the settings for the agent, such as which metrics and logs to collect, where to send the data, and other configuration options. We previously setup the configuration for CloudWatch agent as part of Systems Manager Parameter store when we installed the agent on our compute instances. When you start accessing the application using the load balancer DNS name, you will start to see custom metrics and application logs being sent to CloudWatch. Our configuration is setup to collect metrics and logs from Amazon EC2 instances or on-premises servers.

Let us understand the different parts of this configuration:

- **Agent Settings**:
  - The agent will collect metrics every 60 seconds.
  - It will log its own activities to a specific file, which in this case is - `"/opt/aws/amazon-cloudwatch-agent/logs/amazon-cloudwatch-agent.log`

- **Metrics Collection:**
  - The metrics will be sent to a custom namespace in CloudWatch called `ReviewAnalyzer`.
  - Monitors basic CPU and memory metrics
  - Adds instance ID and environment as dimensions
  - Collects logs from **/var/log/application.log**

You can also send custom metrics from an EC2 instance to Amazon CloudWatch using the AWS CLI. Here is how to do this:

- First, ensure that the AWS CLI is installed on your EC2 instance and properly configured with the necessary permissions to send metrics to CloudWatch.

- The main command you will use is **aws cloudwatch put-metric-data**. This command allows you to send custom metric data to CloudWatch.

Here is a basic structure of the command:

```
aws cloudwatch put-metric-data --namespace "CustomMetricNamespace" --metric-name "CustomMetricName" --value <value> --timestamp <timestamp> --dimensions Name=InstanceId,Value=$(curl -s http://169.254.169.254/latest/meta-data/instance-id)
```

- **--namespace**: This is where you specify a custom namespace for your metric.

- **--metric-name**: The name of your custom metric.

- **--value**: The value of the metric you're sending.

- **--timestamp**: The time of the datapoint (optional, defaults to current time if not specified).

- **--dimensions**: Additional data to categorize the metric. In this example, we're adding the EC2 instance ID as a dimension.

You can also send multiple datapoints in a single call using the **--metric-data** option:

```
aws cloudwatch put-metric-data --namespace "CustomMetricNamespace" --metric-
data    "MetricName=CPU_Usage,Dimensions=[{Name=InstanceId,Value=$(curl    -s
http://169.254.169.254/latest/meta-data/instance-id)}],Unit=Percent,Value=80"
"MetricName=Memory_Usage,Dimensions=[{Name=InstanceId,Value=$(curl    -s
http://169.254.169.254/latest/meta-data/instance-id)}],Unit=Megabytes,Val
ue=1024"
```

You must ensure that your EC2 instance has an IAM role with permissions to send metrics to CloudWatch. The policy should include the **cloudwatch:PutMetricData** action. By using this method, you can send any custom metric from your EC2 instance to CloudWatch, allowing you to monitor and create alarms based on these metrics.

In our sample application, we have created a simple custom metric for you to test with. Here we use the boto3 SDK to send custom metrics to CloudWatch. Here is a sample code for this:

```python
def track_sentiment_metrics(sentiment):
    cloudwatch.put_metric_data(
        Namespace='ReviewAnalyzer',
        MetricData=[{
            'MetricName': 'SentimentDistribution',
            'Value': 1,
            'Unit': 'Count',
            'Dimensions': [
                {'Name': 'SentimentType', 'Value': sentiment}
            ]
        }]
    )
```

When you analyze the review sentiment in your application a few times with different types of reviews, you will see your custom metric flow to CloudWatch under the *ReviewAnalyzer'* namespace, with the metric name *SentimentDistribution*. You can plot the metrics for further analysis. For example, the following graphic shows the sum of all occurrences of each sentiment in a 1-hour period, as shown:

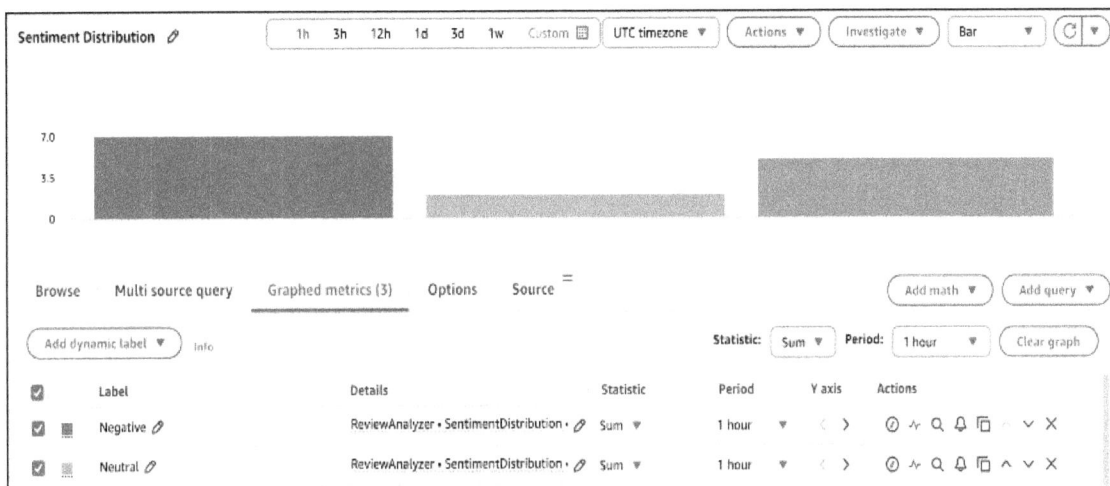

Figure 7.4: Custom metric for review sentiments analyzed in CloudWatch

Our CloudWatch agent is also configured to send per instance system metrics for memory. Memory metrics are not available in CloudWatch by default for EC2 instances. This is because memory usage is an OS-level metric that requires access to the operating system's internals. AWS can only collect metrics that are visible from the hypervisor level by default (like CPU, network, disk I/O). Memory usage can only be accurately measured from within the instance itself. The CloudWatch agent runs inside the instance with proper permissions to access OS-level metrics and hence is able to collect and send these metrics to CloudWatch. The following figure shows how per-instance memory metrics collected by the agent based on our configuration, can be plotted in CloudWatch for analysis. For each instance, we are sending available memory and percentage of used memory.

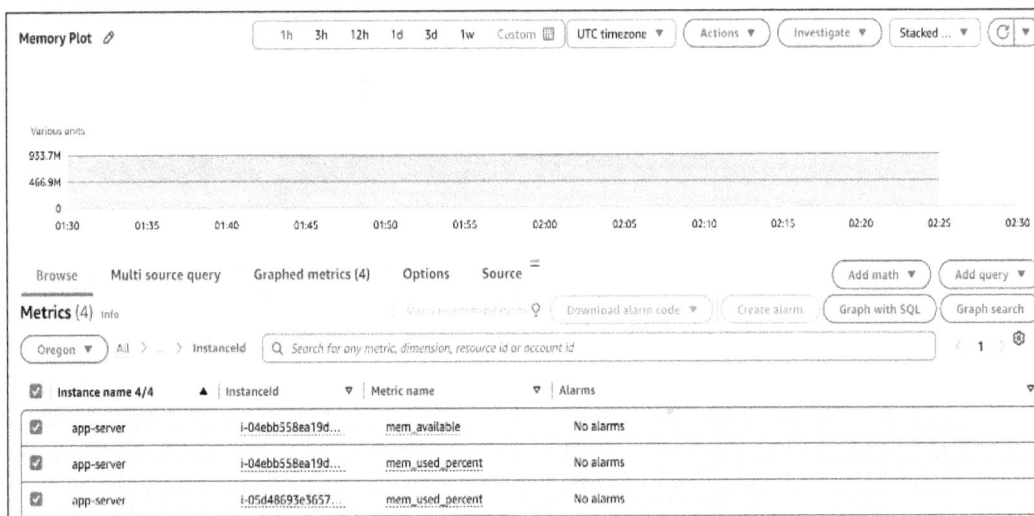

Figure 7.5: Memory metrics collected by CloudWatch agent and sent to CloudWatch service

Lastly, our CloudWatch agent also sends application logs from the local log files on EC2 instances to CloudWatch logs. Once in CloudWatch Logs, you can:

- Search and filter log entries using keywords

- Create metric filters to extract and monitor specific patterns

- Set up alerts based on log content

- Analyse log data for troubleshooting

- Create dashboards for log-based metrics

- Retain logs for long-term storage and compliance

Our configuration sends the application logs to a log group with the name **review-analyzer-logs**. Within this log group, you will find separate log streams created for each EC2 instance that you have running for this workload.

You can see how the logs appear in a log stream within this log group:

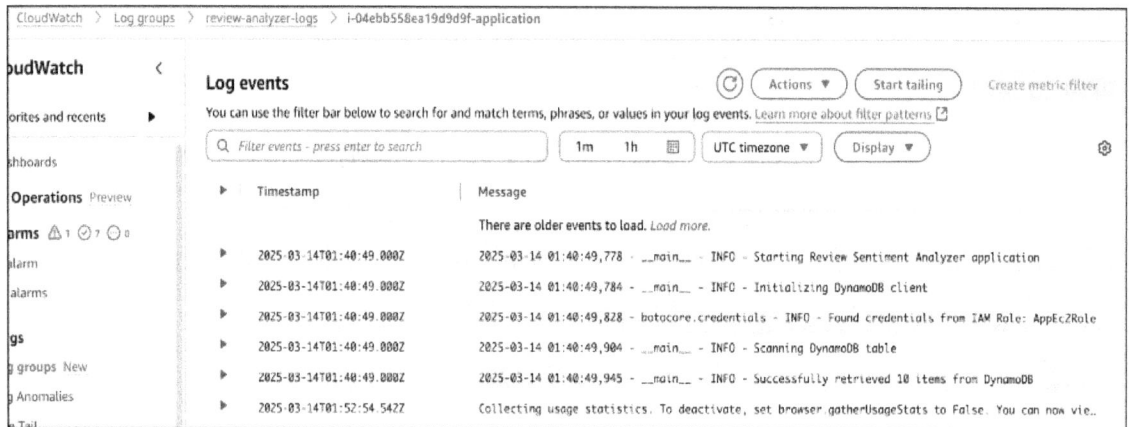

Figure 7.6: Application logs piped by CloudWatch agent to CloudWatch logs

Metric streams

CloudWatch Metric Streams is a feature that allows you to continuously stream CloudWatch metrics to destinations of your choice in near real-time. This feature is particularly useful for large-scale monitoring, analytics, and alerting use cases. Metric streams allow integration with third-party monitoring and analytics tools such as DataDog, New Relic, Sumo Logic, and more. CloudWatch natively provides Quick Setup options for some partner integrations. Metric streams typically stream metrics within a minute of them being published, providing low latency delivery. You can stream all metrics or filter for specific namespaces. It supports JSON and OpenTelemetry formats. In a multi-account setup, you can set up metric streams to stream metrics to a centralized monitoring account. Amazon Kinesis Data Firehose is the primary supported destination for metric streams. From here, you can send metrics to Amazon S3, Amazon Redshift, Amazon OpenSearch Service, or supported partner services. By default, metric stream includes MAX, MIN, SUM, and SAMPLECOUNT statistics, but you can also configure additional statistics, like percentiles, to be included in the streams.

Metric streams can be created and managed via the AWS Management Console, AWS CLI, or AWS SDKs. To set up a metric stream using the AWS CLI, you can use the put-metric-stream command.

Here is a basic example:

```
aws cloudwatch put-metric-stream \
    --name "SampleMetricStream" \
    --firehose-arn "arn:aws:firehose:region:account-id:deliverystream/delivery-
stream-name" \
    --role-arn "arn:aws:iam::account-id:role/MetricStreamRole" \
    --output-format "json"
```

In the command above, we create a metric stream with the name **SampleMetricStream**. The command includes a **firehose-arn**. This represents the Kinesis Firehose delivery stream which will receive the metrics. This delivery stream must already exist in the same account. **Role-arn** represents the IAM role which will be used by the metric stream to access the Kinesis Data Firehose.

CloudWatch Metric Streams provides a powerful way to integrate CloudWatch metrics with your broader monitoring and analytics ecosystem, enabling more comprehensive and timely insights into your AWS environment.

Embedded Metric Format

CloudWatch **Embedded Metric Format** (**EMF**) is a powerful JSON specification that enables you to ingest complex application metadata and extract actionable metrics directly from your log data, effectively bridging the gap between logging and metrics collection in AWS environments. By embedding metric data within structured log events, EMF eliminates the need for separate metric publishing code and infrastructure, allowing you to generate both detailed logs and high-resolution CloudWatch metrics from the same source while maintaining dimensional context that traditional metrics often lack. You can adopt EMF to significantly reduce operational overhead, decrease metric ingestion costs compared to custom metric publishing, gain deeper insights through high-cardinality dimensions. This can be prohibitively expensive with standard CloudWatch metrics. It enables seamless correlation between metrics and logs for enhanced troubleshooting capabilities. The format's integration with AWS Lambda and container environments makes it particularly valuable for serverless and microservice architectures, where traditional instrumentation approaches might introduce unacceptable performance overhead or require complex agent deployments, ultimately providing developers with a streamlined path to comprehensive observability while maintaining application performance. Here is a very simple example of CloudWatch EMF:

```
{
  "_aws": {
    "Timestamp": 1634324376000,
    "CloudWatchMetrics": [
      {
        "Namespace": "CustomNamespace",
        "Dimensions": [["Application", "Env"]],
        "Metrics": [
          {
            "Name": "RequestLatency",
            "Unit": "Milliseconds"
          },
          {
            "Name": "RequestCount",
            "Unit": "Count"
          }
        ]
      }
    ]
  },
  "Application": "SampleApplication",
  "Env": "Prod",
  "RequestLatency": 135.42,
  "RequestCount": 1,
  "RequestId": "abc-123-xyz-789",
  "UserId": "user-456"
}
```

This EMF log entry:

- **Defines two metrics**: `RequestLatency` and `RequestCount.`

- **Includes dimensions**: `Application (SampleApplication)` and `Env (Prod).`

- Publishes metrics to the **`CustomNamespace`** namespace.

When this JSON is written to a CloudWatch Logs stream, CloudWatch automatically extracts the metrics while preserving the complete log entry.

Here are some key considerations for effectively using CloudWatch metrics:

- **Choose the right metrics**: Select metrics that are relevant to your workload and provide meaningful insights into its performance. For example, if you're monitoring an EC2 instance, you might choose metrics like CPU utilization, memory usage, and network traffic.

- **Understand the units of measurement**: Different metrics have different units of measurement (e.g., Percent, Bytes, Seconds, Count). Understanding these units is essential for interpreting metric data accurately.

- **Use dimensions to filter data**: Dimensions provide additional context for your metrics, allowing you to filter and analyze data based on specific criteria. For example, you might use the InstanceID dimension to filter metrics for a specific EC2 instance.

- **Set appropriate alarm thresholds**: Configure alarms to trigger when metrics exceed or fall below specified thresholds. This can help you proactively identify and address potential issues.

- **Analyze trends over time**: Look for trends in your metrics to identify patterns and anomalies. This can help you identify potential problems and take corrective action.

- **Correlate metrics with other data**: Consider correlating metrics with other data sources, such as logs or traces, to gain a more complete picture of your workload's health.

- **Leverage CloudWatch features**: Take advantage of CloudWatch features like dashboards, anomaly detection, and metric math to enhance your analysis capabilities.

By following these guidelines, you can effectively use CloudWatch metrics to monitor the health of your workload and ensure that your applications are performing as expected.

Anomaly detection

CloudWatch anomaly detection is a feature provided by Amazon CloudWatch that uses machine learning algorithms to analyze metrics of your AWS resources and applications continuously. It helps identify unusual patterns or behaviors without requiring manual setup of thresholds. This feature automatically detects anomalies in your metrics. This helps identify potential issues or unusual behavior in your systems and reduces the need for manual threshold setting and alarm management. As an SRE function, this is invaluable, as there may be occasions when a new problem may be occurring for the very first time, for which you do not have the necessary controls in place.

Anomaly detection uses machine learning to analyze historical data. It creates a model of expected values for a metric and continuously evaluates incoming metric data against this model. It identifies data points that fall outside the expected range and surfaces them as anomalies that may need your attention. It uses adaptive learning, and the model is continuously updated or retrained based on new data. It also handles seasonal and cyclical patterns in metrics. It can be used to create dynamic alarms, which are based on the metric's expected value. These alarms do not need any static thresholds.

Anomaly detection can be enabled through the AWS Management Console, AWS CLI, or AWS SDKs. It allows customization of the anomaly detection threshold and supports excluding specific time periods from the model training. Anomaly detection bands can be displayed on CloudWatch graphs. This helps visualize normal ranges alongside actual metric values.

To get started with CloudWatch anomaly detection, you can use the AWS Management Console or the AWS CLI.

Here is a basic example of how you might create an anomaly detector using the AWS CLI:

```
aws cloudwatch create-anomaly-detector \
    --namespace "AWS/EC2" \
    --metric-name "CPUUtilization" \
    --stat "Average" \
    --dimensions Name=InstanceId,Value=i-1234567890abcdef0
```

This command creates an anomaly detector for the **CPUUtilization** metric of a specific EC2 instance.

When implementing anomaly detection, it is important to consider the specific characteristics of your applications and metrics to ensure the most effective use of this feature. It is particularly useful for systems with dynamic workloads or seasonal patterns where static thresholds might not be effective.

CloudWatch Logs Anomaly Detection is a feature of Amazon CloudWatch that uses machine learning to automatically analyze log data and identify potential anomalies or unusual patterns. This feature was introduced relatively recently to help users more easily detect and investigate issues in their applications and systems. It automatically identifies unusual patterns in log data and helps quickly spot potential issues in CloudWatch logs. It reduces the need for manual log analysis. This feature uses machine learning algorithms to analyze log patterns. It establishes baselines of typical log content and continuously evaluates incoming logs against these baselines. It flags log entries or patterns that deviate significantly from the norm while also continuously updates its understanding of *normal* behavior. Log anomaly detection can be enabled for specific log groups, and you can also configure anomaly detection thresholds. Specific time periods can be excluded from analysis. Anomalies can be viewed in the CloudWatch console and can be used to trigger CloudWatch alarms.

You can use this to detect sudden increases in error messages, identify unusual application behavior, spot potential security incidents, and monitor for unexpected changes in log patterns. It reduces time to detect and respond to issues, minimizes the need for manual log review, and helps catch issues that might be missed by traditional threshold-based alerting. The feature analyzes log data as it is ingested, so it starts working on new log entries after you enable it.

It typically requires about two weeks of historical data to establish reliable baselines. You can view detected anomalies in the CloudWatch console or query them using CloudWatch Logs Insights. Anomaly detection is included in the standard CloudWatch Logs ingestion and analysis charges.

To enable CloudWatch logs anomaly detection using the AWS CLI, you can use a command like this:

```
aws logs create-log-anomaly-detector \
    --log-group-arn "arn:aws:logs:us-west-2:123456789012:log-group:/aws/lambda/
my-function:*" \
    --anomaly-detection-threshold 0.5
```

This command creates an anomaly detector for the specified log group with a detection threshold of 0.5.

CloudWatch logs anomaly detection is particularly useful for complex systems where manual log analysis is time-consuming and error prone. It can help operations teams quickly identify and respond to potential issues, improving overall system reliability and performance.

AWS X-Ray

Distributed Tracing is a critical tool for understanding the performance and behavior of modern, complex applications that are distributed across multiple services and components. It provides a way to track requests as they flow through a distributed system, helping to identify performance bottlenecks, errors, and dependencies.

Here are some key benefits of distributed tracing:

- **Performance bottlenecks**: In distributed systems, performance issues can arise from various components. Distributed tracing helps pinpoint the exact location of bottlenecks, whether it's a slow database query, a network latency issue, or a faulty service.

- **Error identification**: When an error occurs, distributed tracing can trace the request's path to identify the root cause. This helps in debugging and resolving issues quickly.

- **Dependency analysis**: Understanding the dependencies between different services is crucial for maintaining system reliability. Distributed tracing visualizes these dependencies, making it easier to identify potential risks and optimize the system.

- **Observability**: Distributed tracing provides a high level of observability into your system, allowing you to understand how different components interact and contribute to the overall performance.

Distributed tracing tracks the flow of requests through a distributed system. It provides a way to visualize the interactions between different components and identify performance bottlenecks.

Here are the key concepts involved in distributed tracing:

- **Trace**: A trace represents a single request or transaction that flows through a distributed system. Each trace has a root span, which is the starting point of the request.

- **Span**: A span represents a single operation or unit of work within a trace. Spans can have parent-child relationships, forming a hierarchical structure that reflects the flow of the request. Spans can have attributes associated with them to provide additional context, such as the operation name, status, and timing information.

- **Distributed context propagation**: Each span is assigned a unique identifier (trace ID and span ID) to track its progress through the system. This identifier is propagated to downstream services or components, allowing them to associate their spans with the original trace.

- **Sampling**: Distributed tracing can introduce overhead, especially in high-traffic systems. To reduce overhead, sampling techniques can be used to selectively trace a subset of requests. Various sampling strategies, such as head sampling or probabilistic sampling, can be employed.

- **Span hierarchies**: Parent-child relationships: Spans can be organized into hierarchical structures to represent the flow of a request. These hierarchies can be visualized using tools like AWS X-Ray to understand the request's journey.

Amazon X-Ray is a service that helps developers analyze and debug production applications. It provides a visual representation of how requests flow through your application's components, making it easier to identify performance bottlenecks and errors. X-Ray helps you identify performance bottlenecks in your distributed applications by visualizing the flow of requests and measuring the time spent in each component. By tracing requests end-to-end, X-Ray can help you pinpoint the root cause of errors and bugs. X-Ray automatically maps the dependencies between different components of your application, making it easier to understand how they interact.

X-Ray integrates seamlessly with other AWS services like AWS Lambda, Amazon ECS, and Amazon EKS, making it easy to monitor and debug your serverless applications. You can create custom metrics to track specific aspects of your application's performance, providing you with more granular insights.

Here is how X-Ray works:

- **Instrumentation**: Instrumentation in AWS X-Ray refers to the process of adding code to your application components to collect data about incoming and outgoing requests. You deploy X-Ray agents to your application components, which collect data about incoming and outgoing requests. This data is then sent to X-Ray for analysis and visualization. X-Ray provides SDKs for various programming languages (e.g., Java, Python, Node.js) that you can integrate into your application. In some cases, X-Ray can automatically instrument common frameworks and libraries, reducing the amount of manual effort required. For custom components or specific use cases, you may need to manually instrument your code to capture the desired data. The instrumentation code collects information such as request IDs, timestamps, and error codes. The collected data is propagated to downstream components, allowing X-Ray to create a complete trace of the request's journey.

- **Tracing**: X-Ray creates a trace for each incoming request, capturing information about the request's journey through your application. Tracing in AWS X-Ray is the process of tracking the flow of requests through your distributed application. It provides a visual representation of how requests are processed by different components, making it easier to identify performance bottlenecks and errors. Each request is assigned a unique trace ID, which is used to track its journey through the application. Spans represent individual operations or functions within a trace. They are organized in a hierarchical structure, with a root span at the top and child spans representing sub-requests. X-Ray measures the time spent in each span, allowing you to identify performance bottlenecks. Spans can have attributes associated with them, providing additional context and information. X-Ray automatically captures errors that occur during the processing of a request.

- **Visualization**: X-Ray provides a visual representation of the trace, showing the flow of requests between components and the time spent in each component. It creates visual representations of your application's architecture, showing how different services and components interact. For each request, X-Ray generates a trace graph that visualizes the flow of the request through your application. The timeline view shows the duration of each span and the overall request duration. You can add annotations to traces to provide additional context or highlight specific areas of interest. X-Ray also provides performance metrics for each span, such as response time, error rate, and throughput. By using X-Ray, you can gain a deeper understanding of your application's behavior and identify areas for improvement.

Here are the key code snippets for instrumenting a Python program with AWS X-Ray:

- **Import X-Ray SDK**:
```
from aws_xray_sdk.core import xray_recorder, patch_all
from aws_xray_sdk.ext.boto3.patch import patch
```

- **Configure X-Ray**:
```
xray_recorder.configure(service='ServiceName')
patch_all()
```

This function patches all supported libraries that the X-Ray SDK can instrument automatically. When you call **patch_all()**, it attempts to patch commonly used Python libraries.

Alternately, you can specify specific libraries (e.g., boto3) that you want to patch.

Here is how you can do it:

```
patch(['boto3'])
```

The instrument a function is as follows:

```
@xray_recorder.capture('function_name')
def your_function():
        # Your code here
```

Create a segment, as follows:

```
with xray_recorder.in_segment('segment_name'):
        # Your code here
```

Create a subsegment, as follows:

```
with xray_recorder.in_subsegment('subsegment_name'):
        # Your code here
```

Add metadata or annotations as follows:

```
xray_recorder.current_segment().put_metadata('key', 'value')
```

```
xray_recorder.current_segment().put_annotation('key', 'value')
```

Begin and end a custom segment manually as follows:

```
segment = xray_recorder.begin_segment('segment_name')
# Your code here
xray_recorder.end_segment()
```

These snippets cover the most common X-Ray instrumentation tasks. Understanding how traces are sent from X-Ray instrumented code to the X-Ray service is crucial for effective implementation and troubleshooting.

Let us break down this process as follows:

- **Instrumented application**: Your X-Ray instrumented Python code generates segments and subsegments as it runs. These segments and subsegments contain timing information, metadata, and annotations.

- **X-Ray SDK:** The SDK collects and buffers these segments in memory. The SDK doesn't send traces directly to the X-Ray service; it relies on the daemon.

- **X-Ray daemon**: The X-Ray daemon is a separate process that runs alongside your application. For containerized applications, it is typical to run the X-Ray daemon as a sidecar container. It is responsible for receiving segment documents from the SDK and forwarding them to the X-Ray service. The daemon acts as a buffer and intermediary, which helps with performance and reliability.

The following section explains the communication between the SDK and daemon:

The SDK sends the buffered segments to the X-Ray daemon via **User Datagram Protocol** (**UDP**). By default, it communicates on localhost (127.0.0.1) and port 2000. The daemon receives these UDP packets. It batches and encrypts the segments. It handles retries and backoff if there are issues communicating with the X-Ray service. The daemon sends the batched and encrypted segments to the X-Ray service over HTTPS. This happens periodically or when a certain batch size is reached. You can configure the SDK to send traces to a different IP or port if the daemon is running on a different host. In containerized environments (like ECS or Kubernetes), you might run the daemon as a sidecar container. For Lambda functions, AWS manages the X-Ray daemon for you. This architecture allows for efficient local processing and buffering while ensuring secure and reliable transmission to AWS. It also provides flexibility in how you deploy and manage the X-Ray components in various environments.

Example of configuring the SDK to use a custom daemon address:

```
from aws_xray_sdk.core import xray_recorder
xray_recorder.configure(
    daemon_address='127.0.0.1:3000',  # Custom IP and port
    context_missing='LOG_ERROR'
)
```

Let us discuss the X-Ray Service.

The X-Ray service receives the segments. It processes and stores them. It makes them available for viewing and analysis in the AWS X-Ray console. The daemon needs the right permissions to send data to X-Ray. The X-Ray service exposes APIs that the daemon uses to send trace data. X-Ray first validates the incoming segments to ensure they're properly formatted and contain required fields. It assembles individual segments into complete traces. A trace represents the path of a request through your application. X-Ray indexes the traces for efficient querying and retrieval. Traces are stored for a default period of 30 days. This retention period can be configured. X-Ray generates a service graph showing the relationships between services and resources in your application. It creates a timeline view of traces, showing the time spent in each service and component. X-Ray provides capabilities to search and filter traces based on various criteria like time range, service names, and annotations. X-Ray can generate insights about your application's behavior, highlighting anomalies or frequent errors.

Our sample application code is already instrumented to send traces to X-Ray using the X-Ray agent installed on EC2 instances as part of the bootstrap user-data script. After you access the application from your browser a few times, you should find the traces being captured in the X-Ray console. Additionally, you should also be able to see a trace map in the X-Ray console, which could look as shown:

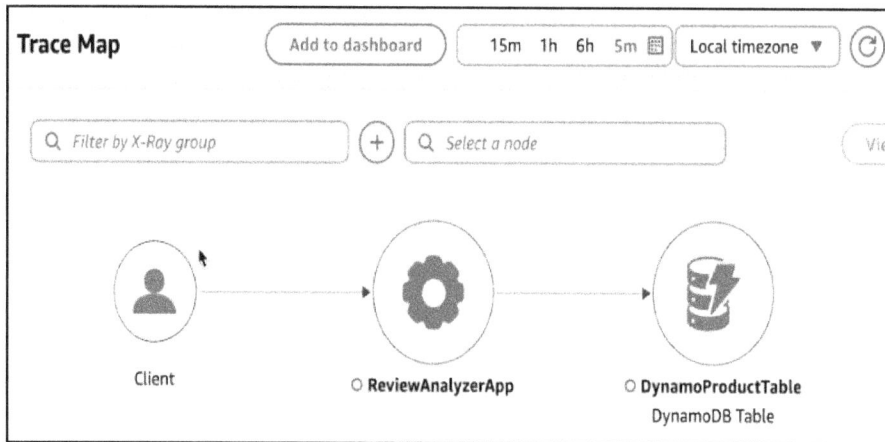

Figure 7.7: Trace map of traces sent from the sample application to X-Ray service

Conclusion

Observability is critical to managing large-scale cloud applications on AWS. It provides essential insights into your systems' health, performance, and behavior, enabling you to detect and address issues proactively. This chapter covered the fundamental concepts, tools, and best practices for implementing observability and monitoring in AWS.

We discussed AWS services like CloudWatch and X-Ray in detail, highlighting their ability to collect and analyze metrics, logs, and distributed traces to gain a comprehensive understanding of your application's performance. CloudWatch is a comprehensive service with several features. We covered the fundamental features of CloudWatch that enhance your SRE team's ability to monitor and respond to issues in a timely manner to ensure optimal performance of your workloads. This allows you to maintain the SLO that you want for your workload.

By implementing a robust observability strategy, you can reduce costs, ensure compliance, and improve the overall reliability and user experience of your AWS applications. The insights gained from observability can inform scaling, caching, and other optimization decisions, leading to more efficient resource utilization. Additionally, observability data can be used to demonstrate compliance with industry regulations and internal policies. In conclusion, the chapter has provided a foundation for understanding the importance of observability and the tools and strategies available in the AWS ecosystem to build reliable, observable applications.

In the next chapter, we will cover how you can automate the resilience of your AWS environment.

Points to remember

- Observability is the ability to understand a system's internal state through its external outputs.

- Logs are text-based records providing insights into events and actions within AWS resources.

- Metrics are numerical measurements that track performance over time.

- Traces show how requests flow through distributed systems.

- CloudWatch is AWS's primary monitoring service for collecting metrics, logs, and setting alarms.

- The CloudWatch agent collects metrics and logs from EC2 instances and on-premises servers.

- AWS X-Ray enables end-to-end tracing of requests through distributed applications.

- CloudWatch anomaly detection uses machine learning to identify unusual patterns automatically.

- Metric math allows combining multiple metrics to create new derived metrics.

Multiple choice questions

1. **What is the primary purpose of observability in cloud operations?**

    a. To provide visibility into the performance and behavior of cloud applications and infrastructure

    b. To automate cloud infrastructure management

    c. To ensure compliance with industry regulations

    d. To reduce cloud costs

2. **Which AWS service is specifically designed for monitoring distributed applications?**

    a. Amazon CloudWatch

    b. AWS X-Ray

    c. AWS Lambda Insights

    d. AWS Config

3. **What are the three main components of an observability strategy according to the chapter?**

    a. Metrics, logs, and distributed tracing

    b. Monitoring, security, and cost optimization

    c. Capacity planning, incident response, and disaster recovery

    d. Infrastructure management, updates/maintenance, and release engineering

4. **Which type of metrics are generated by the applications themselves, rather than by AWS services?**

    a. System metrics

    b. Application metrics

    c. Custom metrics

    d. All of the above

5. **What is the primary benefit of using distributed tracing tools like AWS X-Ray?**

    a. Identifying performance bottlenecks in distributed applications

    b. Automating infrastructure provisioning

    c. Enforcing security policies

    d. Reducing cloud costs

6. **Which AWS service provides general-purpose monitoring capabilities for a wide range of resources?**

    a. Amazon CloudWatch

    b. AWS X-Ray

    c. AWS Lambda Insights

    d. AWS Config

7. **What is the relationship between observability and monitoring?**

    a. Observability and monitoring are the same thing

    b. Observability is a subset of monitoring

    c. Monitoring is a subset of observability

    d. Observability and monitoring are independent concepts

8. **Which of the following is not considered a key component of an observability strategy according to the chapter?**

    a. Metrics

    b. Logs

    c. Distributed tracing

    d. Capacity planning

9. **What is the primary purpose of using custom metrics in an observability strategy?**

    a. To track specific data points that are important to the business

    b. To reduce the cost of monitoring

    c. To comply with industry regulations

    d. To automate infrastructure management

10. **What is the primary purpose of using CloudWatch metric math?**

    a. To combine and transform existing metrics to create new, derived metrics

    b. To automatically aggregate data across AWS Regions

    c. To enable custom dashboards and alarms based on metric data

    d. To reduce the cost of monitoring by pre-aggregating metric data

Answers

1.	a
2.	b
3.	a
4.	b
5.	a
6.	a
7.	c
8.	d
9.	a
10.	a

Join our Discord space

Join our Discord workspace for latest updates, offers, tech happenings around the world, new releases, and sessions with the authors:

https://discord.bpbonline.com

CHAPTER 8
Automating Resilience

Introduction

As an essential concern for SRE, resilience ensures that systems can withstand and recover from failures, maintaining service availability and performance even in the face of adversity. This chapter looks into the critical aspects of automating resilience on AWS, exploring strategies and tools that enable organizations to build robust, fault-tolerant applications. From architectures for **high availability** (**HA**) to planning **disaster recovery** (**DR**), we will examine how AWS services can be leveraged to create systems that not only survive disruptions but continue to thrive. For SREs, automating resilience is paramount in achieving and maintaining **service level objectives** (**SLOs**), reducing toil, and ensuring that systems can gracefully handle unexpected events. By embracing automation in resilience strategies, SREs can proactively mitigate risks, minimize downtime, and ultimately deliver a more reliable and consistent user experience.

Structure

The chapter covers the following topics:

- Defining resilience
- High availability and disaster recovery
- Achieving high availability on AWS

- DR planning and testing
- Additional considerations

Objectives

By the end of this chapter, you will learn how to define resilience. You will understand the differences between HA and DR and see how they are complementary to each other. You will gain information about how to achieve HA for your AWS workloads using the services offered by AWS. You will learn about the different DR strategies and how to pick the right one based on the needs of your workloads and your business. You will also learn how to apply trade-offs in picking your DR solution.

Defining resilience

Resilience is the ability to withstand adversity and recover. It is an important characteristic of any IT infrastructure. In the cloud era, where businesses rely on cloud-based services increasingly for their operations, resilience has become even more essential. Cloud resilience refers to the ability of cloud-based systems to remain operational and functional in the face of disruptions, such as hardware failures, software issues, network outages, or security breaches.

A resilient cloud infrastructure is designed to minimize downtime, reduce data loss, and ensure business continuity. It involves a combination of technical, organizational, and operational measures that are aimed at preventing, mitigating, and recovering from disruptions. One of the key components of cloud resilience is redundancy. This involves creating multiple copies of data and applications across different physical locations or virtual environments. Redundancy ensures that if one component fails, another can take over its functions, minimizing the impact of the disruption. For example, cloud providers often use techniques like replication and mirroring to create redundant copies of data across multiple data centres.

Another important aspect of cloud resilience is fault tolerance. Fault tolerance refers to the ability of a system to continue operating even if individual components fail. This can be achieved through techniques like clustering, load balancing, and automatic failover. Clustering involves grouping multiple servers together into a single logical unit, allowing the system to continue operating even if one or more servers fail. Load balancing allows distributing traffic across multiple servers, preventing a single server from causing a performance bottleneck by being overloaded. Automatic failover ensures that if a server fails, another server can automatically take over its functions.

In addition to technical measures, cloud resilience also requires organizational and operational best practices. You should develop comprehensive DR plans that outline how you will respond to disruptions. These plans should include procedures for backing up data, restoring systems, and communicating with stakeholders. Additionally, you should implement robust security measures to protect your cloud infrastructure from cyberattacks or potential breaches.

Cloud providers like AWS play a significant role in ensuring cloud resilience. They invest heavily in building redundant infrastructure, implementing fault-tolerant systems, and providing DR services. However, as this is a shared responsibility between AWS and customers who build applications on AWS, it is important for organizations to understand the extent of resilience provided by cloud providers and take steps to protect their own data and applications.

One of the challenges of achieving cloud resilience is the complexity of modern cloud environments. Cloud infrastructures can be highly distributed and interconnected, making it challenging to identify and address potential modes of failure. Additionally, the rapid pace of technological change can make it essential to keep up with the latest best practices for cloud resilience. Despite these challenges, cloud resilience is essential for businesses that rely on cloud-based services. By investing in redundancy, fault tolerance, and organizational best practices, you can minimize the impact of disruptions and ensure business continuity. As the cloud continues to evolve, the importance of cloud resilience will only grow.

High availability and disaster recovery

HA and DR are often used interchangeably, but they serve distinct purposes within the IT infrastructure. While both aim to ensure uninterrupted service, they employ different strategies and prioritize different objectives. In my experience of working with AWS customers, I have come across situations where customers treat HA as DR and DR as HA. This can be problematic, as they have distinct purposes and solve different challenges.

HA is an architectural approach focused on maximizing system uptime and ensuring continuous operation of production workloads by eliminating single points of failure throughout the infrastructure stack. It involves implementing redundant components at multiple levels - from hardware elements like servers, storage systems, and network devices, to software components such as application instances and databases. It also requires incorporating intelligent health checking and automated failover mechanisms to ensure seamless operation even when failures occur. This redundancy can be achieved through several strategies, including clustering multiple nodes to work together as a single system, ensuring redundancy across **Availability Zones** (**AZs**), load balancing to distribute the load across multiple resources while monitoring their health, and automated failover mechanisms. HA solutions also incorporate design patterns like circuit breakers, retry mechanisms, and graceful degradation to handle transient failures, while implementing monitoring and alerting systems to quickly identify and respond to potential issues before they impact service availability. The goal is to create a self-healing system that can automatically recover from failures without human intervention, maintaining consistent performance and availability even during component failures, planned maintenance, or unexpected operational issues. This ultimately delivers on strict SLOs that modern applications require.

DR is a comprehensive strategy that ensures business continuity when faced with potentially catastrophic events. These events can include natural disasters, cyber-attacks, infrastructure failures, or human errors that severely impact primary operations. DR focuses on maintaining business-critical functions and protecting essential data through systematic planning and infrastructure redundancy. It requires establishing one or more secondary sites in geographically distant locations to avoid shared risks with the primary site. These secondary sites can be cold (backup only), warm (partially running), or hot (fully operational), depending on business requirements. DR plans must define clear **Recovery Time Objectives (RTO)** and **Recovery Point Objectives (RPO)** based on business impact analysis.

DR planning should include detailed procedures for failover, testing, and failback operations. Regular testing of DR procedures is essential to validate their effectiveness and identify gaps. DR solutions often incorporate automated data replication, backup systems, and orchestrated recovery processes. The goal is to minimize data loss and operational disruption while enabling rapid recovery when disaster strikes. Modern DR strategies also consider application dependencies, data consistency, and the human factors involved in executing recovery procedures. Success in DR requires ongoing maintenance of procedures, regular training of personnel, and continuous adaptation to evolving business needs.

The following figure depicts a representation of HA and DR. Some characteristics of HA include independent storage for primary and secondary copies of data within the same site. Clustering of the compute, usually across AZs for load balancing and redundancy. Synchronous replication of data to ensure strongly consistent writes. For DR, the data is copied asynchronously to ensure that the latency of cross-site data copying does not impact the performance of the application. This also means that the data in your backup site will eventually be consistent.

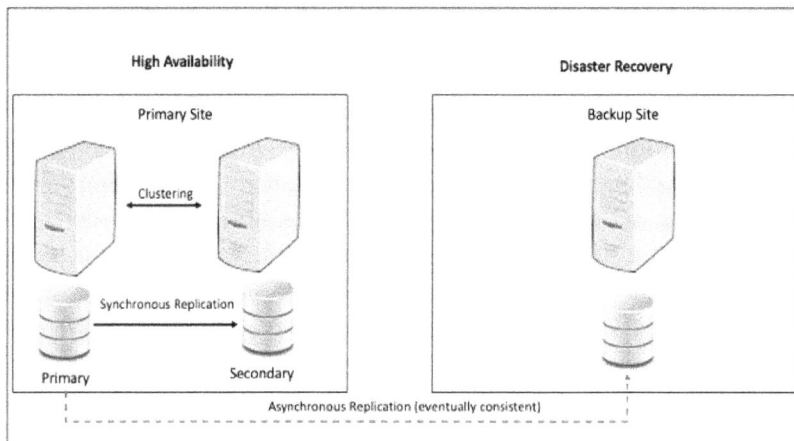

Figure 8.1: HA vs DR

While HA and DR are complementary, they have different scopes and priorities. HA focuses on preventing minor outages, which can impact the availability of a system, while DR focuses on recovering from major disasters that could affect the entire organization. HA solutions are typically implemented within a single site, although multi-site HA is not uncommon, or DR solutions involve establishing a secondary site that may be located outside of the organization's primary geographic region, possibly separated by several miles.

HA or DA is not a choice, and you will likely always need both. For organizations providing a service, guaranteeing a certain level of availability is always important. A service's true value is measured by its reliability when customers depend on it most. This makes HA solutions essential. Organizations also need the ability to be able to provide continuity of business in the face of catastrophic events. If your service is not available for a significant period, irrespective of the cause, your customers could leave for a competitor and never return. So, really, you need a combination of HA and DR to ensure adequate quality of service and continuity of business under all circumstances.

In recent years, cloud computing has emerged as a powerful tool for implementing HA and DR solutions. Cloud providers like AWS offer a variety of services, such as virtual machines, storage, networking, and managed services that can be used to create highly available and disaster-tolerant infrastructure. For example, cloud-based replication can be used to replicate data across multiple regions, ensuring that it is protected against regional disasters. Additionally, failover mechanisms can be used to automatically switch over to a secondary site in the event of a failure.

The specific techniques and technologies used to implement HA and DR solutions will vary depending on the organization's size, industry, and risk profile. However, the underlying principles remain the same: redundancy, replication, and failover. By carefully considering the organization's needs and implementing appropriate HA and DR solutions, it is possible to minimize downtime and protect against catastrophic events.

HA and DR are both essential components of a robust infrastructure. While they serve distinct purposes, they are complementary and can be used together. By understanding the differences between HA and DR, you can make well-informed decisions on how to protect your IT systems and data.

Achieving high availability on AWS

HA is a critical requirement for modern applications, ensuring minimal downtime and uninterrupted service. AWS offers a range of tools and features to help you achieve HA for your applications. Let us explore some common approaches to achieving HA on AWS.

Multi-AZ deployment

Multi-AZ deployment is a fundamental strategy for achieving HA on AWS. It involves distributing your application across multiple AZs within a region. Each AZ is a distinct geographic location with independent power, cooling, and networking. By deploying components in different AZs, you can protect against failures that could affect a single AZ. Some common causes of failures are hardware failures, such as issues with servers, storage, or networking equipment within an AZ. Power outages are another common cause of failures. Natural disasters such as earthquakes, floods, or hurricanes can also impact your infrastructure within a specific AZ or even the entire region.

With a multi-AZ setup, your application and your data are replicated across multiple regional sites. Replicating data across multiple AZs ensures data durability and protection against data loss. This ensures that if there is a single AZ failure, the application and data can be accessed from another AZ. This offers fault tolerance and allows you to continue providing service in the event of a failures that impact one of the AZs from which your workload runs. AWS offers a variety of services that support multi-AZ deployments, providing HA and fault tolerance. Here are some prominent examples. This list is not exhaustive, but it gives you a good sampling of services that provide the ability to distribute your applications and data across multiple AZs for HA:

- **Regional Services (Multi-AZ by default):**
  - o **Amazon DynamoDB**: DynamoDB tables are automatically replicated across multiple AZs within a single AWS Region. This ensures HA and durability, as even if one AZ experiences a failure, your data remains accessible. This provides seamless multi-AZ replication for HA and durability.

  - o **Amazon S3**: Amazon S3 replicates data across a minimum of three AZs within a single AWS Region. This redundancy significantly enhances data durability and availability. Amazon S3 creates multiple copies of your data and stores them in different physical locations to protect against data loss due to hardware failures, power outages, or other unforeseen events.

  - o **Amazon Simple Queue Services (SQS)**: SQS queues are replicated across multiple AZs within a single AWS Region. This redundancy ensures HA and durability, as even if one AZ experiences a failure, the queue can continue to operate seamlessly.

- **Regional services with Multi-AZ configuration option:**
  - o **Amazon Elasticache for Valkey**: Amazon Elasticache for Valkey allows distributing your Valkey nodes across multiple AZs within a single AWS Region, and you can protect against failures that may affect a single AZ. The serverless configuration for this service automatically stores your data across multiple AZs redundantly.

  - o **Amazon RDS**: With Amazon RDS, your database instances can be replicated across multiple AZs within a single AWS Region. This significantly enhances the availability and durability of your database, as it can automatically fail over to a standby instance in a different AZ in case of a failure. This ensures data replication and automatic failover.

  - o **Amazon OpenSearch Service**: Amazon OpenSearch Service enhances the availability and durability of your OpenSearch clusters by distributing data and nodes across multiple AZs within a single AWS Region. By using a multi-AZ deployment, you can significantly reduce the risk of downtime caused by infrastructure failures or other unforeseen events.

- **Global services:**

  - **Amazon CloudFront**: Amazon CloudFront is a global service for **content delivery network** (**CDN**) that helps deliver data, images, videos, applications, and APIs to customers globally with low latency, high transfer speeds, and increased security. CloudFront operates a vast network of edge locations around the world, caching content to improve performance for users by reducing latency.

  - **Amazon IAM**: AWS **Identity and Access Management** (**IAM**) is a global service, meaning it is accessible from any AWS Region. This global nature ensures that your IAM policies and user identities can be used to manage access to resources across all your AWS accounts, regardless of their region.

  - **Amazon Route 53**: Amazon Route 53 is a global service that provides a scalable **Domain Name System** (**DNS**) web service that is highly available. This means it is accessible from anywhere in the world and uses a globally distributed network of DNS servers to ensure fast and reliable DNS resolution.

By leveraging these multi-AZ services, you can significantly enhance the availability and resilience of your applications on AWS.

Autoscaling

Autoscaling is another essential component of HA on AWS. It allows you to automatically adjust the capacity of your application based on demand. By scaling up or down as needed, you can ensure that your application has the resources it requires to handle varying workloads. Autoscaling helps you avoid overprovisioning or under-provisioning resources. By scaling up during peak demand, you can maintain high performance levels. Autoscaling can help you reduce costs by only paying for the resources you need. You can define scaling policies that specify how and when your application should scale up or down. You can monitor key metrics, such as CPU utilization, memory usage, and network traffic, to make scaling decisions. Different scaling strategies, such as step scaling, target tracking, scheduled scaling, and predictive scaling, can be applied to achieve autoscaling. Here is a quick introduction to each of these strategies:

- **Target tracking**: Maintains a specific metric at a desired target value. The scaling policy adjusts the capacity to keep the metric at a desired target value. The scaling policy determines the appropriate action based on the deviation from the target. For example, if the metric exceeds the target threshold, the policy might trigger an increase in instances to handle the increased load. Conversely, if the metric falls below the target, the policy might decrease the number of instances to optimize resource utilization. Target tracking is particularly effective for applications where maintaining a consistent level of performance or resource utilization is important.

- **Step scaling**: Adjusts the capacity of your application in discrete steps based on specific thresholds. For example, if CPU utilization exceeds 60%, the scaling policy might add ten instances. This allows you to quickly scale up your capacity in increments that make sense for your workload's traffic surges. It is best suited for applications with predictable workload patterns and sudden spikes in demand.

- **Scheduled scaling:** is a proactive approach to capacity management that allows you to adjust your application's resources based on a predetermined schedule. This is particularly useful for applications with predictable, recurring workload patterns, such as daily or weekly peaks. By anticipating and planning for these surges in traffic, you can ensure that your application can handle the increased demand by providing necessary capacity, preventing performance bottlenecks, and maintaining a positive user experience. Scheduled scaling empowers you to optimize resource utilization, reduce costs, and enhance the overall reliability of your application.

- **Predictive scaling:** leverages historical data and sophisticated machine learning algorithms to forecast future demand for your application. By analysing past trends, patterns, and anomalies, predictive scaling models can anticipate fluctuations in workload and proactively adjust your application's capacity to meet those demands. This intelligent approach is particularly valuable for applications with complex and dynamic workload patterns that are challenging to predict using traditional methods. Predictive scaling enables you to optimize resource utilization, avoid performance bottlenecks, and ensure a consistent user experience, even during periods of peak demand or unexpected surges.

Multi-AZ deployment and autoscaling can complement each other to provide a robust HA solution. Multi-AZ deployment ensures that your application can continue to operate in the event of a failure, while autoscaling helps you optimize resource utilization and maintain performance. By combining multi-AZ deployment with autoscaling, you can ensure HA. Autoscaling can help you adjust the capacity of your application to meet demand, even in the event of a failure. This helps with the performance of your application. By scaling down during periods of low demand, you can reduce your overall costs.

Application-level high availability

Application-level HA involves implementing redundancy and fault tolerance within your application code. This can include techniques such as circuit breakers and retries. For example, exponential backoff is a technique used to handle transient errors or temporary failures when interacting with AWS services through their SDKs or APIs. It involves retrying a failed operation multiple times, with each retry attempt waiting for a longer interval than the previous one. This exponential increase in waiting time helps to avoid overwhelming the service or introducing a feedback loop that could make the problem worse. The general process of exponential backoff with retries involves making the initial request to the AWS service. If the request fails due to a transient error (e.g., network issues, service throttling), the waiting time for the next retry is determined based on the number of previous attempts. The waiting time typically increases exponentially with each retry. If the retry fails again, they are tried again after waiting for a calculated period, until a maximum number of retries is reached or the request succeeds. Transient errors like network timeouts, throttling errors, or temporary service disruptions are usually good candidates for retries.

Additional considerations for high availability

Here are some other factors to consider when achieving HA on AWS:

- **Backup and recovery**: Implement regular backups of your data and applications to ensure that you can recover from data loss or system failures.

- **Monitoring and alerting**: Monitor your application's health and performance, and set up alerts to notify you of any issues.

- **Testing and failover drills**: Regularly test your HA procedures to ensure that they are effective.

By carefully considering these factors and implementing the appropriate strategies, you can build highly available and resilient applications on AWS. HA is a foundational requirement for achieving SLOs. HA ensures that an application is available to users for a significant portion of the time. This directly contributes to meeting uptime SLOs. Redundancy and fault tolerance in HA architectures can help minimize response times by distributing load across multiple instances, AZs, or regions. This helps meet response time SLOs. While a multi-AZ deployment is a powerful tool for achieving HA, it can become insufficient under certain circumstances. *Everything fails, all the time* is an often-cited quote from the *Chief Technology Officer of Amazon, Dr. Werner Vogels,* which addresses the reality of the fact that you cannot rely on any system having 100% uptime, all the time. A widespread outage affecting an entire region can impact both AZs, rendering the multi-AZ setup ineffective. This is where a multi-region deployment can provide additional resilience. Although rare, issues at the data centre level, such as power failures or network disruptions, can affect multiple AZs within a region. Misconfigurations or accidental deletions can impact both AZs, especially if they are centrally managed.

Consider a workload that needs a 99.99 % availability SLO. This is also known as the four 9s of availability. In terms of time, this translates to about 53 minutes of unavailable time over the course of a year. The amount of time it can take to detect a failure (on average about five minutes) and the time it takes for somebody to respond to a failure (an average of 10 minutes) leaves you with less than 40 minutes to recover from the failure. If this SLO is further attached to an SLA that can lead to reputational or financial losses, a regional problem that impacts multiple AZs together can prove to be a loss. In such a situation, it makes sense to evaluate the cost of running the workload in a highly available manner in multiple regions and compare it with the cost of the damages that can result from a regional outage through SLA misses. Some AWS services provide cross-region replication and deployment capabilities that you can leverage to achieve multi-region HA:

- **Amazon S3:** S3 offers a cross-region replication feature, which allows you to automatically replicate objects from one S3 bucket in one region to one or more destination buckets in different regions. This ensures data redundancy and enables you to access your data from multiple locations

- **Amazon Aurora:** Amazon Aurora offers a Global Database feature, which provides multi-region capability by replicating data across multiple AWS Regions within seconds. This allows you to have a primary region where your data resides and one or more secondary regions where data is replicated. You can continuously send reads to replicas in secondary regions for cross-regional HA. In case of a regional outage, you can also promote a replica in the secondary region to become the primary within a short amount of time to start accepting writes.

- **Amazon DynamoDB:** Amazon DynamoDB's Global Tables feature provides a fully managed, multi-region, and multi-active database solution. It enables you to replicate your DynamoDB tables across multiple AWS Regions, ensuring cross-region HA through asynchronous replication. Each Region can independently read and write data, providing low-latency access for users located in different parts of the world.

HA measures like redundancy and failover can reduce the likelihood of errors due to hardware failures or network issues, contributing to lower error rates. HA can improve throughput by ensuring that the application can handle increased traffic without performance degradation. This helps meet throughput SLOs. By ensuring that an application is resilient to failures and can handle varying workloads, HA helps deliver a consistent and reliable user experience, which is essential for meeting the expectations set by SLOs.

DR planning and testing

DR on AWS is a tailored approach that varies depending on an organization's specific needs and risk tolerance. A one-size-fits-all solution is not feasible due to factors like financial obligations through SLA defined in contracts, the possibility of reputational loss and customer churn, and data sensitivity. RPO and RTO are crucial metrics used to define the acceptable data loss and system downtime in the event of a disaster.

Let us understand these concepts:

- **Recovery Time Objective (RTO):** RTO is the maximum acceptable time your business can tolerate a service being down. It answers the question *How soon must we recover?* For example, if your RTO is four hours, your systems must be restored and operational within four hours of a disruption. A shorter RTO means faster recovery but typically requires more investment in infrastructure and automation. An online payment system might need an RTO of minutes, while an internal human resources portal may be able to tolerate an RTO of hours.

- **Recovery Point Objective (RPO):** RPO defines the maximum acceptable amount loss in data loss, as measured by time. This answers the question *How much data can we afford to lose?* For example, if your RPO is one hour, you must ensure your backup or replication system captures data at least every hour. A shorter RPO means less data loss but requires more frequent backups or continuous replication. A financial trading system might require an RPO of seconds, while a content management system might accept an RPO of 24 hours.

While it is tempting to target an aggressive RTO or RPO of minutes, organizations must perform a thorough cost-benefit analysis before committing to such stringent recovery objectives. The infrastructure, tools, and operational overhead required to achieve near-immediate recovery can increase costs exponentially.

Let us revisit the question of what a disaster is in the context of DR. In the realm of IT and business continuity, a disaster is any event that significantly disrupts normal operations, causing potential data loss and system downtime. These disasters can be natural, such as hurricanes, earthquakes, or floods, or human-made, such as cyberattacks, fires, or power outages.

Declaring a disaster and initiating recovery

The process of declaring a disaster and initiating recovery involves a combination of automated systems and human intervention. Here is a general outline:

- **Monitoring and alerting:**
    - o Continuous monitoring systems detect anomalies or critical events, such as system failures, data loss, or security breaches.
    - o Alert systems notify relevant personnel about the incident.

- **Incident response team activation:**
    - o A designated incident response team is activated to assess the situation and initiate the recovery process.
    - o Declaring a disaster is an intensive process and requires investment of time from many members of your operations team and IT leadership. Such a decision should be made after careful consideration.

- **Damage assessment:**
    - o The team evaluates the extent of the damage, including affected systems, data loss, and potential impact on business operations.

- o If the issue is caused by an AWS service outage, you should consult with AWS support and your AWS Technical Account Manager (if one is available) to understand the impact of the outage and how long they expect the resolution to take. If the problem is resolved within your RTO and RPO needs, then there is no need to declare a disaster.

- **Activation of the DR plan:**

  - o This can usually involve escalating up the chain of the IT leadership to make the call to declare the situation a disaster. This means all other options have been evaluated for a recovery within the primary site, and a failover to a backup site is the only option left.

  - o Your organization's DR plan is activated, outlining specific procedures for recovery.

  - o You test the health of your backup site to ensure that it is ready to start accepting traffic from your customers. If your preferred backup site is also affected by the disaster, further assessment may be needed.

- **Execution of recovery procedures:**

  - o Technical teams execute the recovery procedures, following the outlined steps in the DR plan.

  - o This may involve restoring data from backups, activating failover systems, or rerouting traffic to redundant infrastructure.

- **Continuous monitoring and evaluation:**

  - o Close monitoring of the recovery process is essential to identify and address any issues. You test the applications from the point of view of your customers to ensure that they provide a satisfactory user experience.

  - o Post-incident reviews are conducted to learn from the experience and improve future DR plans.

By having a well-defined DR plan and effective monitoring systems, organizations can minimize the impact of disasters and ensure business continuity.

To achieve optimal DR, AWS offers several strategies. The following figure depicts them and organizes them based on the level of availability they provide, and the cost involved in implementing the strategy:

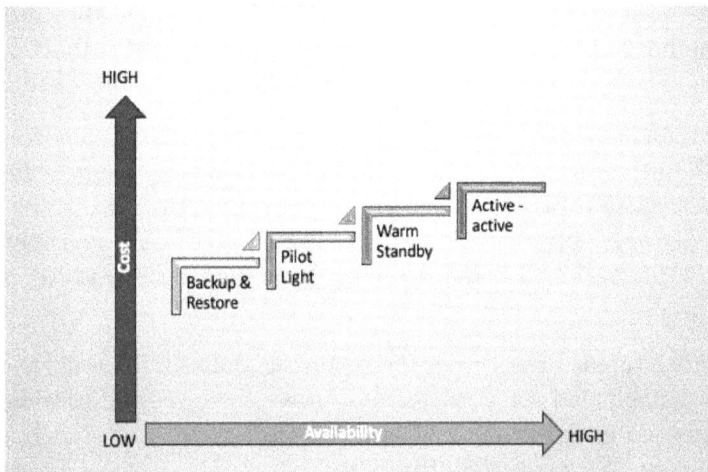

Figure 8.2: DR strategies by cost and availability

Now, let us look at each of the elements mentioned in the figure.

Backup and restore

The backup and restore strategy involve creating regular backups of data and applications and restoring them to a new environment, usually a different AWS Region, in the event of a disaster. This approach is suitable for applications with higher RTO and RPO requirements, where a longer recovery time and some data loss can be tolerated. The RPO/RTO hours for this strategy usually run into hours or days. This is also the most cost-effective DR strategy among the four.

The key considerations are as follows:

- **Backup frequency**: You must determine the optimal frequency for backups based on data sensitivity and business needs. The lower your RTO and RPO targets are, the more frequent backups you will need. For highly sensitive data like financial records or transaction data, frequent backups (e.g., hourly, multiple times a day, daily) are essential to minimize data loss. For less important data, longer backup timeframes could suffice. Change rate also plays an important part. For databases and applications with frequent updates, more frequent backups (e.g., hourly or multiple times daily) are necessary to capture the latest changes. For static data, less frequent backups (e.g., weekly or monthly) may be sufficient.

- **Backup storage**: You should choose a reliable and secure storage solution like Amazon S3 to store backups. Many AWS services intrinsically use Amazon S3 for storing backups, including RDS, EBS, and S3 itself. This provides the necessary reliability and durability for your backups. You can use services like AWS Backup to copy your backups to another region for DR purposes. In some cases, there may even be a case to copy the backup to a separate AWS account meant specifically for backups. This account can have extra security protections to ensure only authorized personnel have access to it, and there is a lower risk of threats like ransomware attacks.

- **Backup retention policy**: You need to define a retention policy to specify how long backups should be retained. Retaining the backups for a shorter time than they are needed will cause a problem when you need to restore from the backup, and the backup is not available. If you retain backups longer than you have a use for them, it can result in a backup sprawl, which is hard to manage and can also increase your backup costs.

- **Restore procedures**: Procedures for restoring data and applications from backups need to be established for your teams. As we have seen, declaring the disaster is a consensus-based process, and all-hands-on-deck coordination is needed within your operations team to execute DR effectively.

- **Testing**: Having a DR plan in place is not sufficient by itself. If the DR process is not tested regularly, it may reveal gaps when it is exercised for a live recovery scenario. It is, hence, a necessary practice to regularly test your backup and restore procedures to ensure their effectiveness.

AWS Services for backup and restore are listed as follows:

- **AWS Backup**: A fully managed service that automates the backup and restore process for various AWS resources.

- **Amazon S3**: A highly scalable and durable object storage service for storing backups.

- **Amazon Glacier**: A cost-effective storage tier of S3 for long-term archiving of backups.

- **AWS CloudFormation**: Can be used to automate the deployment of infrastructure in the recovery environment.

By leveraging these AWS services and implementing a well-defined backup and restore strategy, organizations can effectively protect their data and applications from potential disasters.

Pilot light

The pilot light strategy is a cost-effective DR approach where a minimal version of the application environment is maintained in a standby region. The term *pilot light* is derived from the concept of a small, continuously burning flame in a gas appliance that ignites the main burner. Similarly, in a pilot light DR strategy, a minimal version of the application is kept running, ready to ignite and scale up in case of a disaster. This analogy highlights the idea of a small, constantly running component that can quickly ignite and expand into a full-fledged application when needed. This environment includes essential components like databases, storage, and networking, but the compute resources (e.g., EC2 instances) are not actively running. Pilot light DR strategy is recommended when your RPO/RTO time is 10s of minutes. This costs more than a backup and restore DR strategy to implement but is still a cost-effective option. The reason for this is that you are not provisioning a major portion of your compute until you need it. Compute tends to form the biggest portion of your cloud spend, and by avoiding spending on compute in the DR region, you save costs on implementing this DR strategy.

The key components of a pilot light strategy are as follows:

- **Data replication**: Critical data is continuously replicated from the primary region to the standby region. This ensures data consistency and enables rapid recovery. Many of the techniques employed in the backup and restore strategy can be used here. However, the frequency of backups is more regular or even continuous.

- **Minimal infrastructure**: A small set of essential infrastructure components, such as load balancers and network configurations, is deployed in the standby region. This enables you to stand up a fully scaled production grade infrastructure in your DR site/ region much faster, as you are not waiting for fundamental parts of your infrastructure to be created and become ready.

- **Automated scaling**: Auto-scaling groups are configured to automatically scale up compute resources as needed during a DR event. The idea with the pilot light strategy is to save on compute costs by not running compute until you actually need it. With AWS Auto Scaling, you can have your compute scaled down to no compute or zero. You can scale out your compute when you decide to.

- **Regular testing**: Regular testing and failover drills are crucial to ensure the effectiveness of the pilot light environment and identify potential issues. The testing process will involve checking both the data recovery and scaling the compute as part of your DR plan.

The AWS implementation is as follows:

- **Amazon RDS and Amazon Aurora**: You would ship your database backups to a secondary region. Additionally, you can consider making use of the cross-region replicas feature offered by RDS and Aurora Global Database feature in Amazon Aurora to continuously replicate data to a secondary region. This allows for even faster recovery speeds, as the data would be current and within seconds of the primary region. The replica instance can be quickly promoted to be the primary in the backup region.

- **Amazon S3**: You replicate your S3 data across multiple regions using S3 cross-region replication. This provides continuous replication and keeps your data current in the backup region.

- **AWS CloudFormation**: In the pilot light strategy, most baseline infrastructure is expected to already be provisioned in your recovery region. However, if there is a need to provision something in just in time as part of the recovery process, it is recommended you do this using IaC like AWS CloudFormation.

- **AWS Auto Scaling**: Auto-scaling plays an important role in the pilot light DR strategy. This is what enables you to go from no compute to fully scaled out compute to service your production traffic when the recovery process is initiated.

By implementing a well-designed pilot light strategy, you can significantly reduce recovery time and minimize the impact of a disaster on your business.

Warm standby

The warm standby strategy involves maintaining a partially provisioned environment in a standby region, ready to be activated quickly. This approach strikes a balance between cost-effectiveness and recovery time. The key components and considerations, and even the services that you use to implement the warm-standby DR strategy, are the same as the pilot light DR strategy. There is, however, a very key difference. Unlike a pilot light, where only essential components are running, a warm standby environment has a scaled-down version of the production environment, including some compute resources. A subset of the production infrastructure, such as database servers, application servers, and network devices, is deployed in the standby region and is always running. AWS Auto Scaling again plays an important role here and handles the job of bringing the DR region in parity with the primary region when the recovery process is initiated. Cost-wise, this is on the higher end of the spectrum and only next to a full-fledged active-active multi-site implementation. The availability provided by this strategy is also very high, as you are running a scaled-down version of the same workload that is running in your primary region. Your secondary region can service a small number of customers at any given time. For that reason, this strategy is recommended for RPO/RTO of minutes. You do not use your warm-standby region until a disaster is declared and you start the recovery process. However, you have the comfort of knowing that your standby region is ready to go at a smaller scale whenever you need it. This is also faster to scale to full production size when compared with the pilot-light strategy, as you are not scaling your compute from zero.

Active-active

The active-active strategy is the most available, but also the most expensive DR strategy. It involves replicating data and workloads across multiple regions, enabling both regions to simultaneously handle live traffic. This approach offers the highest level of availability and DR, making it ideal for critical applications with near real-time RTO and RPO requirements.

The key characteristics of an active-active strategy are as follows:

- **Zero-downtime**: In the event of a failure in one region, traffic can be seamlessly shifted to the other region, with no downtime. You can use health checks on the primary region to decide if you want to failover to the active backup region, which is already configured to serve traffic with the same configuration as the primary region.

- **Enhanced performance**: By distributing the workload across multiple regions, active-active can improve application performance for users in the same region by reducing latency. This strategy to make use of infrastructure that is running in another region to actively serve traffic to a portion of your use base is a good strategy to get return on investment for the cost of the infrastructure.

The AWS implementation is as follows:

- **Multi-region deployment**: Deploying your application and data across multiple AWS Regions.

- **Data replication:** Ensuring consistent data replication between regions using services like Amazon S3 Cross-Region Replication, Amazon Aurora Global Database, and DynamoDB Global Tables.

- **Global load balancing**: Using Amazon Route53 or AWS Global Accelerator to distribute traffic across multiple regions based on factors like latency and availability.

- **Failover mechanisms**: Implementing automatic failover mechanisms to route traffic to healthy regions in case of failures.

- **Consistent configuration**: Maintaining consistent configurations across all regions.

While active-active is a powerful strategy, it requires careful planning and implementation. It is crucial to consider factors like data consistency, network latency, and synchronization mechanisms to ensure seamless operation.

By carefully evaluating RTO, RPO, and other factors, organizations can select the most appropriate DR strategy for their specific needs. AWS provides a flexible platform that enables organizations to implement robust DR solutions, ensuring business continuity and minimizing downtime in the event of a disaster.

Considerations for cross-region backup copies

There are cost implications to copying your backups to another region. You need to consider the storage costs for storing backups in multiple regions. Your storage costs will be a multiple of the number of additional regions you copy your backups to. This cost can be controlled by setting the right retention policies on your backups in all regions, so they can either be archived to lower cost storage or be permanently expired.

You should also be aware of the data transfer costs associated with copying backups across regions, especially for large datasets. Inter-region data transfer in AWS has a cost per GB, which varies by the regions the data is being transferred to. The data transfer is charged in each direction it is transferred. When a backup is copied to a new AWS Region for the very first time, AWS Backup makes a full copy of the backup. Any further copies of the backup in the same AWS Region will be incremental. Meaning you will only be charged for the amount of data that has changed after the original full copy of the backup is made and copied.

When your backups are copied to a new region, AWS Backup handles re-encryption of backups during cross-region copying differently depending on whether the resource type has full AWS Backup management support. AWS Backup automatically encrypts the copies with the target backup vault's KMS key. This happens even if the original backup was unencrypted. The re-encryption is handled automatically as part of the copy process. For resources without full AWS Backup management, cross-region copies are encrypted using the destination region's default AWS-managed key for that service. For example, if you are copying an EBS snapshot to us-east-1, it will use the aws/ebs key in us-east-1. The copy does not use the AWS Backup vault's KMS key.

For enhanced security, it is advisable to use customer-managed keys instead of AWS-managed keys. You must ensure proper IAM permissions for both source and destination KMS keys. You can monitor the encryption operations through AWS CloudTrail. You can use backup policies in AWS Backup to enforce encryption.

AWS Backup policies

AWS Backup policies are JSON documents used within AWS Organizations to manage and enforce backup requirements across multiple AWS accounts centrally. These policies define backup rules, including frequency, backup windows, retention periods, and which resources to back up based on tags. When attached to **organizational units** (**OUs**) or individual accounts, backup policies combine through inheritance, policies from the root, parent OUs, and the account level merge to create an effective policy for each account. Once applied, these policies automatically create immutable backup plans in AWS Backup that appear in each account's AWS Backup console. The backup plans created from these policies cannot be modified directly in the member accounts, ensuring consistent backup strategies and compliance across the organization. AWS Backup then uses the specified IAM role to automatically perform backups according to the defined schedules and retention rules.

Here is an example AWS Backup policy:

```
{
    "plans": {
        "ProdServerBackups": {
            "regions": {
                "@@assign": [
                    "us-east-1",
                    "us-west-2"
                ]
            },
            "rules": {
                "DailyBackups": {
```

```
                        "target_backup_vault_name": {
                            "@@assign": "DailyBackupVault",
                            "encryption": {
                                "@@assign": "arn:aws:kms:region:account:key/
key-id"

                            }
                        },
                        "schedule_expression": {
                            "@@assign": "cron(0 5 ? * * *)"
                        },
                        "start_backup_window_minutes": {
                            "@@assign": "60"
                        },
                        "complete_backup_window_minutes": {
                            "@@assign": "480"
                        },
                        "lifecycle": {
                            "move_to_cold_storage_after_days": {
                                "@@assign": "30"
                            },
                            "delete_after_days": {
                                "@@assign": "120"
                            }
                        },
                        "target_backup_vault_arn": {
                                    "@@assign": "arn:aws:backup:*:*:backup-
vault:DailyBackupVault"
                        },
                        "copy_actions": {
                         "arn:aws:backup:eu-west-1:*:backup-vault:secondary-
vault": {
                                    "target_backup_vault_arn": {
                                        "@@assign": "arn:aws:backup:eu-west-
1:*:backup-vault:secondary-vault"
                                    },
```

```
                                            "lifecycle": {
                                                "move_to_cold_storage_after_days": {
                                                    "@@assign": "30"
                                                },
                                                "delete_after_days": {
                                                    "@@assign": "120"
                                                }
                                            }
                                        }
                                    }
                                },
                                "selections": {
                                    "tags": {
                                        "Environment": {
                                            "iam_role_arn": {
                                                "@@assign": "arn:aws:iam::*:role/BackupRole"
                                            },
                                            "tag_key": {
                                                "@@assign": "Environment"
                                            },
                                            "tag_value": {
                                                "@@assign": [
                                                    "Production"
                                                ]
                                            }
                                        }
                                    }
                                }
                            }
                        }
                    }
```

The explanation of this backup plan is as follows:

- **Regions configuration:**
  - o Backups will run in us-east-1 and us-west-2
  - o Primary backups will be stored in these regions
  - o The backup vault is encrypted with a KMS key. By default, AWS Backup uses the AWS managed key (aws/backup), using a **customer-managed key (CMK)** provides more control and auditability. The KMS key ARN must be in each region where backups are stored.

- **Backup schedule:**
  - o Runs daily at 5:00 AM UTC (cron(0 5 ? * * *))
  - o Has a 60-minute window to start (start_backup_window_minutes)
  - o Allows 8 hours total to complete (complete_backup_window_minutes: 480)

- **Lifecycle rules:**
  - o Primary backups move to cold storage after 30 days.
  - o Backups are deleted after 120 days
  - o Cross-region copies follow the same lifecycle rules

- **Cross-region copy:**
  - o Copies are made to eu-west-1 region
  - o Uses a vault named "secondary-vault"
  - o Applies same lifecycle rules (30 days transition to cold, 120 days to deletion)

- **Resource selection:**
  - o Selects resources tagged with "Environment=Production"
  - o Uses BackupRole IAM role for permissions

Cell-based architecture on AWS for HA and DR

A cell-based architecture is a design pattern where an application is divided into independent, isolated units or cells. Each cell is a self-contained unit with its own infrastructure and resources. Each cell is designed such that it shares nothing. Each cell gets its own load balancer, compute nodes, database instances, and any storage. Anything that the workload needs for its functioning should be included in the cell for the cell-based architecture to be successful. For example, if your architecture uses services like **Amazon Elastic Container Services (Amazon ECS)** or **Amazon Elastic Kubernetes Services (Amazon EKS)**, each cell would have its own ECS or EKS cluster. No two cells would share a common cluster. This is what makes a cell in cell-based architecture self-contained and complete on its own.

The following figure illustrates how a typical cell-based architecture can be achieved. As you can see, each cell receives its own copy of the resources required for the application, allowing each cell to operate independently:

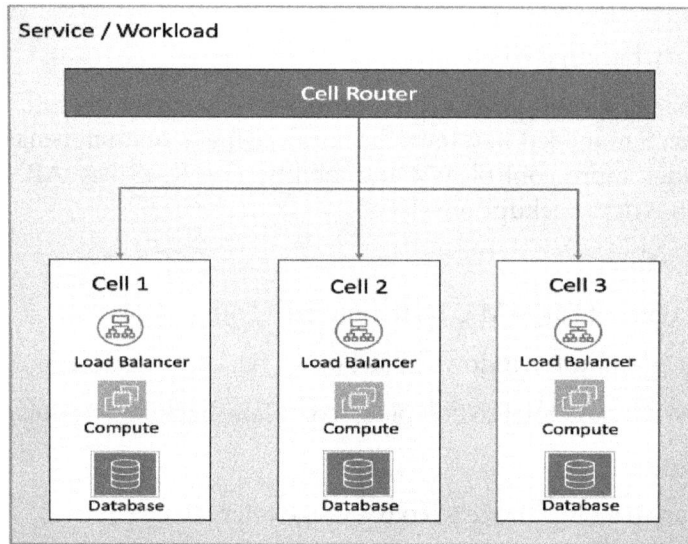

Figure 8.3: Cell-based architecture example

This architectural approach can significantly enhance the availability and resilience of applications on AWS and can help with both HA and DR.

Here are some advantages provided by cell-based architecture for HA and DR:

- **HA advantages:**

  o **Fault isolation:** By dividing the application into isolated cells, a failure in one cell is less likely to impact the entire system. This reduces the blast radius of failures, improving overall system availability.

  o **Scalability**: Each cell can be scaled independently, allowing for better resource utilization and faster recovery from increased load or unexpected spikes.

  o **Redundancy**: Cells can be deployed across multiple AZs or regions, providing redundancy and fault tolerance.

- **DR advantages:**

  o **Rapid recovery**: The modular nature of cell-based architecture allows for faster recovery from disasters. Failed cells can be quickly replaced or rebuilt, minimizing downtime. Also, by isolating your clients to different cells, you can prevent from a faulty or rogue activity in one of the cells from impacting other clients sending traffic to other cells.

- o **Geographical distribution**: By deploying cells in multiple regions, you can mitigate the impact of regional failures.

- o **Data replication:** Data is replicated across multiple cells or regions, ensuring data redundancy and enabling quick recovery in case of data loss.

Implementing cell-based architecture on AWS includes the following stages:

- **Identify cells:** Break down your application into logical units based on functionality or data boundaries.

- **Deploy cells:** Cells can be deployed in various configurations to achieve different levels of availability and scalability.

  - o **Single-AZ deployment:** Cells are deployed within a single AZ. This offers a simple setup and keeps your costs low. The disadvantage of this strategy is that a single AZ failure can impact all cells within that AZ.

  - o **Multi-AZ deployment:** Cells can be deployed across multiple AZs within a region. This provides enhanced fault tolerance and HA. On the other hand, it increases complexity and cost, as along with duplicating your infrastructure components across cells, you further distribute parts of it across AZs, which can lead to more costs.

  - o **Multi-region deployment:** Cells can also be deployed across multiple AWS Regions. This provides you with global redundancy, improved DR, and improved performance for users in different regions. The cons again are that your costs multiply based on how many different regions you deploy your cells to. Your routing also increases in complexity as you have to route between multiple regions.

- **Thin routing layer:** In a cell-based architecture, a thin routing layer acts as a traffic director, routing incoming requests to the appropriate cell. It is designed to be as simple and lightweight as possible, focusing solely on routing decisions. It should have minimal functionality beyond routing requests. The routing layer itself should be highly available, often implemented using redundant components and load balancing. It should be able to handle increasing traffic loads and scale accordingly. The routing layer must also be secure and protected from unauthorized access and common attacks by using something like a **Web Application Firewall (WAF)**, which can defend against them.

- **Monitor and alert:** You must implement a robust monitoring and alerting system to detect and respond to failures promptly. For example, if one of the cells fails, you should investigate if the problem is likely to impact other cells. If not, you should consider redeploying the impacted cell so that the clients impacted through the failure in the cell can be serviced again. Normally, you would distribute your clients across multiple isolated cells, so that there is redundancy even if one of their cells is impacted by a failure.

Conclusion

In conclusion, automating resilience is a critical aspect of building robust and reliable applications on AWS. This chapter has explored various strategies for achieving HA and implementing effective DR plans. From multi-AZ deployments and autoscaling to more advanced approaches like pilot light, warm standby, and active-active configurations, AWS offers a range of tools and services to meet diverse resilience requirements. The choice of strategy depends on factors such as RPO, RTO, and cost considerations. Regular testing and continuous improvement of DR plans are essential to ensure their effectiveness. By leveraging AWS services and following best practices, organizations can significantly enhance their ability to withstand and recover from disruptions, ultimately ensuring business continuity and maintaining customer trust in an increasingly digital world.

In the next chapter, we will understand how you can automate responses to incidents that you observe in your AWS environment.

Multiple choice questions

1. **What is the primary purpose of a multi-AZ deployment in AWS?**
    a. To distribute the application across multiple AZs for HA
    b. To reduce costs by using fewer resources
    c. To increase application performance
    d. To simplify database management

2. **Which AWS service automatically replicates data across multiple AZs within a single region?**
    a. Amazon EC2
    b. Amazon DynamoDB
    c. Amazon CloudFront
    d. AWS Lambda

3. **What is the main benefit of using autoscaling in AWS?**
    a. To automatically adjust capacity based on demand
    b. To reduce network latency
    c. To improve data encryption
    d. To simplify database queries

4. **Which of the following is NOT a type of autoscaling strategy in AWS?**
    a. Target Tracking
    b. Manual Scaling

   c.   Step Scaling

   d.   Predictive Scaling

5. **What does RPO stand for in the context of DR?**

   a.   Recovery Point Objective

   b.   Recovery Process Optimization

   c.   Rapid Performance Optimization

   d.   Resilience Planning Operation

6. **Which DR strategy maintains a minimal version of the application environment in a standby region?**

   a.   Pilot light

   b.   Warm Standby

   c.   Active-Active

   d.   Backup and Restore

7. **What is a key advantage of an Active-Active DR strategy?**

   a.   Lowest cost

   b.   Simplest to implement

   c.   Highest level of availability

   d.   Least amount of data replication

8. **Which AWS service is commonly used for global load balancing in an Active-Active strategy?**

   a.   Amazon EC2

   b.   Amazon RDS

   c.   Amazon S3

   d.   AWS Global Accelerator

9. **What is a key consideration when implementing a backup and restore strategy?**

   a.   Backup frequency

   b.   Number of active regions

   c.   Real-time data replication

   d.   Continuous compute scaling

10. **Which DR strategy is typically recommended for RPO/RTO of minutes?**

    a. Warm standby

    b. Backup and restore

    c. Pilot light

    d. Active-active

Answers

1.	a
2.	b
3.	a
4.	b
5.	a
6.	a
7.	c
8.	d
9.	a
10.	a

Join our Discord space

Join our Discord workspace for latest updates, offers, tech happenings around the world, new releases, and sessions with the authors:

https://discord.bpbonline.com

CHAPTER 9
Incident Response Automation

Introduction

We have learned several techniques so far that allows us to design our workloads on AWS to be highly resilient and withstand failures. There will however invariably be situations where things do not go as planned and you must quickly respond to investigate or recover from it. Incident response is a primary concern for SRE, that requires careful planning and automation to ensure that it is achieved in a systematic manner without delays that can lead to a wider spread outage.

Structure

The chapter covers the following topics:

- Principles of incident response
- Responding to events with Amazon EventBridge
- Using runbooks for incident response
- Automating with multi-step workflows
- Testing recoverability

- Chaos engineering
- AWS Fault Injection Service

Objectives

By the end of this chapter, you will learn the principles of incident response and why it is important to automate the response to incidents. You will learn about different types of incidents that you may encounter while running workloads on AWS. You will learn about AWS services such as Amazon EventBridge and how it can be combined with other services like Amazon SNS and AWS Lambda for effective incident response automation. Lastly, you will also be introduced to chaos engineering and how you can continuously test your workloads for anomalous situations by simulating conditions that can occur in the real-world.

Principles of incident response

Incident response is a discipline that needs to be implemented and improved on continuously for best results. Every incident response without proper automation and documentation creates two problems: the one you are currently solving, and the one you are creating for the next person who encounters this issue. The temporary success of solving production fires quickly fades when you are facing the same alerts three months later, wondering what worked last time. In this section, we will understand the principles that make up incident response:

- **Preparation**: This stage for incident response on AWS prepares you to handle unexpected events effectively through multiple integrated components. It begins with developing detailed runbooks that provide step-by-step procedures for addressing various scenarios, from service disruptions to security incidents, while ensuring these procedures align with AWS Well-Architected best practices. You will also continuously review and refine these runbooks as you discover new patterns. The stage implements robust monitoring and alerting systems using AWS native services, including CloudWatch, Config, CloudTrail, GuardDuty, and Security Hub, creating a multi-layered detection framework that provides real-time visibility into your security posture. Automation plays a crucial role here, through the use of Lambda functions, Step Functions workflows, and Systems Manager Automation runbooks, enabling immediate responses to predefined triggers while reducing human error and response times. The preparation framework incorporates regular testing through controlled incident simulations using tools like AWS **Fault Injection Simulator** (**FIS**) and game days, allowing you to validate your response procedures, identify gaps, and refine approaches. We will discuss FIS later in this chapter as part of the chaos engineering section.

  This stage also emphasizes the importance of proper access management through AWS IAM, maintaining up-to-date asset inventories, establishing clear communication channels, and ensuring team members are adept in both AWS services and incident response procedures. Additionally, it includes developing relationships with AWS Support and maintaining current contact information for key stakeholders, while also implementing proper logging and forensics capabilities to support post-incident analysis. This prepares you well to respond to incidents with confidence, precision, and speed.

- **Detection**: In the detection stage of incident response on AWS, you set up your monitoring and alerting systems, with Amazon CloudWatch serving as the key enabler. As we saw in *Chapter 7, Observability for Reliable Operations*, CloudWatch continuously collects and analyses metrics, logs, and events from across the AWS infrastructure, providing a comprehensive view of your resource health and performance. CloudWatch's integration with Amazon EventBridge further enhances its capabilities, allowing for real-time event-driven detection of potential incidents. This enables you to create a set of rules to identify patterns or abrupt changes indicative of security threats, performance issues, or service disruptions. As data flows through your systems, machine learning algorithms embedded in services like CloudWatch anomaly detection can establish baselines and flag deviations to offer an additional layer of intelligent monitoring. By configuring alerts for a wide range of scenarios, from simple threshold breaches to complex multi-metric anomalies, you can ensure that potential incidents do not go unnoticed. These alerts, delivered through channels such as SNS topics or integrated with incident management platforms, serve as your first line of defense, prompting immediate investigation and response. The detection stage also leverages other AWS services like GuardDuty for threat detection, Config for compliance monitoring, and VPC Flow Logs for network traffic analysis, providing a multi-faceted approach to incident detection. This comprehensive detection framework not only helps in identifying known threats but also in uncovering subtle, emerging issues. This significantly reduces the mean time to detection, enabling faster, more effective incident response in the AWS environment.

- **Containment**: In the containment stage of incident response on AWS, speed and precision become important as you take the necessary steps to isolate and neutralize threats before they can spread. This phase leverages security features on AWS to create a barrier around affected systems. Security Groups and Network ACLs serve as the first line of defense, allowing you to implement granular traffic restrictions and cordon off compromised resources from the rest of the infrastructure. This enables you to create adaptive security perimeters, adjusting access controls in real-time as the incident unfolds. Implementing circuit breakers can protect against cascading failures, automatically severing connections or shutting down services when predefined thresholds are breached. This prevents a localized issue from evolving into a wider system failure. For web applications, AWS WAF offers an additional layer of protection by filtering malicious web traffic and blocking common attack patterns. This approach can be further enhanced by the use of AWS Lambda functions, which can be triggered to automatically respond to security events, perhaps by revoking IAM credentials or isolating EC2 instances through network controls. You can also use

AWS Organizations to implement **Service Control Policies (SCPs)**, restricting certain actions across multiple accounts. These options allow your incident response team to isolate the threat without causing undue disruption to critical business operations. This containment strategy, orchestrated with AWS's native security features and complemented by custom automation, prevents the spread of incidents. This buys valuable time to investigate and eradicate the root cause of the problem.

- **Eradication**: The eradication stage can also be viewed as the root cause analysis stage in AWS incident response. It is a phase that extends to both security incidents and a wide spectrum of potential failures that can impact your infrastructure. In this stage, you will discuss the issue, whether it is a security breach, service outage, performance degradation, or a **disaster recovery (DR)** scenario. By leveraging AWS's suite of diagnostic tools, you can dissect the incident and piece together the sequence of events that led to the failure. For security incidents, this might involve using Amazon GuardDuty, Amazon Detective, VPC Flow Logs, and CloudTrail logs to trace the attacker's path through the system to identify compromised resources. For service failures, CloudWatch logs and metrics, combined with X-Ray distributed tracing, help investigate the situation that led to the outage. For performance issues, you can use RDS Performance Insights for database analysis or use EC2 Systems Manager to gather detailed system-level metrics. In DR scenarios, you need to have an understanding of the extent of data loss and the effectiveness of backup and replication strategies, often utilizing AWS Backup and S3 versioning. You may employ AWS Config to understand changes in resource configurations that might have contributed to the incident. The goal is not just to identify what went wrong but to understand why it went wrong and how existing controls may have proven insufficient. This phase will often involve cross-team collaboration, bringing together experts from various domains to interpret the data and form a comprehensive understanding of the incident. As the root cause emerges, you can begin formulating strategies for permanent remediation. This may involve patching vulnerabilities, redesigning system architectures for better resilience, updating policies and procedures, or enhancing monitoring and alerting capabilities. This thorough analysis and eradication process serves as the foundation for preventing similar incidents in the future, transforming each incident into an opportunity for enhancing the overall robustness and security of your AWS environment.

- **Recovery**: The recovery stage in AWS incident response brings systems back to a stable, secure state. As you initiate the recovery process, you can leverage AWS backup and recovery tools, such as AWS Backup, which provides a centralized solution for managing and automating backups across various AWS services. This stage often begins with a careful assessment of the backup integrity, ensuring that the data and configurations to be restored have not been compromised. You can utilize IaC tools like AWS CloudFormation or Terraform to recreate the affected infrastructure rapidly in a clean, controlled environment. This approach not only accelerates the recovery process but also ensures consistency and eliminates human error that could introduce new vulnerabilities. As services are gradually brought back online, AWS

Auto Scaling plays a crucial role in managing the increased load often associated with recovery operations, dynamically adjusting resource capacity to meet demand spikes without overwhelming the recovering systems. Throughout this process, you should continuously validate system integrity using tools like AWS Config and Security Hub to ensure that the restored environment adheres to security best practices and compliance standards. You might employ AWS Step Functions to orchestrate intricate recovery workflows across multiple services in more complex scenarios. The recovery stage concludes with a comprehensive review, where you document lessons learned and refine your recovery processes.

- **Post-incident analysis**: The post-incident analysis stage in AWS incident response provides opportunities for growth and improvement. After recovering from the incident, your teams can gather in a blameless manner to conduct a comprehensive post-mortem analysis. This process begins with a thorough review of the incident timeline, piecing together events using data from AWS CloudTrail, CloudWatch Logs, and other monitoring tools. You will review each decision made and action taken, evaluate their effectiveness, and identify areas for improvement. You will discuss the root causes, examining the technical failures and any procedural or cultural factors that may have contributed to the incident. As insights emerge, you document them as a post-mortem report, which becomes a valuable resource for future reference. This document captures not only what went wrong but also what went right, celebrating successful interventions and innovative solutions that emerged during the incident response. The lessons learned from this analysis can lead to a series of improvements across the organization. Runbooks are updated to incorporate new scenarios and refined procedures, while automation scripts are enhanced to address newly identified vulnerabilities or failure modes. You may discover architectural changes, such as implementing more robust failover mechanisms or enhancing security controls. Knowledge can be shared across the organization with insights from the incident through internal tech talks, blogs, wikis, or updated training materials. This approach ensures that the lessons learned extend beyond the immediate incident response team, fostering a culture of continuous improvement and shared responsibility for system reliability and security. The post-incident analysis stage may also spark broader initiatives, such as revisiting DR plans, refining incident classification criteria, or investing in new tools for enhanced monitoring and automated response. As the process concludes, your teams emerge not only with a stronger, more resilient AWS environment but with a deeper understanding of your systems.

- **Automation**: Automation emerges as a key strength in incident response by transforming reactive measures into proactive safeguards. Automation uses the ecosystem of AWS services to detect, respond to, and mitigate incidents in a timely manner. Amazon EventBridge serves as an important piece of the puzzle here by constantly monitoring for patterns and anomalies across the AWS environment. When it detects a pattern indicating a potential incident, it can trigger AWS Lambda functions that can execute predefined actions, such as isolating compromised instances or revoking suspicious IAM credentials. AWS Step Functions can be employed for more complex scenarios to orchestrate multi-step response workflows spanning multiple services and account for various contingencies. These workflows might involve escalating alerts, controlling scaling behavior, initiating backup processes, or even automatically failing over to DR sites. EventBridge can integrate with AWS Config to automatically take remedial actions or alert teams when resource configurations deviate from predefined compliance and security standards. You can also use AWS Systems Manager Automation to standardize and execute complex operational procedures across large-scale environments consistently and reliably. This might include patching vulnerabilities, updating configurations, or running diagnostic routines. The result is a self-improving incident response ecosystem that not only reacts to threats with speed but also evolves to anticipate and prevent future incidents, creating a more resilient and secure AWS infrastructure.

- **Notification**: The principle of effective notification in incident response ensures that the right information reaches the right people at the right time. At the core of this notification strategy lies Amazon **Simple Notification Service (SNS),** a versatile and scalable pub/sub messaging service that serves as the central hub for alerting. When incidents occur, SNS orchestrates notifications, delivering tailored messages across various channels. These could range from emails and text messages to Slack channels and custom applications. However, notifications go beyond just message delivery. It must also strike a fine balance between keeping stakeholders informed and avoiding alert fatigue. You must carefully craft notification rules and filters, leveraging the power of Amazon EventBridge in conjunction with SNS to reduce the signal-to-noise ratio. This employs sophisticated logic to ensure that only truly actionable alerts make their way to responders, preventing burnout and ensuring that critical incidents do not get lost amidst low-priority notifications. As an incident progresses, the notification strategy will need to evolve as well. Initial alerts can be terse and targeted, designed to alert SRE teams to respond quickly. More detailed updates can be made available through carefully segmented communication channels. This ensures that technical teams, management, and affected customers all receive information appropriate to their needs and level of technical understanding. Transparency is important, with regular status updates providing a clear picture of the incident's impact, ongoing mitigation efforts, and expected resolution timelines. These updates, when automated through integration with incident management platforms, help maintain trust and manage expectations during critical periods. The notification system serves not just as an alert mechanism but as a collaborative tool, facilitating real-time communication among response teams and enabling rapid decision-making. This ensures that all stakeholders remain aligned through the incident lifecycle. By the time an incident is resolved, the notification trail provides rich insights for post-incident analysis and continual improvement of the response process. In this way, the notification stage in AWS incident response transcends simple alerting. It becomes a sophisticated, adaptive system that guides you through critical incidents with assurance.

- **Continuous improvement**: The principle of continuous improvement serves as the driving force behind organizational resilience and adaptability. This phase transcends any specific incident, and is an ongoing process touching different aspects of operations. It involves a commitment to a regular and thorough review of incident response plans, identifying areas of strength and opportunities for enhancements. The feedback gathered from these sessions feed into a continuous refinement loop. Here, you can iteratively improve your processes, fine-tune your automation scripts, and update your response playbooks to reflect new learnings. This culture of improvement must extend beyond internal processes, with teams staying informed of the latest AWS guidelines and feature releases. Successful SRE teams attend AWS conferences, participate in webinars, and consult with AWS solution architects to ensure their incident response strategies leverage best in class options from AWS's evolving toolkit. The ethos of continuous improvement also drives cross-functional collaboration, breaking down silos between development, operations, and security teams. This approach ensures that lessons learned from incident response inform architectural decisions, security policies, and development practices, creating a virtuous cycle of enhancement that elevates your organization's cloud maturity. This intentional pursuit of improvement and not being satisfied with the status quo transforms each incident into a stepping stone towards greater resilience, agility, and expertise in managing AWS environments.

Responding to events with Amazon EventBridge

In this section, we are going to discuss Amazon EventBridge. Amazon EventBridge forms the backbone of incident response on AWS. An event bus in Amazon EventBridge is a central serverless component that acts as a conduit for event-driven architectures in AWS. An event bus receives events from various sources and routes them to target services or applications based on defined rules. It serves as the primary mechanism for event management and distribution in AWS. Event buses can be shared across AWS accounts, enabling multi-account architectures. EventBridge comes with a default event bus, which is automatically created for you in your AWS account. EventBridge also allows you to create multiple custom event buses in addition to the default bus for your custom event-driven architectures. You can build event-driven applications specific to your business domain, which make use of these custom event buses.

The default bus automatically receives events from AWS services. This is key to the ability of being able to use EventBridge as the enabler of incident response workflows on AWS.

Let us understand how event buses function:

- **Event ingestion**: Event buses ingest events from various sources, including AWS services, custom applications, and SaaS providers. You can create rules associated with event buses, which matches events arriving on the bus.

- **Rule matching**: When an event is received, the bus checks it against all associated rules. When there is a match found for the incoming event with the rule, the event is routed to the registered targets. Multiple targets could be registered per rule. However, to keep the architecture simple to understand and troubleshoot, it is recommended to set up one target per rule. When you need to use more than one target, it is usually better to create a different rule for each target you want to send the event to.

- **Event filtering**: Rules can filter events based on their content or pattern before they are sent to targets. This can be used to ensure that targets only receive the necessary events. This can also be useful to control costs, especially when the target you are invoking has a cost associated with it, like a Lambda function invocation.

- **Target invocation**: If an event matches a rule, the bus routes it to the specified targets (for example, Lambda functions, SNS topics). The target processes the events, which it receives in JSON format.

The following figure depicts how AWS services or cron-based events flow through EventBridge to common targets. We will learn about custom events in the subsequent sections. (Custom events also take a similar path).

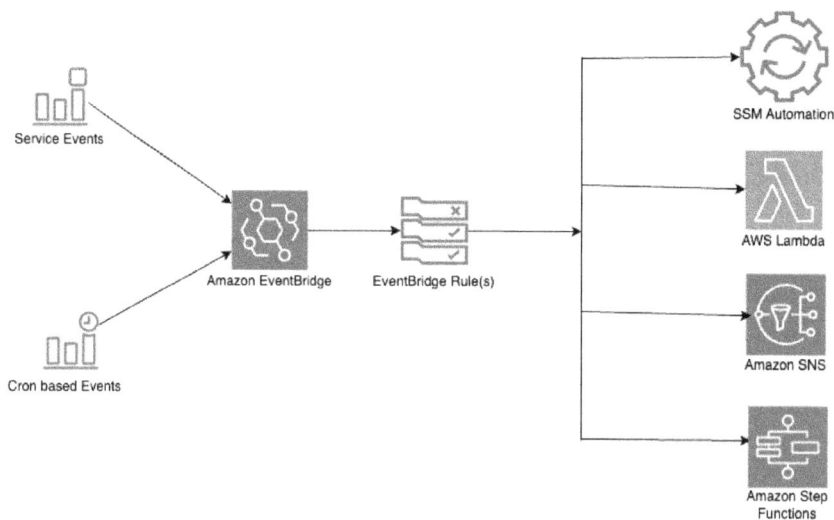

Figure 9.1: Event flow from EventBridge to different targets

Amazon EventBridge seamlessly consumes events from a vast array of AWS services, creating a robust foundation for real-time incident response in cloud environments. As AWS services generate events, such as EC2 instance state changes, S3 bucket modifications, or CloudTrail API call, they make their way to EventBridge. EventBridge automatically ingests these into its default event bus without a need for any additional configuration. This native integration allows for immediate visibility into the operational state and security posture of your AWS infrastructure. In the context of incident response, this capability becomes invaluable. For instance, sudden spikes in failed login attempts captured by CloudTrail events could trigger an automated response through EventBridge, instantly alerting security teams or initiating predefined remediation workflows.

Similarly, unexpected changes in resource configurations detected through AWS Config events can prompt immediate investigation or rollback procedures. By leveraging EventBridge's rule-based event routing, you can create sophisticated incident response systems that react to potential security threats or operational anomalies in near real-time. This might involve automatically isolating affected resources, scaling up defensive measures, or notifying relevant personnel through integration with services like AWS Lambda, SNS, or third-party incident management platforms. The ability of EventBridge to consume and act upon events from across the AWS ecosystem transforms incident response from a reactive process into a proactive, automated strategy. This significantly reduces response times and minimizes the potential impact of security incidents or operational disruptions.

Let us look at an example of how you can configure an EventBridge rule for AWS services and use it for incident response. For this example, we will pick an example of an EC2 state change and a notification going out to the SRE team. We will use Amazon SNS to send the notification. We will also see how you can use the event to take remedial action using a Lambda function.

Let us go through these using CLI commands instead of CloudFormation. This will give you an opportunity to understand the different steps involved in configuring this.

Note: **As your EC2 instances are part of an auto scaling group (ASG), when you try to stop one of them using the example that follows, the ASG may respond to your instances temporarily reporting as unhealthy and start new instances.**

We want to use our Lambda function to restart the stopped EC2 instance. To achieve this, you can temporarily pause autoscaling by running this command:

```
aws autoscaling suspend-processes --auto-scaling-group-name <<asg-name>>
```

You can retrieve the name of your ASG from the list of resources that your CloudFormation template has created by viewing it in the AWS Console.

When you have completed the example as shown, you can resume autoscaling by running the command:

```
aws autoscaling resume-processes --auto-scaling-group-name <<asg-name>>
```

The following are the steps to be undertaken:

1. Let us first create an SNS topic that will receive notifications and store the topic ARN in a variable:

```
aws sns create-topic --name ec2-incident-response
export SNS_TOPIC_ARN=$(aws sns create-topic --name ec2-incident-response
--query 'TopicArn' --output text)
```

2. Create an IAM role for the Lambda function. Follow each command listed in the following one by one:

```
cat << 'EOF' > trust-policy.json
{
  "Version": "2012-10-17",
  "Statement": [
    {
      "Effect": "Allow",
      "Principal": {
        "Service": "lambda.amazonaws.com"
      },
      "Action": "sts:AssumeRole"
    }
  ]
}
 EOF
aws iam create-role    --role-name lambda-ec2-role    --assume-role-
policy-document file://trust-policy.json

aws iam attach-role-policy    --role-name lambda-ec2-role    --policy-
arn arn:aws:iam::aws:policy/service-role/AWSLambdaBasicExecutionRole

cat << 'EOF' > policy.json
{
    "Version": "2012-10-17",
    "Statement": [
        {
            "Effect": "Allow",
            "Action": [
                "ec2:StartInstances",
                "ec2:DescribeInstances"
            ],
            "Resource": "*"
        },
        {
            "Effect": "Allow",
            "Action": [
                "sns:Publish"
```

```
                    ],
                    "Resource": "arn:aws:sns:*:*:*"
              },
              {
                    "Effect": "Allow",
                    "Action": [
                         "logs:CreateLogGroup",
                         "logs:CreateLogStream",
                         "logs:PutLogEvents"
                    ],
                    "Resource": "*"
              }
         ]
    }
    EOF
    aws iam create-policy      --policy-name lambda-ec2-custom-policy
    --policy-document file://policy.json
    aws iam attach-role-policy      --role-name lambda-ec2-role      --policy-
    arn arn:aws:iam::012345678901:policy/lambda-ec2-custom-policy
```

3. Create a Lambda function for remediation using the commands in the following:

```python
cat << 'EOF' > index.py
import boto3
import os
def lambda_handler(event, context):
    # Extract instance information from the event
    instance_id = event['detail']['instance-id']
    state = event['detail']['state']
    ec2 = boto3.client('ec2')
    sns = boto3.client('sns')

    if state == 'stopped':
        try:
            # Start the instance
            ec2.start_instances(InstanceIds=[instance_id])
            message = f"Remediation action taken: Starting instance
{instance_id}"
```

```
      # Send notification about remediation
      sns.publish(
        TopicArn=os.environ['SNS_TOPIC_ARN'],
        Message=message,
        Subject='EC2 Incident Response - Remediation Taken'
      )
    except Exception as e:
      sns.publish(
        TopicArn=os.environ['SNS_TOPIC_ARN'],
        Message=f"Failed to start instance {instance_id}:
{str(e)}",
        Subject='EC2 Incident Response - Remediation Failed'
      )
EOF

zip function.zip index.py

aws lambda create-function    --function-name ec2_remediate_function
--runtime python3.11    --handler index.lambda_handler    --role
arn:aws:iam:: 012345678901:role/lambda-ec2-role  --timeout 180   --zip-
file fileb://function.zip
```

4. Create an environment variable on the Lambda function with the right ARN of your SNS topic. This will allow your Lambda function to reference the SNS topic, without the need to hardcode the topic ARN in the function body:

```
aws lambda update-function-configuration --function-name ec2_remediate_
function --environment "Variables={

SNS_TOPIC_ARN=arn:aws:sns:us-west-2:012345678901:ec2-incident-response
    }"
```

5. Create the EventBridge rule using AWS CLI. First, create a file named:

```
event-pattern.json

cat << 'EOF' > event-pattern.json
{
    "source": ["aws.ec2"],
    "detail-type": ["EC2 Instance State-change Notification"],
    "detail": {
        "state": ["stopped"]
    }
}
EOF
```

6. Create the EventBridge rule using the CLI:

```
aws events put-rule \
            --name "ec2-incident-response-rule" \
            --event-pattern file://event-pattern.json \
--description "Monitor EC2 instance stops & trigger incident   response"
```

7. Add targets to the rule (both SNS and Lambda). Create a file named **targets.json**. Replace the placeholders for SNS topic **Amazon Resource Name** (**ARN**) and Lambda function ARN with their correct values that you previously obtained when you created them:

```
[
  {
    "Id": "SendToSNS",
    "Arn": "<SNS_TOPIC_ARN>",
    "InputTransformer": {
      "InputPathsMap": {
        "instance": "$.detail.instance-id",
        "state": "$.detail.state",
        "time": "$.time"
      },
      "InputTemplate": "\"EC2 instance <instance> changed state to
<state> at <time>\""
    }
  },
  {
    "Id": "TriggerLambda",
    "Arn": "<LAMBDA_FUNCTION_ARN>"
  }
]
```

8. Add the targets to the rule:

```
aws events put-targets \
            --rule ec2-incident-response-rule \
            --targets file://targets.json
```

9. Grant necessary resource permissions to allow EventBridge to invoke the Lambda function and send notifications to the SNS topic:

```
aws lambda add-permission \
            --function-name ec2-incident-response \
```

```
          --statement-id EventBridgeInvoke \
          --action lambda:InvokeFunction \
          --principal events.amazonaws.com \
          --source-arn $(aws events describe-rule --name ec2-
incident-response-rule --query 'Arn' --output text)
aws sns set-topic-attributes --topic-arn arn:aws:sns:us-west-2:
01234567890:ec2-incident-response      --attribute-name Policy
--attribute-value '{
        "Version": "2012-10-17",
        "Statement": [
    {
            "Sid": "EventBridgeToTopic",
            "Effect": "Allow",
            "Principal": {
                "Service": "events.amazonaws.com"
            },
            "Action": "sns:Publish",
            "Resource": "arn:aws:sns:us-west-2:01234567890:ec2-incident-
response"
        },
    {
            "Sid": "LambdaToTopic",
            "Effect": "Allow",
            "Principal": {
                "Service": "lambda.amazonaws.com"
            },
            "Action": "sns:Publish",
            "Resource": "arn:aws:sns:us-west-2:01234567890:ec2-incident-
response"
        }

    ]
    }'
```

10. Add an email subscription to the SNS topic to see that you are being notified when you stop one of the EC2 instances. Replace it with the following:

```
aws sns subscribe \
    --topic-arn arn:aws:sns:us-east-1:01234567890:ec2-incident-response
```

```
\
    --protocol email \
  --notification-endpoint john.doe@example.com
```

This setup will:

a.   Monitor for EC2 instances that enter a **stopped** state.

b.   Send a notification to the SNS topic with formatted message.

c.   Trigger a Lambda function that attempts to restart the instance.

d.   Send another notification about the remediation action.

EventBridge simplifies the process of building event-driven architectures. While we do not focus on building even-driven applications with custom event buses in this chapter, this is another use case for EventBridge. Since this book is focused on SRE, we used EventBridge to receive events from AWS services and take necessary incident response or recovery actions. This foundational example illustrates EventBridge's core functionality. As an SRE, you will find this pattern useful across multiple operational use cases, particularly in automation and event-driven operations.

Using runbooks for incident response

Normally, a Lambda function works well when you have to take isolated actions that are completed within a reasonable amount of time. Lambda functions can run for a fixed period of time and are good for performing one task really well. When you have multi-step actions or workflows, it is better not to overload a Lambda function but to look at other alternatives. The first alternative we will explore for this purpose is **Systems Manager Automations (SSM Automations)**. We have already covered Systems Manager Automations in *Chapter 5, Automating Infrastructure Maintenance.* Here, let us understand when it may be a more suitable option than Lambda functions for incident response automation. SSM Automations can help you build runbooks for automating actions on your SSM-managed nodes and AWS services.

The following are some common scenarios where you can use SSM Automations:

*   **Complex infrastructure management tasks**: SSM Automations are designed for infrastructure management and can execute complex, multi-step operational tasks more efficiently than Lambda functions. This is particularly useful for scenarios like coordinated patching across multiple instances, complex application deployments, or orchestrating actions across various AWS services.

*   **Long-running operations**: Lambda functions have a maximum execution time of 15 minutes, which can be limiting for lengthy operations. Systems Manager Automations do not have this constraint, making them better suited for tasks that may take longer periods to complete.

- **Predefined operational runbooks**: AWS provides a library of pre-built Automation runbooks for common operational tasks. These can be used as is without much effort. They are also rigorously tested, so they are less error-prone than writing equivalent Lambda functions from scratch.

- **Cross-account and cross-region operations**: Systems Manager Automations can more easily perform actions across multiple AWS accounts and regions. While this is also something you can achieve with AWS Lambda, it can be more effort to set up.

- **Reduced development overhead**: While SREs are generally adept with programming, those from a traditional operations background tend to favour command line-based scripting. Creating and maintaining Automation runbooks may be more accessible than developing and updating Lambda functions.

- **Rate management**: SSM Automations offer robust rate-limiting capabilities, providing you with fine-grained control over the execution of automation workflows across your AWS infrastructure. These rate-limiting features allow you to specify the number of concurrent executions that can run simultaneously, as well as the number of accounts and regions where the automation can execute concurrently. This level of control is particularly advantageous in managing resource utilization, preventing potential overload on target systems, and ensuring compliance with service quotas.

- **Cost considerations:** Although this may differ based on specific scenarios, the cost model for SSM automations could be more efficient than Lambda functions for complex automations. SSM automation costs are based on the number of steps beyond a monthly free tier and a per-second cost for aws:executeScript action step. Whether there is a cost advantage or not will require a deeper evaluation of your automation scenario and a comparison of Lambda costs vs SSM Automation costs.

Note: **The cost advantage should not be your only reason to pick one over the other. Picking the right option based on suitability for the automation task should take higher precedence. Single-step automations with a known duration of executions, which fall within the limits offered by Lambda functions, are best suited for AWS Lambda. For longer-running, multi-step automations that could span across AWS accounts and regions, you may want to consider SSM Automations.**

Automating with multi-step workflows

AWS Step Functions is a powerful serverless workflow orchestration service that can significantly enhance incident response automation in cloud environments. By leveraging Step Functions, you can create sophisticated, multi-step workflows that coordinate various AWS services and external systems to respond to security incidents swiftly and effectively. For example, a Step Function workflow could be triggered by an Amazon CloudWatch alarm or a security event detected by Amazon GuardDuty. The workflow could then automatically isolate affected resources by modifying security groups, initiate forensic data collection using

AWS Lambda functions, and create snapshots of compromised instances for later analysis. It can even trigger human approval steps for important decisions that require manual oversight. Step Functions' ability to handle long-running processes, retry failed steps, and maintain state throughout the execution makes it ideal for managing complex incident response procedures that may involve multiple services and timeframes. Its visual workflow designer and detailed execution history provide transparency and auditability, which are crucial aspects of effective incident response. By automating these processes with Step Functions, SRE teams can significantly reduce response times, minimize human error, and ensure consistent execution of incident response protocols, ultimately improving your organization's overall resiliency posture.

The following are some scenarios where you can employ Step Functions for your incident response:

- **Complex orchestration**: Step Functions excel at orchestrating complex, long-running workflows that involve multiple services and decision points. If your process requires intricate branching logic, parallel execution, or complex error handling, Step Functions may be more suitable.

- **Visual workflow design**: Step Functions provide a visual workflow designer, making it easier to design, understand, and maintain complex processes, especially for teams that prefer visual representations of their workflows.

- **Integration with a wider range of AWS services**: While Systems Manager Automations are great for infrastructure management, Step Functions can integrate with a broader range of AWS services and can easily incorporate and orchestrate custom Lambda functions for additional flexibility.

- **Fine-grained control over execution**: Step Functions offer more granular control over the execution of each step, including retry policies, error handling, and state transitions.

- **Human interaction in workflows**: While Systems Manager Automations support approval workflows, Step Functions offer more flexible options for human interaction within workflows, including integration with Amazon SNS for notifications and approvals.

- **Standardized workflow patterns**: Step Functions provide standardized workflow patterns (like Map state for parallel execution) that can be more efficient and easier to implement than creating equivalent logic in Systems Manager Automations.

- **Execution history and debugging**: Step Functions provide detailed execution histories and visual representations of workflow executions, making it easier to debug and analyze complex processes.

- **Cost advantage for certain workflows**: Step Functions can be more cost-effective for certain types of workflows, especially those with long idle periods between steps, as you only pay for the state transitions.

While Systems Manager Automations remain excellent for infrastructure-focused tasks, Step Functions are generally better suited for complex, application-level workflows that span multiple services and require sophisticated orchestration. The choice between the two often depends on the specific use case, the complexity of the workflow, and whether the focus is more on infrastructure management or application logic.

Let us implement a Step Function example that you can test with our sample workload. We will use a CloudFormation template to deploy this. In this example, we will use a combination of EventBridge and Step Functions to change our Auto Scaling configuration. We set up a cron-based event, which scales up the capacity of your ASG during peak hours (mornings) and scales it down during off-peak hours (evenings). Here is an excerpt of the CloudFormation template for this. The full version of this template will be available in the code examples shared with this book.

You can create your CloudFormation stack with the following template, as discussed in the previous chapters:

```
AWSTemplateFormatVersion: "2010-09-09"
Description: "Step Functions state machine for ASG capacity management"

...
Resources:
  ...
  CapacityManagementStateMachine:
    Type: AWS::StepFunctions::StateMachine
    Properties:
      RoleArn: !GetAtt CapacityManagementRole.Arn
      Definition:
        Comment: "State machine for managing ASG capacity"
        StartAt: CheckTime
        States:
          CheckTime:
            Type: Choice
            Choices:
              - Variable: "$.timeOfDay"
                StringEquals: "peak"
                Next: ScaleUpForPeak
              - Variable: "$.timeOfDay"
                StringEquals: "offPeak"
                Next: ScaleDownForOffPeak
          ScaleUpForPeak:
```

```
          Type: Task
          Resource: arn:aws:states:::aws-sdk:autoscaling:updateAutoScalingGr
oup
            Parameters:
              AutoScalingGroupName: !ImportValue ASG-Name
              MinSize: !Ref PeakTimeMinSize
              MaxSize: !Ref PeakTimeMaxSize
              DesiredCapacity: !Ref PeakTimeDesiredCapacity
            Retry:
              - ErrorEquals:
                  - States.ALL
                IntervalSeconds: 3
                MaxAttempts: 3
                BackoffRate: 2
            End: true
        ScaleDownForOffPeak:
          Type: Task
          Resource: arn:aws:states:::aws-sdk:autoscaling:updateAutoScalingGr
oup
            Parameters:
              AutoScalingGroupName: !ImportValue ASG-Name
              MinSize: !Ref OffPeakMinSize
              MaxSize: !Ref OffPeakMaxSize
              DesiredCapacity: !Ref OffPeakDesiredCapacity
            Retry:
              - ErrorEquals:
                  - States.ALL
                IntervalSeconds: 3
                MaxAttempts: 3
                BackoffRate: 2
            End: true
  MorningScaleUpRule:
    Type: AWS::Events::Rule
    Properties:
      Description: "Trigger scale up at start of business hours"
      ScheduleExpression: "cron(0 8 ? * MON-FRI *)"
```

```
      State: ENABLED
      Targets:
        - Arn: !Ref CapacityManagementStateMachine
          Id: "MorningScaleUp"
          RoleArn: !GetAtt EventsRole.Arn
          Input: '{"timeOfDay": "peak"}'
  EveningScaleDownRule:
    Type: AWS::Events::Rule
    Properties:
      Description: "Trigger scale down at end of business hours"
      ScheduleExpression: "cron(0 18 ? * MON-FRI *)"
      State: ENABLED
      Targets:
        - Arn: !Ref CapacityManagementStateMachine
          Id: "EveningScaleDown"
          RoleArn: !GetAtt EventsRole.Arn
          Input: '{"timeOfDay": "offPeak"}'
...
```

When the Step Function executes during the cron scheduled for the evening, it will scale down the capacity for your ASG to only one instance. If you observe the execution details for the Step Function state machine in your AWS Console, you should see the following figure in the execution details:

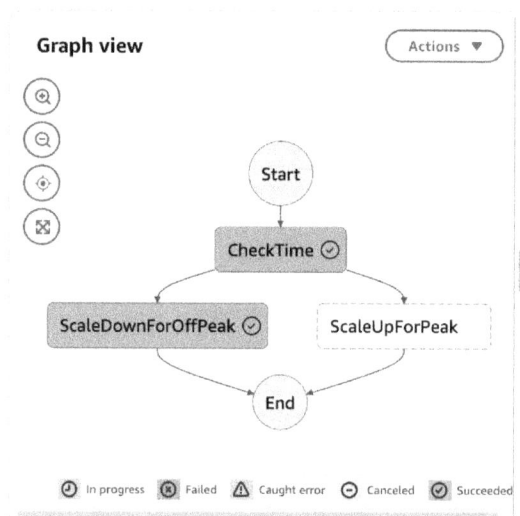

Figure 9.2: Step Function execution to scale down capacity

Similarly, when the Step Function executes during the cron scheduled for the morning, it will scale up the capacity for the ASG to our original auto-scaling configuration. If you observe the execution details for the Step Function state machine in your AWS Console, you should see this figure in the execution details:

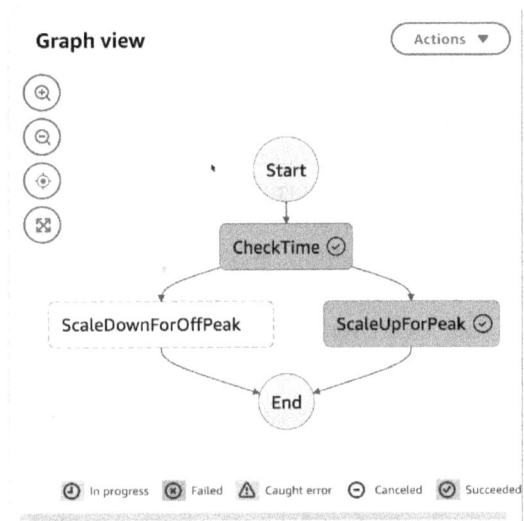

Figure 9.3: Step Function execution to scale up capacity

AWS Step Functions serve as a powerful option in SRE's toolkit, offering a systematic approach to orchestrating complex operational workflows. Its visual interface, built-in error handling, and integration with AWS services make it particularly valuable for automating routine operations, incident response, and system maintenance tasks. While the initial learning curve may require investment in understanding state machine concepts, the long-term benefits of reduced manual intervention, improved reliability, and consistent execution of operational procedures make it worthwhile. By leveraging Step Functions, SREs can transform manual runbooks into automated, auditable workflows that execute reliably at scale. The ability to iterate and improve these workflows over time, combined with detailed execution histories and built-in observability, aligns perfectly with SRE principles of reducing toil and maintaining system reliability.

Testing recoverability

Testing recoverability for incident response on AWS is crucial for ensuring business continuity and minimizing downtime in case of unexpected events. Incidents can occur in different forms, and there are specific ways in which you would react to each of these situations. Following are various ways to test recoverability in AWS:

- **Disaster recovery (DR) drills**: To ensure robust DR preparedness, it is essential to conduct full-scale DR drills that simulate a complete failure of primary systems. These drills should include testing the failover process to secondary regions or accounts, which is crucial for maintaining business continuity. Additionally, it is important to validate both data integrity and application functionality after the failover has been completed. This comprehensive approach helps identify any potential issues and ensures your organization can effectively recover from a major disruption with minimal impact on operations.

- **Chaos engineering**: To enhance system resilience and test DR capabilities, you can leverage tools like AWS **Fault Injection Service** (**FIS**) to introduce controlled chaos into your environments. This approach allows for the simulation of various failure scenarios, such as EC2 instance termination, network latency, or I/O errors. By deliberately creating these controlled disturbances, you can closely observe system behaviour under stress and validate the effectiveness of their recovery processes. This proactive method of testing helps identify weaknesses in the infrastructure and ensures that systems can withstand and recover from unexpected disruptions, ultimately improving overall reliability and performance.

- **Backup and restore testing**: An essential component of a robust DR strategy is the regular testing of backup restoration processes, such as those from Amazon S3 or AWS Backup. These tests should be conducted systematically to ensure that data can be successfully recovered when needed. During these restoration exercises, it is crucial to thoroughly validate the integrity and completeness of the restored systems, confirming that all critical data and configurations are accurately reproduced. Additionally, these tests provide an opportunity to measure and verify the actual **Recovery Time Objectives** (**RTO**) and **Recovery Point Objectives** (**RPO**) against the established targets. By consistently performing these backup and restore tests, you can identify any gaps in their recovery processes, refine their procedures, and gain confidence in your ability to swiftly and effectively recover from potential data loss scenarios.

- **Configuration drift detection**: To maintain system integrity and ensure consistent performance, it is important to implement robust configuration drift detection mechanisms. Leveraging AWS Config is an effective way to achieve this, as it allows you to detect and receive alerts on any configuration changes across your AWS environment. This service will be discussed in more detail in the last chapter of this book. This proactive monitoring helps identify unauthorized or unintended modifications that could potentially impact system stability or security. Furthermore, it is essential to regularly test the ability to revert to known-good configurations. This ensures that in the event of a non-compliant change, you can quickly restore systems to a stable state, minimizing downtime and potential data loss. By combining continuous monitoring with the capability to roll back changes, you can significantly enhance their overall resilience and maintain optimal system configurations.

- **Automated recovery testing**: Automated recovery testing is essential to maintaining a resilient and responsive cloud infrastructure. A key aspect of this testing involves implementing and rigorously evaluating auto-scaling policies designed to handle sudden traffic spikes. These policies ensure that the system can dynamically adjust its resources to meet unexpected demands, maintaining performance and availability under varying loads. Validation of auto-healing mechanisms is important as well, such as those found in ASG instance replacement. These mechanisms automatically detect and replace unhealthy instances, minimizing downtime and maintaining service continuity. By thoroughly testing both auto-scaling and auto-healing capabilities, organizations can ensure their systems are capable of autonomously responding to and recovering from a wide range of potential issues, thereby enhancing overall system reliability and reducing the need for manual intervention during critical events.

- **Database failover testing**: Database failover testing ensures high availability and DR readiness, particularly for services like Amazon RDS. This process involves thoroughly testing the failover mechanisms to read replicas or multi-AZ deployments, simulating scenarios where the primary database becomes unavailable. During these tests, it is essential to closely monitor and validate application behaviour both during the failover process and after it is completed. This approach helps identify any potential issues in the failover procedure, such as data inconsistencies, connection problems, or performance degradation. By regularly conducting these tests, you can fine-tune your failover processes, minimize downtime during actual failures, and ensure that applications remain responsive and functional even when database infrastructure changes occur. This significantly enhances the overall resilience and reliability of database-dependent systems.

- **Load testing**: Load testing is important for testing system reliability and performance under stress. It involves conducting comprehensive tests to verify that systems can effectively handle unexpected traffic spikes without compromising functionality or user experience. AWS Load Balancer helps distribute traffic efficiently across multiple resources, which also enables the simulation of various failover scenarios. By systematically increasing the load and monitoring system behaviour, you can identify performance bottlenecks, determine scaling requirements, and validate the effectiveness of auto-scaling policies. This proactive approach to load testing allows fine-tuning your infrastructure, optimize resource allocation, and ensure systems remain responsive and available even during periods of peak demand or when facing unforeseen traffic surges. Ultimately, regular and thorough load testing contributes significantly to building robust, scalable, and resilient cloud-based applications.

- **Security incident response**: Security incident response preparedness requires regular, hands-on practice to be effective. Conducting simulated security breaches to test and refine your incident response procedures ensures that teams are well-prepared for real-world threats. These simulations should encompass a wide range of scenarios, from data breaches to malware infections, allowing security teams to practice their detection, containment, and eradication strategies. A critical component of these exercises is the practice of swiftly isolating compromised resources to prevent further spread of the threat. Equally important is the process of recovering clean systems, which involves restoring from verified backups or rebuilding systems from scratch using secure baselines. By regularly engaging in these realistic drills, you can identify gaps in their response plans, improve team coordination, and significantly enhance your ability to quickly and effectively mitigate the impact of actual security incidents when they occur.

- **API throttling and circuit breaking**: API throttling and circuit breaking are critical aspects of building resilient cloud-based applications, particularly when interacting with AWS services. It is essential to thoroughly test application behaviour when AWS API calls are subject to throttling, simulating scenarios where request limits are reached or exceeded. This testing helps ensure that applications can gracefully handle rate limiting without crashing or degrading user experience. Equally important is the implementation and validation of circuit breakers, which are designed to prevent cascading failures across interconnected services. These mechanisms temporarily disable calls to failing components, allowing them time to recover and protecting the overall system stability. By rigorously testing both API throttling responses and circuit breaker functionality, organizations can build more robust applications that maintain performance and reliability even when facing service constraints or partial outages. This proactive approach to handling API limitations and service failures significantly enhances the overall resilience of cloud-based systems.

- **Multi-region failover**: For those operating globally distributed applications, implementing and testing multi-region failover capabilities is essential to ensuring continuous service availability. This process involves conducting comprehensive tests to verify the ability to seamlessly transition operations between different AWS Regions in the event of a regional outage or disaster. A key component of this strategy is the validation of DNS failover mechanisms using Amazon Route 53, which enables automatic rerouting of traffic to healthy endpoints across multiple regions. By regularly simulating regional failures and assessing the effectiveness of failover procedures, you can identify and address potential bottlenecks or inconsistencies in their multi-region architecture. This approach enhances the overall resilience of the application and also helps maintain optimal performance, while minimizing downtime for users across different geographical locations.

The goal is not just to pass these recovery tests but to continuously improve your incident response capabilities. Regular testing, coupled with thorough post-mortem analyses, will help refine your recovery strategies and increase overall system resilience.

Chaos engineering

Chaos engineering is the practice of intentionally introducing controlled failures into a system to test its resilience and identify weaknesses. It involves building a hypothesis about the steady-state behavior of your system. You then test the system's resilience by deliberately introducing controlled disturbances that mimic real-world events, such as server crashes or unexpected traffic spikes. This methodology advocates for running experiments directly in production environments to assess system behavior under genuine conditions accurately. To ensure ongoing vigilance and adaptation, these experiments are often automated to run continuously, allowing for the detection of vulnerabilities that may emerge over time due to system changes or evolving external factors. However, an important characteristic of chaos engineering is the careful management of the **blast radius**, limiting the potential negative impact of these experiments. This is achieved through focused planning and implementation of safeguards. It ensures that while the tests are meaningful and revealing, they do not pose undue risk to the overall system stability or user experience. Thus, you can systematically improve your workload's resilience and build confidence in your ability to withstand unforeseen challenges.

Here are some key benefits of chaos engineering:

- Improved system resilience

- Increased confidence in system capabilities

- Better incident response preparedness

- Identification of hidden issues

AWS Fault Injection Service

AWS FIS is a fully managed service that makes it easier to perform chaos engineering experiments on AWS workloads. It allows you to introduce faults into your applications in a controlled manner.

Let us explore some key features of AWS FIS:

- **Experiment templates**: Pre-defined templates for common fault scenarios

- **Actions**: Specific faults you can inject (for example, stopping EC2 instances)

- **Targets**: Resources that will be affected by the actions

- **Stop conditions**: Criteria for automatically stopping an experiment

- **IAM integration**: Fine-grained access control for running experiments

- **CloudWatch integration**: Monitoring and logging of experiment activities

The following are some common fault injection scenarios that you can simulate with FIS:

- **Compute layer:**
  o EC2 instance termination
  o CPU stress testing
  o Memory pressure simulation
  o Instance state changes (stop or restart)

- **Network layer:**
  - Increased latency
  - Packet loss simulation
  - DNS failure simulation
  - API throttling

- **Storage layer:**
  - EBS volume errors
  - IO performance degradation
  - Volume detachment

Some common challenges with chaos engineering involve balancing the need for realistic tests with minimizing customer/business impact. You must ensure that business users do not find the chaos experiments intrusive or disruptive, even though they are being performed with the right intent. Chaos experiments must comply with security and governance controls within your organization and must not risk elevating privileges or exposing sensitive information. Monitoring and managing the costs associated with running experiments is also important so that the **return on investment (ROI)** of chaos engineering is realized.

The following are some key considerations for ensuring success with chaos engineering:

- Start small and gradually increase complexity.
- Always have stop conditions.
- Monitor both infrastructure and application metrics.
- Have clear rollback procedures.
- Test during off-peak hours.
- Notify stakeholders before experiments.
- Test in staging first.
- Have backup procedures ready.
- Keep experiments time-boxed.
- Document learnings and improvements.

By systematically implementing chaos engineering using AWS FIS, you can significantly improve your system's resilience, identify hidden dependencies, and build more robust cloud architectures. Remember, the goal is not just to break things but to learn from controlled failures and continuously improve your systems.

Conclusion

Incident response automation is a critical component of modern cloud operations that enables you to respond quickly and effectively to various types of incidents. Through the use of AWS services like Amazon EventBridge, AWS Systems Manager Automation, and AWS Step Functions, you can build sophisticated automated response workflows that reduce mean time to recovery and minimize human error during critical situations.

The key to successful incident response automation lies in careful preparation, including developing comprehensive runbooks, implementing proper monitoring and alerting systems, and regular testing through chaos engineering practices. AWS FIS provides a controlled environment to test and validate recovery procedures, ensuring that automated responses work as intended when real incidents occur.

By following the principles of incident response from preparation and detection through containment, eradication, and recovery, and combining them with automation capabilities, you can build more resilient systems that can withstand and recover from failures with minimal impact on business operations.

In the next chapter, you will understand the importance of auditing your AWS environments and staying aware of your AWS costs.

Points to remember

- Incident response requires careful planning and automation to ensure systematic handling of issues, key principles such as preparation, detection, containment, eradication, recovery, post-incident analysis, automation, notification, and continuous improvement.

- Amazon EventBridge serves as a central component for incident response automation, allowing you to route events from AWS services to appropriate targets based on defined rules and patterns.

- AWS Systems Manager Automation is better suited for complex infrastructure management tasks and long-running operations compared to Lambda functions, especially when dealing with multi-step actions across accounts and regions.

- AWS Step Functions excel at orchestrating complex, multi-step workflows with visual representation, making it ideal for sophisticated incident response procedures that require multiple services and decision points.

- Testing recoverability is crucial and should include various approaches such as DR drills, backup/restore testing, configuration drift detection, and automated recovery testing to ensure system resilience.

- Chaos engineering, implemented through AWS FIS, helps test system resilience by introducing controlled failures in a systematic way, while carefully managing the blast radius of experiments.

- Successful incident response automation requires a combination of well-documented runbooks, proper monitoring systems, and regular testing through controlled experiments to minimize impact during actual incidents.

Multiple choice questions

1. **What is the primary purpose of Amazon EventBridge in incident response?**

   a. To store event logs

   b. To route events to appropriate targets based on rules

   c. To create backups

   d. To monitor network traffic

2. **Which stage of incident response involves isolating and neutralizing threats before they spread?**

   a. Detection

   b. Preparation

   c. Containment

   d. Recovery

3. **What is a key benefit of using AWS Systems Manager Automation over Lambda functions?**

   a. Lower cost

   b. Faster execution

   c. No time limit constraints

   d. Simpler implementation

4. **In chaos engineering, what does blast radius refer to?**

   a. The scope of potential damage from an experiment

   b. The size of the infrastructure

   c. The number of affected users

   d. The duration of the test

5. **Which AWS service is specifically designed for chaos engineering experiments?**

   a. Amazon CloudWatch

   b. AWS Systems Manager

   c. AWS Fault Injection Service

   d. AWS Config

6. **What is NOT a principle of incident response mentioned in the chapter?**

   a. Preparation

   b. Detection

   c. Marketing

   d. Recovery

7. **When creating EventBridge rules, what is the recommended practice regarding targets?**

   a. Set up multiple targets per rule

   b. Set up one target per rule

   c. Always use Lambda as target

   d. Always use SNS as target

8. **What is a key characteristic of the post-incident analysis stage?**

   a. Blame assignment

   b. Quick fixes

   c. Blameless review

   d. Minimal documentation

9. **Which AWS service is best suited for complex, multi-step incident response workflows?**

   a. AWS Lambda

   b. AWS Step Functions

   c. Amazon SNS

   d. Amazon SQS

10. **What is a primary consideration when implementing chaos engineering?**

    a. Maximizing system damage

    b. Testing only in production

    c. Starting small and gradually increasing complexity

    d. Running experiments without monitoring

Answers

1.	b
2.	c
3.	c
4.	a
5.	c
6.	c
7.	b
8.	c
9.	b
10.	c

## CHAPTER 10

Auditing, FinOps and Miscellaneous Automation

Introduction

We have arrived at the final chapter of this book. Here, we will wrap up our understanding of options to automate SRE and operational tasks on AWS by learning about some topics that we have not covered in detail so far. We will begin by learning about auditing. Auditing allows you to track actions by users and the state of your AWS resources. Next, we will learn about FinOps, which is short for Financial Operations. This helps you track and attribute your cloud spending accurately. Lastly, we will briefly discuss some other operations tasks related to security, network, and data.

Structure

The chapter covers the following topics:

- Auditing on AWS
- Auditing activities with AWS CloudTrail
- Infrastructure auditing with AWS Config
- FinOps and cost management on AWS
- Miscellaneous automation

Objectives

By the end of this chapter, you will learn the principles of auditing on AWS, tracking activities by users and systems making API calls, and also recording AWS resources, how they change, and understanding the impact of resource changes on compliance of your AWS environment. Next, we discuss how AWS CloudTrail and AWS Config can be used for auditing. We understand the practice of FinOps and why it is essential to prevent cost overruns and maximize value from cloud investments. We conclude this chapter by discussing some additional categories of operational tasks.

Auditing on AWS

Auditing in AWS environments is an essential discipline to maintain system governance, security, and compliance. Auditing provides visibility into system behavior, security, and performance. It enables SREs to detect issues, ensure compliance, optimize resources, and conduct effective incident response. Auditing diligently records every action in your AWS account and acts like your organization's digital surveillance camera. Through comprehensive auditing, SREs can continuously improve upon infrastructure and processes, ultimately supporting better service delivery and user experience.

Auditing is essential in AWS for the needs described in the following:

- **Security**: Auditing your AWS environment helps detect and investigate potential security breaches, unauthorized access attempts, and suspicious activities across your AWS environment. By maintaining detailed logs of user actions and system events, auditing enables rapid incident response and forensic analysis.

- **Compliance**: Many industries are subject to strict regulatory requirements (for example, **Health Insurance Portability and Accountability Act (HIPAA)**, **Payment Card Industry Data Security Standard (PCI DSS)**, **General Data Protection Regulation (GDPR)**. AWS auditing tools provide the necessary documentation to demonstrate compliance during audits and avoid potential legal and financial penalties.

- **Operational insights**: Auditing provides valuable data on resource usage, performance, and configuration changes. This information is crucial for optimizing costs, improving system performance, and making informed decisions about capacity planning and resource allocation.

- **Change management**: By tracking all changes made to your AWS resources, auditing supports effective change management processes, helping to maintain system stability and enabling quick rollback of problematic changes if needed.

- **Accountability**: Auditing ensures that all actions within the AWS environment can be traced back to specific users or processes, promoting responsible use of resources and helping to prevent insider threats.

By leveraging AWS's native auditing capabilities, you can maintain a secure, compliant, and efficient cloud environment, ultimately supporting better business outcomes and reducing operational risks.

There are different types of audits you can perform on AWS that address different aspects. Auditing activities and auditing resource configurations in AWS are two distinct but complementary aspects of maintaining a secure and compliant cloud environment. Additionally, you can also perform security audits and audit your network traffic using VPC flow logs and access logs such as ALB access logs and CloudFront access logs. Let us briefly understand each of these types of audits:

- **Auditing activities**: This refers to monitoring and recording user actions, API calls, and service events within your AWS account. It focuses on *who did what, when, and where* in your AWS environment. This type of auditing is essential for maintaining security, ensuring compliance, and supporting forensic analysis. AWS CloudTrail serves as the primary service for this purpose, capturing a detailed history of API calls made to AWS services, including those made through the AWS Management Console, AWS SDKs, command-line tools, and higher-level AWS services. CloudTrail logs provide valuable information such as the identity of the API caller, the time of the API call, the source IP address, the request parameters, and the response elements returned by AWS services.

- **Auditing resources**: This involves assessing the configuration, state, and compliance of your AWS resources. It focuses on *what exists and how it is configured* in your AWS environment. You will audit configurations within an AWS account or your AWS Organization, focusing on what exists in the environment and how these resources are configured. AWS Config serves as the primary service for this purpose, providing a detailed inventory of AWS resources and their configurations, including historical changes. It allows for the creation of custom rules and the use of pre-built rules to evaluate resource configurations against best practices and compliance standards. Additionally, AWS Systems Manager can be used to maintain a detailed inventory of software and applications running on EC2 instances and on-premises servers. These services collectively enable organizations to maintain a clear understanding of their AWS resource landscape, ensure compliance with internal policies and external regulations, optimize resource utilization, and enhance overall security posture.

- **Security and network audit:** Security and network audits on AWS can be performed using a combination of native AWS services and third-party tools to ensure comprehensive coverage. Audit capabilities offered by AWS CloudTrail and AWS Config allow for the assessment of compliance with security policies over time. In addition to this, Security Hub offers a centralized view of security alerts and compliance status across multiple AWS accounts, integrating findings from various AWS services and partner solutions. It automatically assesses your resources against security industry standards and best practices, such as CIS AWS Foundations Benchmark, providing a compliance score and detailed recommendations for improvement. Security Hub also aggregates and prioritizes security findings from services like GuardDuty, Inspector, and Macie, allowing for efficient triage and response to potential threats. For network-specific auditing, VPC Flow Logs capture IP traffic data, enabling the analysis of network patterns and potential security issues. ALB access logs capture detailed information about requests sent to the load balancer, including the client's IP address, request processing time, backend response, and more. This data is invaluable for understanding traffic distribution, identifying performance bottlenecks, and detecting unusual access patterns that might indicate security threats. Similarly, CloudFront access logs provide detailed records of every user request that CloudFront receives. Network security can be further audited using AWS Network Firewall logs and AWS WAF logs to review traffic patterns and potential attacks. Additionally, regular penetration testing (with AWS approval) and vulnerability scans using Amazon Inspector or third-party tools can identify weaknesses in the infrastructure.

The following figure gives an overview of the different AWS services that can be used for the purposes of auditing your AWS environment:

AWS
CloudTrail

AWS
Config

Auditing on AWS

AWS
Security
Hub

VPC Flow
Logs

Figure 10.1: *Auditing services on AWS*

By implementing a comprehensive auditing strategy that encompasses these elements, SREs can significantly enhance the security, reliability, and compliance posture of their AWS environments. Remember that auditing is not a one-time setup but an ongoing process that requires continuous attention and refinement.

Auditing activities with AWS CloudTrail

AWS CloudTrail is the primary service for auditing and monitoring activity within an AWS environment. CloudTrail provides invaluable data for incident identification, alerting, and response in the context of SRE. Following are some key features of CloudTrail:

- **Event history**: CloudTrail maintains a 90-day history of account activity accessible via the AWS Management Console, API, or CLI. This event history provides a wealth of detailed information about each recorded event. Each event record in CloudTrail includes these details:

  o **Event time**: The precise timestamp of when the action occurred, accurate to the millisecond.

  o **User identity**: Details about who performed the action, including the user name, AWS account ID, IAM user or role ARN, and the identity type (for example, IAM user, federated user, AWS service).

  o **Event name**: The specific API action that was performed (for example, CreateBucket, DeleteUser).

  o **Event source**: The AWS service that was accessed (for example, s3.amazonaws.com, iam.amazonaws.com).

  o **AWS Region**: The AWS Region where the action was performed.

  o **Source IP address**: The IP address from which the request originated.

  o **User agent**: Information about the client or tool used to make the API call (for example, AWS Management Console, SDK, CLI).

  o **Request parameters**: The parameters that were passed with the request, which can include resource names, configurations, or other relevant details.

  o **Response elements**: The response returned by AWS for the API call, which may include resource IDs or other pertinent information.

  o **Error code and message**: If applicable, any error information is returned by the API call.

  o **AWS account ID**: The ID of the AWS account in which the activity occurred.

  o **Resource names**: The names or ARNs of the resources involved in the event.

  o **Read-only flag**: Indicates whether the event was a read-only operation or if it modified resources.

  o **Event category**: Classifies the event as either a management event, data event, or Insights event.

  o **Event version**: The version of the CloudTrail event format.

  o **Recipient account ID**: For cross-account actions, the ID of the account that received the request.

  This comprehensive set of details allows for thorough analysis and auditing of AWS account activity, enabling SREs to reconstruct sequences of events, investigate anomalies, and maintain a clear understanding of changes within their AWS environment.

- **Trail creation**: The 90-day retention period for the event history provides a substantial window for routine monitoring and initial incident investigation. However, longer-term storage may be required for an extended look-back period or compliance reasons. This can be achieved by configuring CloudTrail to deliver logs to an S3 bucket for longer retention and analysis. You can use Amazon Athena to analyse your CloudTrail logs in S3 buckets.

Following is how you would write boto3 Python code to create a custom trail with CloudTrail. Replace placeholders for S3 bucket name and AWS account Id with values specific to your environment:

```
trail_name = 'custom_trail'
bucket_name = <your unique S3 bucket name>
database_name = 'cloudtrail_logs'
table_name = 'cloudtrail_events'
account_id = <your account id>
s3_bucket_location = f's3://{bucket_name}/AWSLogs/{account_id}/
CloudTrail'
# Create CloudTrail client
cloudtrail = boto3.client('cloudtrail')
try:
    # Create the trail
    response = cloudtrail.create_trail(
        Name=trail_name,
        S3BucketName=bucket_name,
        IsMultiRegionTrail=True,
        EnableLogFileValidation=True
    )

    # Start logging for the trail
    cloudtrail.start_logging(Name=trail_name)
    print(f"Successfully created trail: {trail_name}")
    return response
except Exception as e:
    print(f"Error creating trail: {str(e)}")
    raise
```

Now that you have the trail in place, we can start configuring Athena to query CloudTrail logs. This involves two stages.

The first is creating a database in Athena and a table to store the logs:

```
# Create Athena client
athena = boto3.client('athena')
# Create database if not exists
create_database_query = f"CREATE DATABASE IF NOT EXISTS {cloud_trail_
db}"
    # Create table for CloudTrail logs
    create_table_query = f"""
CREATE EXTERNAL TABLE IF NOT EXISTS {database_name}.{table_name} (
    eventVersion STRING,
    userIdentity STRUCT<
        type: STRING,
        principalId: STRING,
        arn: STRING,
        accountId: STRING,
        userName: STRING>,
    eventTime STRING,
    eventSource STRING,
    eventName STRING,
    awsRegion STRING,
    sourceIpAddress STRING,
    userAgent STRING,
    requestParameters STRING,
    responseElements STRING,
    errorCode STRING,
    errorMessage STRING,
    requestId STRING,
    eventId STRING,
    eventType STRING
)
PARTITIONED BY (region string, year string, month string, day
string)
ROW FORMAT SERDE 'org.apache.hive.hcatalog.data.JsonSerDe'
STORED AS INPUTFORMAT 'com.amazon.emr.cloudtrail.
```

```
CloudTrailInputFormat'
    OUTPUTFORMAT 'org.apache.hadoop.hive.ql.io.
HiveIgnoreKeyTextOutputFormat'
    LOCATION '{s3_bucket_location}'
    TBLPROPERTIES (
        'projection.enabled'='true',
        'projection.region.type'='enum',
        'projection.region.values'='us-east-1,us-west-2',
        'projection.year.type'='integer',
        'projection.year.range'='2024,2025',
        'projection.year.digits'='4',
        'projection.month.type'='integer',
        'projection.month.range'='1,12',
        'projection.month.digits'='2',
        'projection.day.type'='integer',
        'projection.day.range'='1,31',
        'projection.day.digits'='2',
        'storage.location.template'='{s3_bucket_
location}/${{region}}/${{year}}/${{month}}/${{day}}'
    )
    """

    # Query to repair table partitions
repair_table_query = f"MSCK REPAIR TABLE {database_name}.{table_name}"

    # Execute each of the queries one by one
    try:
        response = athena.start_query_execution(
            QueryString=create_database_query,
            ResultConfiguration={'OutputLocation': f's3://{s3_bucket_
location}/athena_results/'}
        )

        response = athena.start_query_execution(
            QueryString=create_table_query,
            ResultConfiguration={'OutputLocation': f's3://{s3_bucket_
location}/athena_results/'}
        )
```

```
response = athena.start_query_execution(
    QueryString=repair_table_query,
    ResultConfiguration={'OutputLocation': f's3://{s3_bucket_
location}/athena_results/'}
)


print(f"Successfully set up Athena table: {table_name}")
return response
except Exception as e:
print(f"Error setting up Athena: {str(e)}")
raise
```

Next, you use Athena to query the logs. For this example, we are specifically querying AWS Console login events in the last 24 hours. AWS services offer different EventNames in CloudTrail that you can query for. Based on your needs, you can pick the ones you want returned as part of your query. The event we are querying for here is **ConsoleLogin**. Let us see how you can do this from the AWS Console. After logging into your AWS Console, you will navigate to the Athena service console. Here, you can open up the Query Editor and run queries against the Database and the Table you have created. Following figure depicts how this would look:

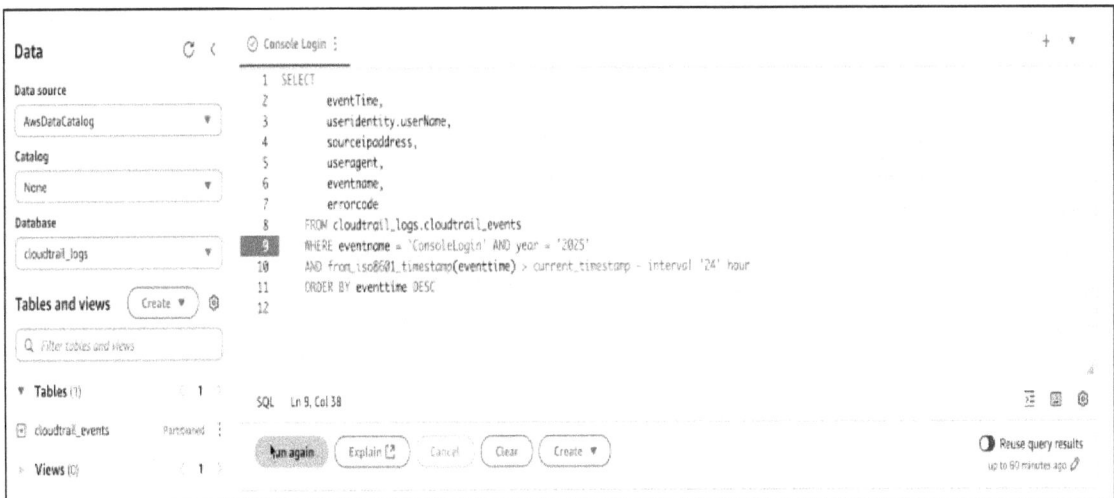

Figure 10.2: Athena query in AWS Console

You also see here that Athena uses standard ANSI SQL syntax. The query we have used above is:

```
SELECT
    eventTime,
```

```
        useridentity.userName,
        sourceipaddress,
        useragent,
        eventname,
        errorcode
    FROM cloudtrail_logs.cloudtrail_events
    WHERE eventname = 'ConsoleLogin' AND year = '2025'
    AND from_iso8601_timestamp(eventtime) > current_timestamp - interval
'24' hour
    ORDER BY eventtime DESC
```

We are picking specific columns in the **SELECT** statement and applying the filter for the **ConsoleLogin** event name in the **WHERE** clause of this SQL query. We have included an additional filter for the year **2025**. This helps reduce the amount of data that is scanned as part of your Athena query. Athena service is billed by the amount of data you scan, so reducing this by applying filters is going to keep costs lower, especially when you have a custom trail in CloudTrail, with events from several years. The final condition in the **WHERE** clause restricts the results to events that have occurred in the past 24 hours.

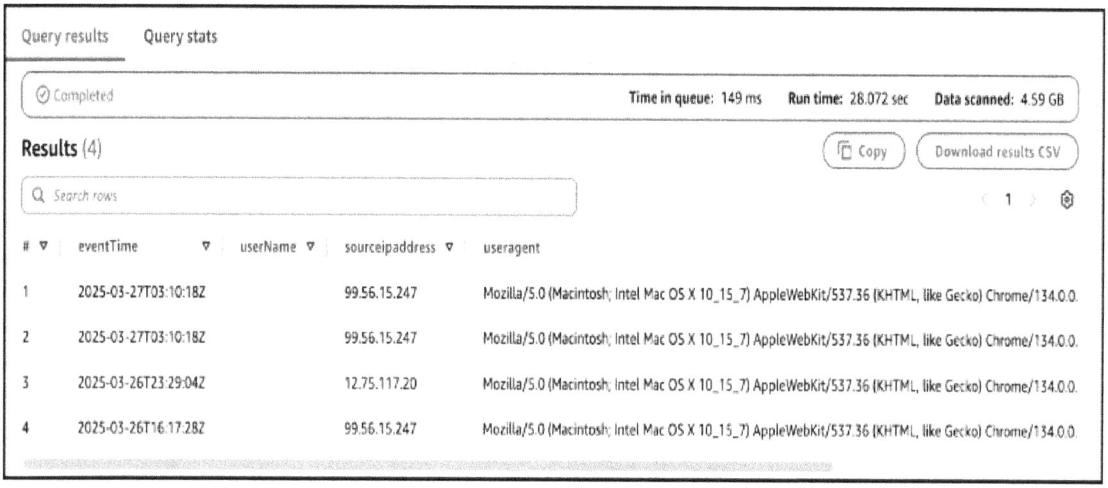

Figure 10.3: Athena query results in AWS Console

Following is how you will see the results of your query appear in the Athena console:

- **Log file integrity validation**: Turning on file integrity validation ensures that log files have not been tampered with after delivery. As you can see in the preceding code example, we turned on file integrity validation with the **EnableLogFileValidation** parameter when we created the trail in CloudTrail.

- **Integration**: CloudTrail works with various AWS services like S3, CloudWatch Logs, and EventBridge. EventBridge is capable of identifying the occurrences of specific API calls within CloudTrail logs and reporting them as Events that you can act on.

Following is a CLI example for setting up an EventBridge rule to look for Console Login events and invoke a Lambda function in response to it.

```
# Create the EventBridge rule
aws events put-rule \
  --name "ConsoleLoginMonitorRule" \
  --event-pattern '{
    "source": ["aws.signin"],
    "detail-type": ["AWS Console Sign In via CloudTrail"],
    "detail": {
      "eventSource": ["signin.amazonaws.com"],
      "eventName": ["ConsoleLogin"]
    }
  }'
# Add the Lambda function as a target
aws events put-targets \
  --rule "ConsoleLoginMonitorRule" \
  --targets "Id"="1","Arn"="<lambda-function-arn>"
```

You can also create CloudWatch alarms by creating custom metrics using events in CloudTrail Logs. A pre requisite for this is creating a CloudWatch Log group associated with your CloudTrail trail. Here is the CLI command you can use for this. You will need to create the CloudWatch Log Group and corresponding IAM role. Once you have done that, you can replace the placeholders in the command with values specific to your environment:

```
aws cloudtrail update-trail \
    --name custom_trail \
    --cloud-watch-logs-group-arn "<CloudWatch Log Group ARN>" \
    --cloud-watch-logs-role-arn "<CloudWatch Log role ARN>"
```

Following is an example of how you would count the number of console logins:

```
# Step 1: Create a metric filter for ConsoleLogin events
aws logs put-metric-filter \
  --log-group-name "/aws/cloudtrail/your-log-group-name" \
  --filter-name "ConsoleLoginCount" \
  --filter-pattern '{ $.eventName = ConsoleLogin }' \
```

```
  --metric-transformations \
    metricName=ConsoleLoginEvents,\
    metricNamespace=CloudTrailMetrics,\
    metricValue=1,\
    defaultValue=0
# Step 2: Create an alarm based on the metric
aws cloudwatch put-metric-alarm \
  --alarm-name "ConsoleLoginFrequencyAlarm" \
  --alarm-description "Alarm when 5 or more console logins occur within
2 hours" \
  --metric-name "ConsoleLoginEvents" \
  --namespace "CloudTrailMetrics" \
  --statistic Sum \
  --period 7200 \
  --threshold 5 \
  --comparison-operator GreaterThanOrEqualToThreshold \
  --evaluation-periods 1 \
  --alarm-actions "arn:aws:sns:region:account-id:your-sns-topic" \
  --treat-missing-data notBreaching
```

Let us wrap up this section about CloudTrail by understanding the applicability of auditing with CloudTrail Application in SRE for Incident Management:

- **Incident identification**: SREs can use CloudTrail logs in several ways to identify incidents. They can analyze logs to spot unusual patterns or unauthorized activities, which helps detect potential security threats. By tracking updates to important resources, you can identify actions that might affect system reliability. Additionally, SREs examine API call patterns to uncover misconfigurations or violations of company policies. These approaches allow SREs to catch and address issues early, maintaining the overall health and security of the AWS environment.

- **Alerting**: CloudTrail integrates with other AWS services to provide effective alerting for SREs. By connecting CloudTrail to EventBridge or CloudWatch alarms, you can set up real-time notifications for specific events. SREs can also create custom CloudWatch metrics based on CloudTrail data, allowing for more detailed monitoring of their environment. These combined capabilities help SREs stay informed about important changes and respond quickly to potential issues in your AWS infrastructure.

- **Incident response**: During incident response, CloudTrail logs are a valuable resource for SREs. These logs help trace the sequence of events that led to an incident, making it easier to identify the root cause. By analysing the affected resources and actions,

SREs can determine how widespread an incident is and what systems it impacts. The detailed information in CloudTrail logs also supports thorough investigations of security incidents, allowing you to understand what happened and how to prevent similar issues in the future. This incident analysis helps SREs resolve problems quickly and improve system reliability over time.

By effectively utilizing CloudTrail, you can significantly enhance your ability to maintain system reliability, security, and compliance. The rich information provided by CloudTrail enables proactive incident prevention, rapid detection of issues, and informed decision-making during incident response. This is required for maintaining high-quality, reliable services in a well-functioning AWS environment.

Infrastructure auditing with AWS Config

AWS Config is a service that provides a detailed view of the configuration of AWS resources in your account. It is another essential tool for SRE to maintain and improve the governance, security, and compliance of your AWS infrastructure through resource auditing.

Let us begin by understanding some key features of AWS Config:

- **Resource inventory**: AWS Config's resource inventory feature provides a comprehensive and continuously updated record of all AWS resources within an account, with detailed information about their configurations, relationships, and historical changes. For each resource, Config records configuration details, such as security group rules for EC2 instances, bucket policies for S3, or permission sets for IAM users. This detailed inventory is not only a static snapshot but a dynamic record that updates as resources are created, modified, or deleted, enabling you to track changes over time and understand the evolution of their infrastructure. The inventory can be queried and filtered, allowing for efficient resource management, compliance checking, and troubleshooting. By integrating this resource inventory with other AWS services like CloudWatch and Lambda, SREs can build sophisticated monitoring and automation systems that react to configuration changes, enforce policies, and maintain the desired state of the infrastructure. This capability is particularly valuable for large-scale or rapidly changing environments, where manual tracking would be impractical, enabling SREs to maintain a clear, up-to-date understanding of your AWS resources and configurations.

- **Configuration history**: AWS Config's configuration history feature provides a detailed, chronological record of changes made to AWS resources over time, offering you a powerful tool for tracking and analysing the evolution of your infrastructure. This feature captures and stores every configuration change, including resource creations, modifications, and deletions, creating a comprehensive timeline of events for each resource. The history includes specific details about what changed, when the change occurred, and who or what initiated the change, allowing SREs to reconstruct past states of your environment. This historical data is valuable for various operational tasks, such as troubleshooting issues by correlating problems with recent changes, conducting security audits to identify unauthorized modifications, and performing compliance checks to ensure resources have consistently met required standards. SREs can use this information to understand trends in resource usage and configuration patterns, inform capacity planning decisions, and validate that infrastructure as code deployments have been executed correctly. Additionally, the configuration history serves as a crucial detail in incident response scenarios, enabling teams to quickly determine what changes might have contributed to an outage or security breach and facilitating faster resolution and more effective post-incident analysis. By maintaining this detailed historical record, AWS Config empowers SREs to enhance system reliability, security, and compliance management across your AWS environment.

- **Configuration snapshot**: AWS Config's configuration snapshot feature allows you to capture and retrieve a comprehensive view of your AWS resource configurations at any given moment, providing an invaluable tool for understanding the current state of their infrastructure. This snapshot includes detailed information about all tracked resources, their settings, and relationships, offering a holistic picture of the AWS environment. SREs can use this feature to perform point-in-time audits, verify compliance with organizational policies, or establish a baseline for comparison during troubleshooting or change management processes. The ability to generate these snapshots on demand is particularly useful when preparing for system upgrades, migrations, or when responding to security incidents, as it allows you to quickly assess the current environment without the need to query multiple services or manually compile resource information. Furthermore, these snapshots can be exported and stored externally, serving as documentation for audits or as a reference for disaster recovery planning. By leveraging configuration snapshots, SREs can maintain a clear and accurate understanding of their AWS infrastructure, enabling more informed decision-making, faster incident response, and improved overall system reliability and security.

- **Compliance checking**: AWS Config's compliance checking feature allows you to assess your AWS resources against a set of rules. These rules can be either AWS-managed (predefined by AWS) or custom (created by you using AWS Lambda functions). When you set up compliance checking, AWS Config continuously monitors your resources and compares their configurations to these rules. If a resource does not meet the requirements set by a rule, AWS Config flags it as non-compliant. You can use this feature to quickly identify and fix misconfigurations, maintain consistent settings across your AWS environment, and demonstrate compliance with various industry regulations or internal policies. When a resource is found to be non-compliant, AWS Config flags it and can trigger notifications or automated remediation actions. This helps SREs maintain consistent configurations across their infrastructure, quickly identify and address misconfigurations, and ensure ongoing compliance with organizational policies and industry standards. Config Rules can cover a wide range of checks, from ensuring that EBS volumes are encrypted to verifying that S3 buckets have proper access controls, making them a versatile tool for maintaining the overall health and security of your AWS environment.

Here is an example of how you can create a custom AWS Config Rule using AWS Lambda. This checks if your EC2 instances have specific required tags. This involves two steps. First, you create the Lambda function that defines the implementation of your Config Rule:

```python
import json
import boto3
import os
from datetime import datetime
def evaluate_compliance(configuration_item, rule_parameters):
    if configuration_item["resourceType"] not in ["AWS::EC2::Instance"]:
        return "NOT_APPLICABLE"

    # Get the required tags from rule parameters
    required_tags = rule_parameters.get("requiredTags", "").split(",")
        # Get the current tags on the instance
    try:
        current_tags = configuration_item["configuration"].get("tags", [])
        current_tag_keys = [tag['key'] for tag in current_tags]
            # Check if all required tags are present
        for tag in required_tags:
            if tag.strip() not in current_tag_keys:
                return "NON_COMPLIANT"
        return "COMPLIANT"
    except Exception as e:
        return "ERROR"
def lambda_handler(event, context):
    # Initialize AWS Config client
    config = boto3.client('config')
        # Parse the invocation event
    invoking_event = json.loads(event['invokingEvent'])
    rule_parameters = json.loads(event.get('ruleParameters', '{}'))
        # Get the configuration item from the invoking event
```

```
    configuration_item = invoking_event.get('configurationItem', {})
        # Check if this is a deleted resource
    if configuration_item.get('configurationItemStatus') ==
'ResourceDeleted':
        compliance_result = 'NOT_APPLICABLE'
    else:
        compliance_result = evaluate_compliance(configuration_item, rule_
parameters)
        # Prepare evaluation response
    evaluation = {
        'ComplianceResourceType': configuration_item['resourceType'],
        'ComplianceResourceId': configuration_item['resourceId'],
        'ComplianceType': compliance_result,
        'OrderingTimestamp': configuration_
item['configurationItemCaptureTime']
    }
        if compliance_result == "NON_COMPLIANT":
        evaluation['Annotation'] = f"Missing required tags: {rule_
parameters.get('requiredTags')}"
    # Put evaluation results
    try:
        config.put_evaluations(
            Evaluations=[evaluation],
            ResultToken=event['resultToken']
        )
    except Exception as e:
        print(f"Error putting evaluations: {str(e)}")
        raise
    return {
        'compliance_status': compliance_result,
        'resource_id': configuration_item['resourceId']
    }
```

Ensure that your Lambda function can be invoked by AWS Config in the Lambda resource policy. Also, provide permission to your Lambda function to PutEvaluations on AWS Config.

Following is how your Lambda permissions should be configured:

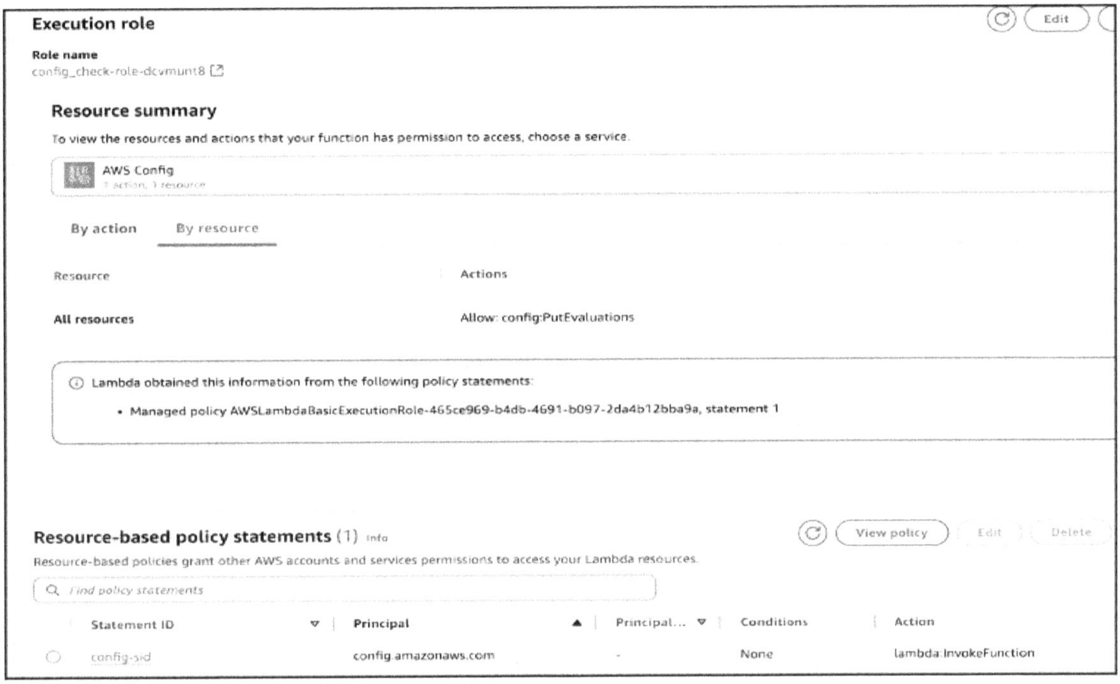

Figure 10.4: Permissions for Config evaluation Lambda

Next, you use boto3 to create a named Config Rule, utilizing the implementation with the Lambda function we defined. This can be another Lambda function or a standalone Python script that you invoke from the CLI, as shown in the following:

```python
import boto3
import json
def main():
    config_client = boto3.client('config')
    response = config_client.put_config_rule(
        ConfigRule={
            'ConfigRuleName': 'required-tags-rule',
            'Description': 'Checks if EC2 instances have required tags',
            'Scope': {
                'ComplianceResourceTypes': [
                    'AWS::EC2::Instance',
                ]
            },
            'Source': {
                'Owner': 'CUSTOM_LAMBDA',
```

```
                    'SourceIdentifier': 'arn:aws:lambda:REGION:ACCOUNT_
ID:function:required-tags-rule-fn,
                'SourceDetails': [
                    {
                        'EventSource': 'aws.config',
                        'MessageType':
'ConfigurationItemChangeNotification'
                    }
                ]
            },
            'InputParameters': json.dumps({
                'requiredTags': 'Environment,Project,Owner'
            }),
            'ConfigRuleState': 'ACTIVE'
        }
    )
    return response
if __name__ == "__main__":
    main()
```

What you have set up here is a Config Rule that evaluates EC2 instances in your AWS account to ensure they are configured with the tags Environment, Project, and Owner. If any EC2 instances are found without these tags, they are marked Non-Compliant. If you set up this custom Config Rule in your AWS account that has our sample workload, you will find that the associated EC2 instances will be marked non-compliant. This is because our EC2 instances are set up to have the tags Env, PatchGroup, and app, but do not have the tags Environment, Project, and Owner. To make these instances compliant, you can either modify the Config Rule above to check for the tags that your EC2 instances are set up to have, or you can add these missing tags to your EC2 instances. You can set up automatic or manual remediation with AWS Config for non-compliant resources. You can do this either with SSM documents or through a combination of EventBridge and Lambda functions, as we have seen before.

Non-compliant resources are displayed in your AWS Console as shown in the following figure:

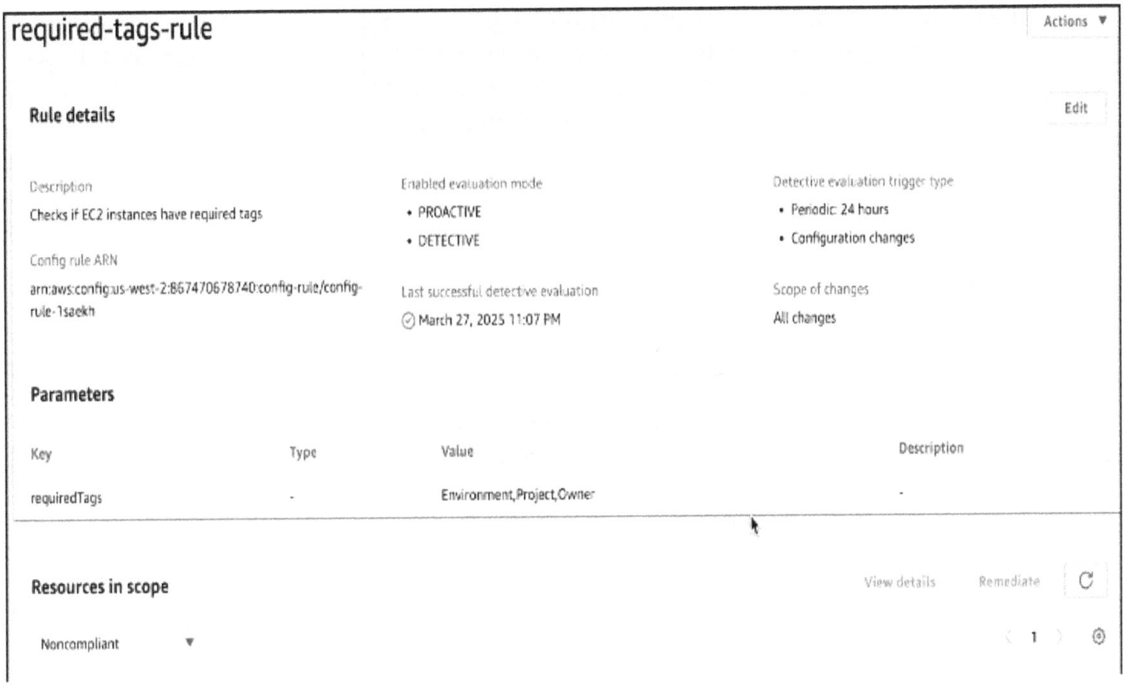

---

required-tags-rule   Actions ▼

Rule details   Edit

Description   Enabled evaluation mode   Detective evaluation trigger type
Checks if EC2 instances have required tags   • PROACTIVE   • Periodic: 24 hours
                                     • DETECTIVE   • Configuration changes
Config rule ARN
arn:aws:config:us-west-2:867470678740:config-rule/config-   Last successful detective evaluation   Scope of changes
rule-1saekh   ⊘ March 27, 2025 11:07 PM   All changes

Parameters

Key	Type	Value	Description
requiredTags	-	Environment,Project,Owner	-

Resources in scope   View details   Remediate   ↻

Noncompliant   ▼   ‹ 1 ›   ⊚

Figure 10.5: Non-compliant resources flagged by the custom Config Rule

The details are as follows:

- **Conformance Packs**: AWS Config Conformance Packs are pre-built collections of AWS Config Rules and remediation actions that help organizations quickly implement governance and compliance controls across their AWS accounts and regions. For SREs, Conformance Packs offer a powerful tool to maintain consistent, secure, and compliant infrastructure at scale. SREs can deploy these packs to assess and enforce best practices for security, operational excellence, and regulatory compliance automatically. The packs cover various domains, such as operational best practices, security controls, and industry-specific regulations like HIPAA or PCI DSS. By using Conformance Packs, you can rapidly implement standardized configurations across your AWS environment, reduce the manual effort in setting up and maintaining compliance checks, and quickly adapt to new compliance requirements. This capability aligns well with SRE principles of automating routine tasks, ensuring consistent configurations, and maintaining high reliability and security standards across the infrastructure.

- **AWS Config advanced queries**: AWS Config advanced queries provide a SQL-like query language that enables you to search and analyze the configuration of AWS resources across your account. Using these queries, you can perform property-based searches against current AWS resource state metadata without making service-specific API calls. The queries support a wide range of AWS resource types and allow you to filter results based on resource configurations, tags, and relationships. You can execute these queries from a single account and region or use configuration aggregators to run queries across multiple accounts and AWS Regions. The query syntax follows a SQL-like structure with **SELECT** statements and **WHERE** clauses and supports various operators for filtering and comparison. While advanced queries are powerful for inventory management, security analysis, and compliance monitoring, they do have some limitations, they do not support complex queries with nested structures, querying of deleted resources, or resources not recorded by the configuration recorder. The service is available in multiple AWS Regions and can be accessed through the AWS Console, CLI, or SDKs.

Here is an example of a query that lists all active DynamoDB tables in your AWS account. If you run this Config query in the AWS account where we have deployed our sample workload, you should see the DynamoProductTable appear in the results, along with any other DynamoDB tables you may have in the same account:

```
SELECT
    resourceId,
    resourceName,
    resourceType,
    tags,
    configuration
WHERE
    resourceType = 'AWS::DynamoDB::Table'
    AND configuration.tableStatus = 'ACTIVE'
```

- **Multi-account, multi-region data aggregation**: AWS Config's multi-account and multi-region data aggregation feature allows you to collect and view configuration and compliance information from multiple AWS accounts and regions in one place. This capability is particularly useful for large organizations or those with complex AWS setups. It enables you to maintain a comprehensive view of your entire AWS infrastructure, regardless of how it is spread across different accounts or geographical regions. With this feature, teams can easily monitor compliance across their organization, identify misconfigurations that span multiple accounts, and ensure consistent policies are applied throughout their AWS environment. This centralized approach simplifies management, improves security oversight, and helps maintain consistent standards across the entire AWS footprint.

Here are different ways in which SRE can utilize AWS Config:

- **Configuration management**: SREs can use AWS Config to maintain a clear view of their infrastructure. You can track changes to resource configurations over time, helping you understand system evolution and troubleshoot issues.

- **Compliance monitoring**: By setting up Config Rules, SREs can continuously check if resources comply with organizational policies or industry standards. This helps in maintaining security and adhering to regulatory requirements.

- **Change detection**: AWS Config can alert SREs about critical changes to their infrastructure. This enables quick response to unauthorized or potentially problematic modifications.

- **Incident investigation**: During incidents, SREs can use Config's historical data to understand what changes might have led to the problem. This speeds up root cause analysis and resolution.

- **Resource optimization**: By analyzing resource configurations, SREs can identify underutilized or misconfigured resources, helping to optimize costs and performance.

- **Security analysis**: Config can help SREs identify security risks, such as overly permissive security group rules or unencrypted storage volumes.

- **Dependency mapping**: Understanding resource relationships helps SREs assess the potential impact of changes and plan maintenance activities more effectively.

- **Automated remediation**: SREs can set up automated remediation actions in response to non-compliant resources using AWS Systems Manager Automation or Lambda functions.

- **Drift detection**: For infrastructure as code, Config can help detect when the actual state of resources drifts from the desired state defined in templates.

- **Audit preparation**: The detailed configuration history maintained by AWS Config is invaluable for preparing for audits and demonstrating compliance over time. AWS Audit Manager is a service that helps gather evidence for your audits. This service uses AWS Config as one of its primary sources of truth, alongside AWS CloudTrail.

By leveraging AWS Config, SREs can maintain a more reliable, secure, and compliant infrastructure. It provides the visibility and control needed to manage complex AWS environments effectively, supporting key SRE principles like reducing toil, enabling self-service, and maintaining system reliability.

FinOps and cost management on AWS

Financial Operations (FinOps) is an important discipline in cloud environments, where the flexibility of cloud resources can lead to unexpected costs if not properly managed. FinOps is often misunderstood as purely a cost saving exercise. It also as much about ensuring your organization is spending on the right things to ensure the growth and success of your business. *"You have to spend money to make money"* is commonly quoted to convey the message that you must invest as part of doing business. Your cloud spend is one of these investments. Ensuring right cost attribution for your workloads and compares it with the revenue the workload is generating is the essence of FinOps.

SRE plays a vital role in implementing FinOps principles and ensuring effective cost controls. SREs are uniquely positioned to bridge the gap between development, operations, and finance through a deep understanding of system architecture, performance metrics, and operational efficiency. By incorporating cost optimization into reliability and performance objectives, SREs can implement automated scaling policies, optimize resource allocation, and identify underutilized or oversized infrastructure. They can also work closely with development teams to promote cost-aware coding practices and architect systems that balance performance, reliability, and cost-effectiveness. SREs can leverage their expertise in monitoring and observability to create comprehensive dashboards that provide real-time visibility into cloud spending, enabling proactive cost management and informed decision-making across the organization. This integration of FinOps principles into SRE practices ensures that cost optimization becomes an integral part of the overall system reliability and performance strategy.

The FinOps foundation defines the principles of FinOps. The following figure depicts these principles:

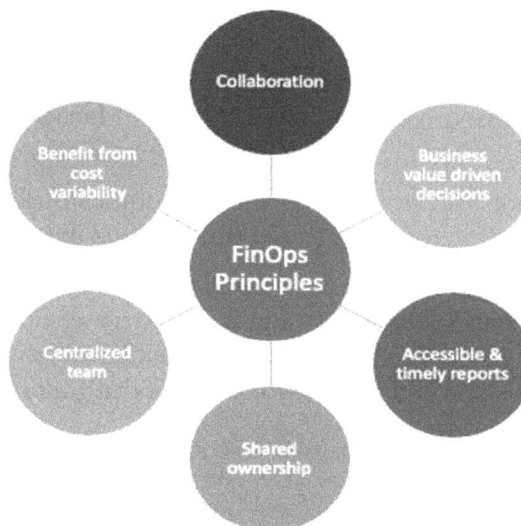

Figure 10.6: FinOps principles

Let us understand these principles and what they mean:

- **Collaboration**: FinOps should unite your finance, technology, product, and business teams, enabling real-time collaboration in the dynamic cloud environment. This cross-functional approach allows for continuous improvement, balancing cost efficiency with innovation as teams jointly optimize resource usage and align cloud spending with business goals.

- **Business value driver decisions:** FinOps prioritizes business value over aggregate spending, using unit economics and value-based metrics to guide decisions. It encourages conscious trade-offs between cost, quality, and speed, viewing the cloud not just as an expense but as an enabler for innovation and competitive advantage.

- **Accessible and timely reports:** FinOps emphasizes real-time, accessible cost data across the organization. Rapid processing and sharing of this information drives better cloud utilization with fast feedback loops and autonomous decision-making. Consistent visibility, along with financial forecasting and trend analysis, enables teams to understand cost fluctuations. The cost benchmarking, internally and against industry peers, allows you to continually improve cloud efficiency.

- **Shared ownership:** FinOps promotes shared cost ownership, sharing accountability with individual teams and engineers. From design to operations, teams are empowered to manage their cloud usage against budgets. This approach integrates cost considerations into the entire software development lifecycle, making it a key efficiency metric alongside traditional technical parameters and fostering cost-effective decision-making at all levels.

- **Centralized team:** While this appears contrary to the idea of shared responsibility, a central team promoting best practices and shared accountability simplifies FinOps implementation. With executive support, this team centralizes rate negotiations and discount optimizations, leveraging economies of scale. This approach allows engineers to focus on usage optimization in their environments while the central team handles broader financial strategies and encourages organization-wide adoption of FinOps principles.

- **Benefit from cost variability:** FinOps leverages the cloud's variable cost model as an opportunity, not a risk. It emphasizes agile, just-in-time capacity planning over static, long-term strategies. This approach advocates for proactive system design with ongoing cloud optimization, replacing infrequent reactive cleanups. The goal is to continuously deliver more value by adapting to changing needs and costs.

FinOps in the AWS cloud revolves around optimizing costs while maintaining the desirable characteristics of your workload, like performance and reliability. Following are some key principles of FinOps in the context of AWS:

- **Visibility and allocation**: Effective FinOps practices in AWS require establishing clear visibility into cloud spending and accurate cost allocation. To achieve this, you can leverage AWS Cost Explorer and AWS Budgets. They provide detailed insights into cloud expenditures and allow for the setting of cost thresholds. It is crucial to implement a comprehensive tagging strategy, enabling the allocation of costs to specific teams, projects, or environments, thus promoting accountability and facilitating more accurate budgeting. For more granular analysis, AWS Cost and Usage Reports offer in-depth data on resource utilization and associated costs. By combining these tools and strategies, you can gain a holistic view of their AWS spending, make informed decisions about resource allocation, and identify opportunities for cost optimization across their cloud infrastructure. Two concepts are central to FinOps cost visibility:

- **Showback:** Showback is a reporting practice where cloud costs are allocated and displayed to different business units or teams to create cost awareness and visibility, but without actually billing those units for their cloud resource consumption.

- **Chargeback**: Chargeback is a financial practice where the actual costs of cloud resources are calculated and directly billed back to the specific business units, teams, or cost centers that consumed them, making each department directly responsible for their cloud spending.

Implementing showbacks and chargebacks are indicators of FinOps maturity in an organization. This drives cost accountability and encourages departments to show profitability while not overspending on cloud costs. Showback often serves as a stepping stone towards implementing a full chargeback model.

- **Optimization**: Optimization is a crucial aspect of FinOps in AWS, and there are several strategies that can be employed to enhance cost efficiency. While not exhaustive, some key optimization techniques include right-sizing EC2 instances using AWS Compute Optimizer, which helps identify the most efficient instance types for your workloads. Leveraging Auto Scaling groups allows for dynamic capacity adjustment, ensuring you are only paying for the resources you need at any given time. For non-critical, interruptible workloads, utilizing spot instances can significantly reduce compute costs. In the realm of storage, implementing lifecycle policies for S3 enables automatic migration of data to more cost-effective storage tiers based on access patterns. It is important to note that these optimization strategies represent just a fraction of the available options, and the most effective approach will vary depending on your specific workload characteristics and the AWS services you are utilizing. A comprehensive FinOps strategy should involve continuous evaluation and adjustment of optimization techniques to align with evolving business needs and AWS offerings.

- **Reserved capacity**: Leveraging reservation and commitment-based discounts is a fundamental strategy in FinOps for AWS cost optimization, particularly for predictable workloads. **Reserved Instances (RIs)** and Savings Plans offer significant cost savings compared to on-demand pricing, with discounts of up to 72% for consistent, long-term usage. It is essential to regularly review and modify these reservations based on evolving usage patterns to ensure optimal coverage and prevent over-commitment. Savings Plans provide more flexibility across instance families, sizes, and even some AWS services compared to RIs, which are more restrictive in nature. For organizations with substantial AWS spending, it is worth noting that you may be able to work with your AWS account team to negotiate commitment-based private pricing agreements. These custom arrangements can potentially offer even more favourable terms tailored to your specific usage patterns and business needs. By strategically employing these reservation and commitment options and maintaining an open dialogue with AWS, you can significantly reduce your cloud costs while maintaining flexibility to adapt to changing requirements.

- **Serverless and pay-per-use**: Embracing serverless and pay-per-use models is a powerful FinOps strategy in AWS that can lead to significant cost reductions when applied appropriately. Services like AWS Lambda allow you to run code without provisioning or managing servers, thereby eliminating idle capacity costs. For database needs, options such as Aurora Serverless or DynamoDB on-demand pricing can efficiently handle variable workloads. Many other AWS services offer a serverless flavor, allowing you to scale down compute during periods of limited activity. Serverless architectures may not always align perfectly with every workload or application design. The decision to adopt a serverless model should be made carefully, considering factors like application architecture, performance requirements, and long-term cost projections. Nevertheless, where going serverless does fit the use case, the potential for cost savings can be substantial. By paying only for the actual compute time or database operations used, organizations can achieve a closer alignment between costs and value delivered, often resulting in notable reductions in overall cloud spend. This pay-per-use model not only optimizes costs but also shifts the focus from infrastructure management to business logic and application development, potentially increasing overall operational efficiency.

- **Governance and control**: Effective governance and control are essential components of a robust FinOps strategy in AWS. At the core of this approach is the implementation of AWS Organizations, which provides a powerful means to manage multiple AWS accounts within an enterprise. This centralized management capability allows for streamlined administration and consolidated billing across business units or projects. To enforce cost-related rules consistently across these accounts, **Service Control Policies (SCPs)** prove invaluable. SCPs enable organizations to set guardrails on AWS service usage, preventing unauthorized or excessive resource provisioning that could lead to unexpected costs. IAM policies also allow for fine-grained access management, particularly in restricting access to high-cost resources. By carefully configuring IAM roles and permissions, you can ensure that only authorized personnel can provision or modify expensive AWS services, thereby reducing the risk of inadvertent overspending. Together, these governance and control measures create a framework for maintaining financial discipline in the cloud, balancing the need for agility with prudent cost management.

- **Continuous monitoring and improvement**: Continuous monitoring and improvement are necessary aspects of an effective FinOps strategy in AWS. A key component of this approach is the regular review of AWS Trusted Advisor recommendations. This service provides real-time guidance to help optimize your AWS infrastructure, offering insights on cost optimization, performance, security, and fault tolerance.

  Setting up AWS Config Rules enables automated, ongoing checks of your resource configurations. These rules can be customized to detect and alert on cost-inefficient setups, such as oversized instances or underutilized resources. This proactive approach allows teams to quickly identify and rectify configuration issues that could lead to unnecessary expenses.

Periodically leveraging the AWS Well-Architected tool adds another layer of thoroughness to your cost optimization efforts. This tool helps you review your workloads against AWS best practices across multiple pillars, including cost optimization. By conducting these assessments regularly, you can ensure your architecture remains aligned with evolving AWS capabilities and FinOps best practices.

Together, these practices foster a culture of continuous improvement in cloud cost management. They provide a systematic approach to identifying cost-saving opportunities, maintaining efficient configurations, and aligning your architecture with best practices.

- **Data transfer optimization**: Network optimization is a crucial yet often overlooked aspect of FinOps in AWS. This begins with a thorough understanding of data transfer costs, particularly between AWS Regions and to the internet, as these can significantly impact overall cloud spending. To mitigate these costs, you should consider implementing AWS Direct Connect for high-volume, consistent data transfers between on-premises infrastructure and AWS. For inter-service communication within AWS, VPC endpoints can be leveraged to keep traffic on the AWS network, thereby reducing or eliminating data transfer costs. Additionally, utilizing Amazon CloudFront as a content delivery network can substantially decrease data transfer costs for serving content to users across the globe. CloudFront's edge locations help reduce the distance data needs to travel, not only improving performance but also potentially lowering costs compared to direct internet data transfer from origin servers. By implementing these network optimization techniques, organizations can achieve substantial cost savings while simultaneously enhancing application performance and user experience. It is important to regularly review network traffic patterns and adjust these optimizations as workloads evolve to ensure continued cost-effectiveness.

- **Collaborative culture**: The collaborative nature of FinOps is key to its success in optimizing cloud costs and driving business value. FinOps requires fostering strong communication channels between finance, engineering, and operations teams. This cross-functional collaboration breaks down traditional silos, enabling a holistic approach to cloud financial management. Regular FinOps review meetings discuss cost trends and identify optimization opportunities. These meetings facilitate a shared understanding of cloud spending patterns, allowing finance teams to gain insights into technical decisions that impact costs while engineering and operations teams become more attuned to the financial implications of their choices. Through this ongoing dialogue, you can develop a culture of cost consciousness, where financial considerations become an integral part of technical decision-making processes. This collaborative approach ensures that cost optimization strategies are not only technically sound but also aligned with broader business objectives. By regularly bringing these perspectives together, companies can make more informed decisions about resource allocation, capacity planning, and technology investments. This leads to more efficient and cost-effective use of cloud resources.

- **Forecasting**: Forecasting is a critical component of FinOps in AWS, enabling organizations to proactively manage their cloud costs and make informed financial decisions. AWS Cost Explorer offers built-in forecasting capabilities that provide valuable insights into future spending based on historical usage patterns. This tool allows teams to project costs over time, helping with budgeting and resource planning. However, for more sophisticated forecasting needs, organizations can leverage the rich data available in AWS Cost and Usage Reports to develop custom forecasting models. These custom models can incorporate business-specific factors, seasonality, and growth projections, offering a more tailored and accurate view of future cloud expenditures. By combining AWS's native forecasting tools with custom analytics, you can create a comprehensive forecasting strategy that aligns closely with your business. This approach not only aids in budget planning but also helps identify potential cost anomalies or areas for optimization before they become significant issues. Regular refinement of these forecasting models, based on actual spending data and changing business conditions, ensures you maintain an accurate and actionable view of your future cloud costs.

- **Anomaly detection**: AWS cost anomaly detection is a feature within AWS Cost Management that uses machine learning to continuously monitor your AWS spending patterns and identify unusual spikes in cost. The service analyzes your historical AWS cost and usage data to establish normal spending patterns, then automatically detects anomalous spending that falls outside these patterns. When an anomaly is detected, the service evaluates its root cause and can send alerts through email or Amazon SNS topics, allowing quick response to unexpected cost increases. You can create custom monitors to analyze specific aspects of your spending, such as individual AWS services, linked accounts, cost allocation tags, or cost categories. The service helps minimize false positives by considering factors like weekly or monthly seasonality and natural growth patterns in your AWS usage. Each alert includes detailed information about the anomaly, including its duration, total cost impact, affected services, and potential root causes, making it easier to investigate and address cost spikes quickly. The service runs multiple times daily and requires minimal setup, though there may be up to 24 hours of delay in anomaly detection due to the underlying cost of data processing time.

Following are some AWS services you can use to observe, report on, and optimize your cloud costs:

- **AWS cost explorer**: This service provides an interactive interface to visualize, understand, and manage your AWS costs and usage over time. It offers detailed cost breakdowns, usage trends, and forecasting capabilities, allowing you to identify cost drivers and optimization opportunities. It allows you to group your costs across various dimensions, while filtering it to specific services, accounts, regions or other attributes of interest.

- **AWS budgets**: Enable you to set custom budgets for cost and usage and receive alerts when you exceed (or are forecasted to exceed) your budgeted amount. This service is crucial for proactive cost management and financial governance. Using AWS Budgets, you can take automated actions in response to certain cost thresholds being breached. For example, you can apply specific IAM policies or stop/terminate EC2/RDS instances. These actions are in addition to being alerted about costs exceeding or projecting to exceed thresholds defined by you.

- **AWS Cost and Usage Report (CUR)**: Provides the most comprehensive set of AWS cost and usage data available. It delivers detailed line items for each unique AWS product, usage type, and operation used by your account, which is invaluable for in-depth cost analysis and custom reporting.

- **AWS trusted advisor**: Offers real-time guidance to help you provision your resources following AWS best practices. It provides recommendations for cost optimization, performance, security, and fault tolerance.

- **AWS Compute Optimizer**: Uses machine learning to analyze your resource configuration and utilization metrics, recommending optimal AWS Compute resources to reduce costs and improve performance.

- **Amazon Athena**: When used in conjunction with the AWS CUR, Athena provides a powerful and flexible way to analyze and gain insights into your AWS costs. This combination allows for custom SQL-based querying of your detailed cost data, enabling deep dives into spending patterns and optimization opportunities.

- **Amazon QuickSight**: QuickSight, along with Amazon Athena and the AWS CUR, forms a powerful foundation for creating comprehensive **Cost Intelligence Dashboards (CID)**. These dashboards provide deep insights into your AWS costs, enabling data-driven decision-making and fostering a culture of financial accountability.

Miscellaneous automation

This section addresses automation opportunities that we have not discussed in other portions of this book. This is the last section of this chapter and the book, and here, we conclude by understanding where you can utilize some of the services, we have already discussed to automate aspects within AWS, such as security operations, network operations, data operations, and ML operations.

While each of these can be detailed chapters on their own, we will limit the scope of discussion on these subjects as these are specialized topics requiring deeper subject matter expertise beyond basic SRE practices:

- **Automating security operations**: Automating security operations on AWS involves leveraging a combination of native AWS services and potentially third-party tools to create a robust, self-managing security ecosystem. At the core of this automation is AWS Security Hub, which provides a comprehensive view of security alerts and compliance status across multiple AWS accounts. Security Hub integrates with services like Amazon GuardDuty for continuous threat detection, Amazon Inspector for automated vulnerability assessments, and Amazon Macie for sensitive data discovery and protection. These services can be configured to automatically send findings to AWS EventBridge, which can then trigger automated responses using AWS Lambda functions or AWS Systems Manager Automation. For example, a GuardDuty finding of a potentially compromised EC2 instance could automatically initiate an isolation procedure using AWS Step Functions, temporarily restricting network access via security groups. AWS Config can be used to continuously evaluate resource configurations against predefined rules, with AWS Systems Manager Automation executing remediation actions for non-compliant resources. IAM Access Analyzer can automatically detect overly permissive resource policies, while AWS Firewall Manager can enforce consistent firewall rules across accounts and VPCs. For network security, AWS Network Firewall can be configured to automatically update rules based on threat intelligence feeds, and AWS WAF can be set to automatically block malicious web traffic patterns. AWS CloudTrail logs all API activity, which can be analyzed in real-time using Amazon OpenSearch Service to detect and respond to suspicious behavior. Amazon CloudWatch can be used to set up alarms and automated actions based on predefined metrics and log patterns. For secrets management, AWS Secrets Manager can automatically rotate credentials on a schedule. Additionally, IaC tools like AWS CloudFormation or Terraform can be used to define and enforce security configurations as code, ensuring consistent and version-controlled security settings across environments. By orchestrating these services and tools, you can create a dynamic, self-healing security posture that continuously monitors, detects, and responds to threats with minimal human intervention. This allows your security teams to focus on higher-level strategy and complex issues such as emerging threat vectors and mitigation strategies.

- **Automating network operations:** Network operations refers to the management and maintenance of computer networks and their associated infrastructure. AWS offers various tools and services to automate network operations, enabling efficient management of complex network infrastructures. You can use Amazon EventBridge to create automated responses to network events, such as VPC changes, Transit Gateway modifications, or Direct Connect status changes. AWS Systems Manager Automation runbooks can be leveraged to automate routine network maintenance tasks, security group updates, and route table modifications. For infrastructure as code, AWS CloudFormation or AWS CDK can define and deploy network resources in a repeatable manner.

VPC Flow Logs integrated with Amazon CloudWatch can trigger automated responses to network traffic patterns or security concerns. AWS Transit Gateway Network Manager enables automated cross-region and cross-account network management, while AWS Network Firewall can automate security policy enforcement. AWS

Step Functions can orchestrate complex network operations workflows, combining multiple AWS services and custom logic. For monitoring and remediation, you can use AWS Config Rules to automatically detect and correct non-compliant network configurations. AWS Organizations can help manage network policies across multiple accounts, while AWS Control Tower can automate network governance at scale. These automation capabilities can significantly reduce manual effort, minimize human errors, improve security posture, and ensure consistent network configurations across your AWS infrastructure.

- **Automating Data Operations (DataOps):** DataOps in the context of AWS refers to the practice of streamlining and automating data management processes using AWS services to improve the speed, quality, and reliability of data analytics. It combines DevOps principles with data management to create more agile and efficient data pipelines. It typically involves data ingestion, data processing, data storage, data analytics, and the automation, orchestration, and monitoring surrounding this.

At the core of this automation is AWS Glue, a fully managed **extract, transform, and load** (**ETL**) service that can automatically discover, catalog, and prepare data for analytics. Glue's Data Catalog serves as a central metadata repository, while Glue ETL jobs can be scheduled to run automatically, transforming data as it arrives. For data ingestion, Amazon Kinesis can be used to automatically collect and process streaming data in real time, with Kinesis Data Firehose handling the automated delivery of this data to destinations like S3, Redshift, or Elasticsearch. Amazon S3 serves as a central data lake, with features like S3 Lifecycle policies automating data tiering and archiving processes. For data processing, Amazon EMR can be configured to automatically scale Hadoop and Spark clusters based on workload, while AWS Lambda can trigger serverless data processing in response to events. Amazon Athena allows for automated querying of data directly in S3 using standard SQL. For data warehousing, Amazon Redshift can automatically optimize query performance and scale compute resources, with Redshift Spectrum enabling querying of exabytes of unstructured data in S3 without loading. Amazon QuickSight can be used for automated business intelligence and visualization, with its ML Insights feature automatically identifying patterns and anomalies in data.

AWS Step Functions can orchestrate complex data processing workflows, automatically managing the execution of multiple AWS services. For data quality and governance, AWS Lake Formation automates the setup of data lakes, including fine-grained access controls. For database operations, Amazon RDS and Amazon DynamoDB offer automated backup, patching, and scaling. Amazon Aurora's serverless option automatically scales database resources based on application demand. By orchestrating these services, you can create a dynamic, self-optimizing DataOps environment that continuously ingests, processes, analyses, and secures data with minimal human intervention, allowing you to focus on deriving insights and driving business value.

- **Automating Machine Learning Operations (MLOps):** MLOps in the context of AWS involves the practices and tools for streamlining machine learning lifecycles, leveraging services like Amazon SageMaker for model development, training, deployment, and inference. It includes data preparation with AWS Glue and SageMaker Data Wrangler, version control via SageMaker Model Registry, orchestration of different steps involved with SageMaker Pipelines or AWS Step Functions, and continuous monitoring with SageMaker Model Monitor. SageMaker Endpoints can be used to provide managed compute for inference as an alternative to self-hosting the models, which can involve a deeper involvement from operations and SRE.

  LLMOps, a specialized subset of MLOps focused on large language models for generative AI, extends these practices to address the unique challenges of working with massive models. In the AWS ecosystem, LLMOps emphasizes prompt engineering and management of prompt library, data management, and content filtering for **Retrieval Augment Generation (RAG)** based architecture, implementing guardrails, invoking inference endpoints, and cost management strategies to ensure your GenerativeAI projects remain within budget. Both MLOps and LLMOps on AWS aim to enhance the reliability, efficiency, and governance of AI/ML systems.

Conclusion

In this final chapter, we explored several crucial aspects of AWS automation that are essential for modern cloud operations. We began by examining the importance of auditing in AWS environments, understanding how services like CloudTrail and AWS Config provide comprehensive visibility into user activities and resource configurations. These auditing capabilities are fundamental to maintaining security, compliance, and operational excellence in cloud environments.

We then discussed FinOps, a discipline that has become increasingly important as organizations seek to optimize their cloud spending while maintaining performance and reliability. The chapter outlined key FinOps principles and practical approaches to implementing cost management strategies using various AWS services. This knowledge is crucial for SREs who need to balance operational excellence with cost efficiency.

The chapter concluded with an overview of miscellaneous automation opportunities across security operations, network operations, data operations, and machine learning operations. These areas represent the frontier of cloud automation, where SREs can leverage AWS services to build sophisticated, self-managing systems that reduce manual intervention and improve reliability.

Throughout this book, we explored numerous aspects of automation in AWS, from basic infrastructure management to sophisticated operational practices. The principles and practices covered in this final chapter brought together various automation concepts and showed how they could be applied to create more efficient, reliable, and cost-effective cloud environments.

As cloud technologies continue to evolve, the ability to effectively implement these automation strategies will become increasingly valuable for SREs and cloud practitioners.

Points to remember

- Auditing in AWS is essential for maintaining security, compliance, operational insights, change management, and accountability, with services like CloudTrail and AWS Config providing comprehensive visibility.

- AWS CloudTrail serves as the primary service for auditing activities, maintaining a 90-day event history and providing detailed information about user actions and API calls across AWS services.

- AWS Config enables infrastructure auditing by providing detailed views of resource configurations, their changes over time, and compliance status against defined rules.

- FinOps principles focus on collaboration, business value-driven decisions, accessible reporting, shared ownership, centralized management, and leveraging cost variability in cloud environments.

- AWS offers various cost management tools, including AWS Cost Explorer, AWS Budgets, AWS CUR, and AWS Trusted Advisor, to help optimize cloud spending.

- Automation opportunities exist across various operational domains, including security operations (SecurityHub, GuardDuty), network operations (VPC, Transit Gateway), data operations (AWS Glue, Kinesis), and ML operations (SageMaker).

Multiple choice questions

1. **What is the primary AWS service used for auditing user activities and API calls?**
   a. AWS Config
   b. AWS CloudTrail
   c. Amazon GuardDuty
   d. Amazon Inspector

2. **Which AWS service provides a detailed view of resource configurations and their changes over time?**
   a. AWS CloudTrail
   b. AWS Config
   c. AWS Systems Manager
   d. Amazon CloudWatch

3. Which of the following is NOT a principle of FinOps according to the FinOps Foundation?

   a. Collaboration

   b. Shared ownership

   c. Maximum cost reduction

   d. Business value driver decisions

4. What AWS service provides interactive visualization of your AWS costs and usage over time?

   a. AWS Budgets

   b. AWS Cost Explorer

   c. Amazon CloudWatch

   d. AWS QuickSight

5. Which AWS service automatically discovers, catalogs, and prepares data for analytics in DataOps?

   a. Amazon S3

   b. Amazon Redshift

   c. AWS Glue

   d. Amazon Kinesis

6. What feature of AWS CloudTrail ensures that log files have not been tampered with?

   a. Log File Integrity Validation

   b. Event History

   c. Multi-Region Trails

   d. CloudWatch Integration

7. Which AWS service is primarily used for creating custom cost and usage alerts?

   a. AWS Cost Explorer

   b. AWS Budgets

   c. Amazon CloudWatch

   d. AWS Trusted Advisor

8. **What is the retention period for CloudTrail's event history?**

    a. 30 days

    b. 60 days

    c. 90 days

    d. 180 days

9. **Which service can be used to analyze CloudTrail logs stored in S3 buckets?**

    a. Amazon Redshift

    b. Amazon DynamoDB

    c. Amazon Athena

    d. Amazon RDS

10. **What AWS service provides automated recommendations for optimal compute resources?**

    a. AWS Systems Manager

    b. AWS Compute Optimizer

    c. AWS Auto Scaling

    d. AWS CloudFormation

Answers

1.	b
2.	b
3.	c
4.	b
5.	c
6.	a
7.	b
8.	c
9.	c
10.	b

Index

www.ingramcontent.com/pod-product-compliance
Lightning Source LLC
Chambersburg PA
CBHW071959220326

41599CB00034BA/6864